MEMORY & COGNITION

MEMORY & COGNITION
An Introduction

John G. Seamon

Department of Psychology
Wesleyan University

New York • Oxford
OXFORD UNIVERSITY PRESS
1980

Copyright © 1980 by Oxford University Press, Inc.

Library of Congress Cataloging in Publication Data

Seamon, John G   1943–
  Memory and cognition.

  Includes bibliographical references and index.
  1. Memory. 2. Cognition. I. Title.
BF371.S46   153.1'2   79-15026
ISBN 0-19-502642-X
ISBN 0-19-502643-8 pbk.

Printed in the United States of America

To my wife, Diane

Preface

This book has grown out of a course I teach at Wesleyan University called *Human Memory*. Over the past seven years, I have sought to broaden the base of this undergraduate course by showing how memory relates to other aspects of human cognition and how an understanding of the principles and concepts of the course have important consequences for events outside of the laboratory. It is in this spirit that I have tried to present the course material in book form. While the book is primarily intended for undergraduate courses beyond the introductory level, it may be used at other levels for the purposes of introduction or review.

What I have attempted to do is present a view of memory within the framework of cognitive psychology that is consistent with a wide variety of experimental and experiential observations. No claim is made for exhaustive coverage. Indeed, if memory is viewed in the larger context of human cognition, much of psychology is potentially relevant and any review attempting exhaustiveness within a single text is doomed to failure. For this reason topics such as concept formation, problem solving, language and communication, as well as research on animal learning and memory, will receive very limited and sometimes only indirect coverage; to do otherwise would expand this book well beyond its present size. In the end, I write about memory because I see it as central to any understanding of human cognition and because it interests me most.

I was assisted indirectly in this endeavor by many people who influenced me at earlier times. Among them I would mention James I. Chumbley and the Cognitive Processes Group of the University of Massachusetts, Amherst, Michael S. Gazzaniga of the New York Hospital-Cornell Medical Center, and William K. Estes of Harvard University. Each of these people has shown confidence in me at some point in time and to each I would like to say thank you.

Middletown, Connecticut   *J. G. S.*
April, 1979

Contents

One   Introduction, 3

Two   Iconic Memory & Visual Experience, 13

Three   Echoic Memory & Auditory Experience, 38

Four   Selective Attention & Immediate Memory, 59

Five   Pattern Recognition Processes, 85

Six   Conceptual Approaches to Memory Formation, 107

Seven   Nonverbal Memory: Pictures, Images, & Faces, 133

Eight   Organizing & Memorizing, 155

Nine   Remembering Events, 173

Ten   Developmental & Pathological Aspects of Memory, 200

References, 221

Name Index, 251

Subject Index, 259

MEMORY & COGNITION

... nature in her unfathomable designs has mixed us of clay and flame, of brain and mind. . . . The two things hang indubitably together and determine each other's being, but how or why, no mortal may ever know.

—William James, 1890

CHAPTER ONE

Introduction

OBJECTIVES

1. *To provide a brief overview of philosophical speculation on memory and cognition—in particular, the relationship between mind and body.*
2. *To distinguish philosophical speculation from experimental methodology and note the early use of the scientific method in the study of memory and cognition in the nineteenth and twentieth centuries.*
3. *To present and define a conceptual approach called information processing.*
4. *To provide a preview of the book by briefly noting the topics to be covered.*

HISTORICAL OVERVIEW

Early Thoughts on Memory and Cognition

The study of memory and cognition is probably as old as the study of man. Although most historical reviews generally begin with the work of the ancient Greek philosophers, no one really knows when man first became interested in mental phenomena. Since memory is based on past experience, some means of preserving the past is necessary. For Plato, the formation and preservation of memory was likened to the imprint of a solid object in soft wax; when the wax hardened, a trace was left behind. Using this example as an analogy, Plato held that experience may similarly leave traces upon an impressionable mind. Memory traces are the records of past experience which occur as a result of learning. They last so long as their imprints are not clouded by new experiences. When that happens the traces are lost, and the experiences which they represented are forgotten.

Aristotle contributed to our understanding of mental processes by compiling a list of conditions which he felt were important for the establishment of memory. Among these were the organization of the material to be remembered and its frequency of presentation. Aristotle extended Plato by arguing that memory traces could be associated so that the remembrance of one experience would lead to the recall of another. While attention to similarities or differences between experiences was necessarily important for Aristotle, temporal and spatial contiguity were the fundamental processes by which associations were formed. Things that were experienced together in time or space were associated in the mind.

Similar ideas were expressed much later, in the seventeenth century, by the British philosopher John Locke. Like Plato and Aristotle before him, Locke proposed that the mind was an impressionable surface, a tabula rasa or blank tablet, upon which experience was recorded. Complex ideas, according to Locke, were based on associations formed among simpler ideas. Our memory for an object such as an apple, for example, is based on the association of simpler ideas which include such aspects as roundness, hardness, and redness. These simpler ideas are associated in our memory of an apple on the basis of contiguity; they are experienced together in time and space.

Partially overlapping in time with John Locke was the seventeenth century French philosopher René Descartes. Following Plato's earlier thoughts on the separation of mind and body, Descartes advocated a dualism in which the body was governed by mechanical forces, while the mind or soul was free of such restrictions. The body was likened to a machine which produced involuntary, reflexive behavior. Sensory information, which passed from the sensory surfaces through the hollow nerves to the brain, was reflected out again to the muscles to produce overt behavior. The body was seen as responding reflexively to external stimulation. The mind, however, while it did interact with the body, was free of external control. Descartes' dualism of mind and body thus served two functions: It enabled Descartes to speculate on behavior in terms of the laws of physics known at that time, and it permitted man to be seen as a spiritual being possessing an immortal soul which was not subject to physical laws. Descartes' use of the word *l'âme*, which means *mind* or *soul* in English, had obvious religious referents. But even if we put aside any discussion of a soul in a religious sense as beyond the scope of this book, we may still discuss a dualism of mind and body in the sense originally intended by Plato. For him, the soul performed mental functions and only later was adopted for religious purposes. So in the sense that soul and mind refer to mental processes, this is the usage that will be adopted.

A dualism of mind and body raises the problem of how both interact within a person. Where is the mind located and how does it affect the body? To say that mind is spirit and related to all parts of the body, as Descartes had argued, does not really further our understanding.

One way of resolving the problem of dualism has been to deny the importance of the mind. If all behavior is viewed as a reflexive response to environmental stimulation, as the nineteenth century Russian physiologist Schenov held, then it becomes possible to study aspects of behavior formerly attributed to the mind. Learning and memory may be seen not as mental processes but as associations between stimuli and responses. It is within this framework that Ivan Pavlov, the Russian physiologist of the nineteenth and twentieth centuries, studied elementary associative learning in dogs.

Pavlov observed that hungry dogs would salivate when food was placed inside their mouth. This was felt to be a normal part of the digestive process and not based on learning and memory for its occurrence. If, however, the food was repeatedly preceded in time by a stimulus such as a bell or a tone, the dogs would eventually salivate to this originally neutral stimulus. The salivation to the bell or tone, according to Pavlov, was a learned response; it was based on the principle of contiguity formulated by Aristotle. Pavlov studied learning and memory in this manner as reflexive behavior and sought to specify controlling stimuli and behavioral responses. There was no need for a concept of mind to understand behavior, and, if we assume that a continuity of learning principles exists across species, the behavioral laws discovered with organisms such as dogs should apply to other species as well. These same assumptions, with slight variation, have survived to the present day in the behavioristic position of some contemporary psychologists whose solution to the problem of dualism has been to ignore the mind (e.g., Skinner, 1974).

Many people, however, would argue strongly that a position which ignores the mind or relegates it to an inconsequential position does so to its own detriment. For many, aspects of the mind present the most interesting phenomena for psychologists to study. William James, for example, in one of the early textbooks of experimental psychology, defined psychology in 1890 as the science of mental life. Instead of denying the mind, James viewed it as an integral aspect of the brain (James, 1890).

Current accounts of the mind-body problem have made use of James' notion of the mind as a component of the brain. Massaro, for example, in his textbook of experimental psychology, views mental phenomena as attributes of the living brain (Massaro, 1975). Mind and body are not considered separate entities in need of an explanation for their interaction; mental experiences such as perceiving, thinking, and remembering are properties of the body's nervous system in the same sense as overt behaviors such as breathing, running, and sleeping. A complete description of man requires an understanding not only of his overt behavior but of his mental experience as well. For this reason, mental phenomena are important and legitimate objects of study. To focus attention on such phenomena as bear on memory and cognition is the main objective of this book.

The Scientific Study of Memory and Cognition

PHILOSOPHICAL SPECULATION VERSUS THE SCIENTIFIC METHOD. Until the nineteenth century, interest in cognitive psychology was confined to philosophical speculation on matters of the mind. Things changed quickly during that century, and a new experimental psychology founded on the scientific method was created. Psychology separated itself from philosophy by adopting the experimental procedures of the sciences to investigate mental phenomena. While both philosophers and psychologists could pose questions about mental events, the psychologists performed experiments in an attempt to formulate and test theories based on empirical observations. Instead of speculating, for example, on how long some experience would be remembered, it was possible to design an experiment which precisely defined the task and measured the duration of retention. By a careful adherence to the procedures that were used, someone else could repeat the task and attempt to verify the observations. This opportunity for testing the reliability of the observations is at the heart of the scientific method. Based on reliable empirical findings, psychologists could now advance and test theories on mental phenomena which heretofore could be approached only on a personal, speculative basis.

EARLY EXPERIMENTAL STUDIES. Exciting discoveries were made in all areas of medicine and science during the nineteenth century, and psychology was no exception. Armed with its new experimental approach to mental phenomena, research began on problems that have continued to interest psychologists to the present time. There were studies with brief visual or auditory signals which sought to determine the existence of memory images and attempted to measure their duration (e.g., Baxt, 1871; Dietze, 1884; Wolfe, 1886). There were studies of digit recall which tried to determine the number of stimuli that could be reproduced following one presentation to measure the memory span (e.g., Jacobs, 1887). And there were studies of digit recall over short periods of time when attention was directed to a second task so as to determine the duration of information no longer held in consciousness (e.g., Daniels, 1895).

Studies of the above type, which focused on trying to determine the limits of human performance, made an early contribution to psychology as a science and have served as a source for much of the research that was to follow. But none had the impact upon psychology that was accorded to Ebbinghaus' studies of verbal memorization. Ebbinghaus began studying learning and memory in 1879 and published his important work in Germany in 1885. This work served as the foundation for much of the research done well into the twentieth century. Among his many discoveries were the following observations: up to seven verbal items could be memorized within a single trial; a list of more than seven items required more than one trial to learn; continued practice after memorization enhanced retention; and forgetting is initially very rapid in the first few minutes after learning and then tapers off in a slow, gradual decline. Ebbinghaus' chief contribution, however, was his application of the scientific method to the study of memory; his findings demonstrated that lawful properties of mental phenomena could be obtained in experimental psychology. For this reason, the study of memory is generally acknowledged as beginning in 1885 with the publication of Ebbinghaus's book, *Memory: A Contribution to Experimental Psychology.*

The experimental study of memory has changed in many respects from the time of Ebbinghaus. Today psychologists are interested in formulating theories of memory phenomena and are increasingly using stimuli found in everyday experience. Ebbinghaus attempted to study memory for stimuli devoid of meaning; he invented nonsense syllables (e.g., DAX) for this purpose. Current psychologists recognize that meaningfulness is an important variable in learning and have sought to make their experimental conditions similar to those of the real world.

One of the earliest investigators to recognize the importance of dealing with real world stimuli was the British psychologist F. C. Bartlett. Unlike Ebbinghaus, Bartlett was more interested in the qualitative than quantitative aspects of memory—the kinds of things that are remembered rather than how long it takes to memorize something. For Bartlett, to understand memory, we must study stimuli that are found in the everyday environment. For this reason, he examined memory for stimuli such as words, objects, faces, and stories. Bartlett's main contribution was made in his book *Remembering* (1932). He found that literal recall was the exception rather than the rule. Under most circumstances we remember only the gist of our experiences; we abstract the meaning of an event, and this is what is remembered. During subsequent recall, we may remember the gist of that earlier experience, but it is unlike a photograph or tape recording. Our remembrances are often vague and incomplete, and we sometimes fill in the gaps unconsciously by making inferences on the basis of what must have been. This is part of the reason why eyewitness testimony is often so variable; perfect memory is not necessary for adequate functioning in most circumstances.

It should be clear from this brief review that there are different ways of studying memory and cognition. We can speculate on the basis of individual past experience or we can use the scientific method and collect empirical data. The present text will follow the latter course and deal with psychology as an experimental science. Within this province, we will attempt to cover both quantitative and qualitative aspects of the subject matter; following Ebbinghaus and Bartlett, each is necessary to understand the topic.

TEXT ORGANIZATION

Mental Events and a Conceptual Framework

The study of memory and cognition is concerned with the acquisition, storage, and retrieval of information. To understand the functioning of memory, we must examine both the processes and content involved. An understanding of memory processes will tell us how information is acquired during learning and remembered during retrieval; an understanding of memory content will tell us what is acquired and retained. To date, no one has a complete understanding of memory processes and content. At best, we currently have some promising leads as to important processes and hints about the nature of memory storage. This book will therefore offer a tentative picture of memory and cognition in light of the conceptual developments in experimental psychology since the time of Ebbinghaus.

One of the most important advances has been the development, over the past fifteen years, of a conceptual framework that has sought to unify the study of perception and memory by viewing both as intimately related aspects of human cognition. The approach, called *information processing*, is concerned with the operations that intervene between a stimulus and a response. By following the flow of information from the point of sensory stimulation to the experience of a perception or the remembrance of an associated experience, we may gain insight into the fundamental operations of the human cognitive system. This necessarily involves dealing with mental processes and information content. The information processing approach seeks to examine the effects of stimulation as it flows through the cognitive system to understand the processes that are in operation at different points in time and how these processes operate on and change the content of the stimulation. We might liken this approach to an attempt to study the processes and content of a complex machine system such as a computer which receives information, performs various operations upon that information, and either stores it for later use or returns it in a modified form based on the operations that have been performed. In this sense, the computer is an information processing device as it acquires, stores, and retrieves information. By describing the operation of these processes and the nature of the information within each stage of processing, we can more fully understand how memory and cognition function in man.

A Preview of Topics

The outline of the book largely follows the information processing approach to cognition. In successive chapters we will follow the flow of information through the system, continually expanding the coverage while attempting to present a unified scheme overall. We start out by examining perceptual processes in Chapters 2 to 5. These chapters will deal with sensory memory for brief stimulus presentations, attention and how selectivity is achieved, and mechanisms by which patterns are interpreted and recognized in the environment. Ideas about informational content and processes will be developed for use in understanding the memory processes to be presented in the chapters that follow.

In Chapters 6 and 7 the operation of the memory system will be reviewed in an attempt to show how it relates to other aspects of cognition and to define the fundamental concepts necessary for an understanding of memory. Chapter 6 will outline a unified account of memory performance which incorporates ideas from both short-term and long-term storage and levels of processing. The levels of processing hypothesis holds that memory is a direct consequence of attention. This view will be expanded in Chapter 7, in a discussion of memory for visual stimuli, to show how facial recognition may be accomplished over long periods of time and despite large changes in appearance.

Attention, however, is not the only important concept for memory. Also important are organization, abstraction, and inference. These concepts will be presented in Chapters 8 and 9, which deal with storage and retrieval processes. Here we will look at the kinds of things we normally remember and why we sometimes forget. Organizational processes will be presented as attempts to bring order to our experiences. Such attempts have been known since antiquity to have beneficial effects upon remembering large bodies of information. *Abstraction* refers to the process of understanding environmental events in terms of their meaning. During remembering, we recall our earlier abstractions, but we also make inferences based on prior knowledge so that what is remembered is frequently a combination of what was and what must have been.

The last chapter of the book will deal with normal and pathological aspects of memory functioning. We will consider how memory develops by examining memory in infants and reviewing how children differ from adults. Pathological aspects of functioning will be considered in terms of psychological and neurological impairments. Among the topics to be considered are various types of amnesia resulting from stress or trauma, memory problems of the aged, and impairments resulting from cerebral surgery. This chapter will conclude by reviewing evidence on the possibility that all experiences produce permanent memory traces. Topics to be covered include electrical stimulation of the brain, hypnotic age regression, and the relearning of a childhood experience. In each instance, normal and pathological performance will be discussed in terms of concepts developed in previous chapters.

SUMMARY

1. There has been much philosophical speculation on the separation of mind and body.

2. Some researchers have resolved the mind-body problem by ignoring the mind and concentrating instead on overt, observable behavior.

3. An alternative approach, and the one adopted for this book, is to view the mind as an attribute of the living brain. An understanding of man requires an understanding of mental experience.

4. Psychology separated itself from philosophy in the late nineteenth century when it adopted the scientific method to study mental phenomena.

5. The scientific method permits experimental observations to be made independent of the particular observer.

6. Early experimental psychologists were interested in defining the limits of human performance. The interest has continued to the present time.

7. Ebbinghaus had a great impact on the young science of psychology with his studies of memorization. He demonstrated that lawful properties of mental phenomena could be observed.

8. Bartlett studied qualitative aspects of memory in the early part of the twentieth century. Using real world stimuli, Bartlett found that literal recall was the exception rather than the rule.

9. Memory is studied in terms of the acquisition, storage, and retrieval of information.

10. Information processing is the name of a conceptual framework which seeks to discover both the content of the infor-

mation as it flows through the cognitive system and the mental processes which intervene between stimulation and response.

11. The organization of the book generally follows the processing of information in man; it begins with perception and ends with remembering.

CHAPTER TWO

Iconic Memory & Visual Experience

OBJECTIVES

1. To demonstrate that a brief iconic memory trace exists for a short period of time following a brief visual stimulus.
2. To define some of the properties of iconic memory, including its duration, its locus in the visual nervous system, and the conditions under which it is likely to occur.
3. To construct a simple information processing model of visual identification and show how the results of studies of iconic memory are relevant to this model.
4. To review the role of iconic memory in visual perception from different perspectives.

INTRODUCTION

Do all of our experiences leave memories behind? The answer to this question appears to depend upon whether permanent memory is implied. Research suggests that while all of our experiences can leave a memory trace behind, all of the traces need not be permanent. Some memories can last a lifetime, some a few days or hours, some perhaps 30 seconds, and some are so brief that they last but a quarter of a second. It is with these brief memories that our study of memory will begin.

13

Imagine a memory that lasts for so little time that it is gone before you can say your name. What kind of memory is this, and what types of evidence are available to document its presence? The kind of memory to be discussed is called *sensory memory*. There are specific sensory memories for the visual and the auditory senses, which take the form of the sense being stimulated. Following visual stimulation there is a brief visual memory trace called an *icon*, and following auditory stimulation there is a brief auditory trace called an *echo* (Neisser, 1967). While the other modalities, such as touch and taste, may have their corresponding sensory memories as well, most is known about vision and audition. The sensory memories for vision and audition will be dealt with separately in Chapters 2 and 3.

DEMONSTRATIONS OF ICONIC MEMORY

Perceptual Color Mixture

Different types of evidence indicate that immediately after a visual stimulus is seen, a short visual trace, an icon, remains available to the observer for further inspection and processing. The first evidence concerns the perceptual phenomenon of color mixture. If two different colored lights are shown simultaneously in the same spatial location, the original two lights will not be seen. What will be seen is a new color, which is a mixture of the two colors being shown. Red and green lights, for example, mix together to produce the experience of seeing yellow. The interesting aspect of color mixture, for the present discussion, is that mixture is also possible under specific conditions if both colors are presented successively (Efron, 1967). Timing is of crucial importance. If the two colors are presented alternately at a slow rate of one second or more each, color mixture is not obtained. The red and green lights are seen simply as alternating reds and greens. However, if the two lights are presented in succession at a very rapid rate so that now each light is shown for only 50 milliseconds, a flickering yellow replaces the alternating reds and greens. Color mixture is obtained with successive presentations if each presentation is very brief.

The results from the color mixture demonstration indicate that perception is not instantaneous; it is a process that occurs over time. Color mixture is not found when red and green lights are successively presented at a slow rate because there is enough time to perceive each color individually. At a fast presentation rate, the same two colors can no longer be perceived individually; they become fused together and produce a new color. But what is being fused? The two lights are presented successively, not simultaneously. When one light is on, the other light is off. It must be that a visual trace of each stimulus remains for a short period of time after that stimulus has terminated. What is fused is the iconic trace of the preceding light with the presentation and trace of the succeeding light. The result is the experience of color mixture under conditions where the two lights are not externally present at the same moment in time.

Moving Slit Viewing

Studies by Parks (1965) and Haber and Nathanson (1968) provide another demonstration of iconic memory in visual perception. A picture of an object is placed behind a nontransparent screen which contains a narrow slit one-eighth of an inch wide down its center. If the screen is held steady, the viewer can see only a narrow band of the picture, and identification is all but impossible. But if the picture is held steady and the slit is moved rapidly back and forth across the picture, the entire picture suddenly becomes visible. Picture perception is possible because each momentary glimpse gives rise to an iconic trace which persists in time. Moving the slit over the picture produces numerous brief glimpses, each of which forms an iconic trace. The aggregate of these brief glimpses and iconic traces is the experience of "seeing" the entire picture— when, in reality, only a small portion is exposed at one time. This demonstration does not require special materials and is easy to verify at home.

Interestingly, if the conditions of the slit demonstration are changed such that the slit is held stationary and the picture is moved rapidly back and forth behind it, identification is extremely difficult. In the first condition, each brief glimpse stimulated a different portion of the light-sensitive retina of each eye to provide a spatial dimension to the picture. The second case destroys the spatial dimension by repeatedly stimulating the same general area of each eye (Haber & Nathanson, 1968). This spatial dimension is an important aspect for normal visual perception. Objects are seen in space; when this quality is destroyed, perception suffers.

PROPERTIES OF ICONIC MEMORY

The preceding demonstrations indicate that iconic traces are obtained with brief visual exposures. To specify more adequately the nature of iconic representations, it is necessary to define some of their properties. Two properties to be reviewed are the duration of an iconic trace and its locus in the human nervous system.

Duration of Iconic Traces

A simple behavioral measure of the duration of iconic memory was obtained in the moving slit study previously discussed (Haber & Nathanson, 1968). If the narrow slit was moved back and forth over the picture at a rate slower than 240 milliseconds (i.e., approximately a quarter of a second), viewers reported that they could not see all of the picture simultaneously. If each brief glimpse gives rise to an iconic trace and the sum of these traces enables the viewer to see the picture in its entirety, then slowing the rate of viewing by moving the slit more slowly permits the iconic traces from previous glimpses to be lost. This technique thus provides an estimate of the duration of iconic memory: In this task, it is the viewing rate at which all of the picture can be seen. The results of this study suggest that iconic traces are lost fairly rapidly; they seem to persist for no more than one-quarter of a second.

Additional support for the finding of a brief trace duration, as well as specification of some of the conditions which can affect duration estimates, was provided by Haber and Standing (1970). Subjects were presented with a light of one of several durations and an auditory click. The light came on periodically at regular intervals. The subjects' task was to align the click of a manual control so that, depending upon instructions, it occurred simultaneously with either light onset or offset. Under conditions when the light was presented for 1 second, the subjects were very accurate at aligning clicks with either light onset or offset. For short light durations of 100–500 milliseconds (1 second = 1000 milliseconds), subjects accurately positioned the clicks only with light onset. At light offset they systematically overestimated the actual duration of the light and had clicks follow the actual offset by as much as half a second.

A schematic diagram of these findings is shown in Figure 2.1 for light-adapted and dark-adapted conditions. The *light-adapted condition* means that the experiment was conducted under normal room lighting, while the *dark-adapted condition* means that the experiment was performed in the absence of room light after the viewer has sufficient time to grow accustomed to the darkness. Perfect performance is indicated by the main diagonal in each graph. If the light was shown for 100 milliseconds, the time between the two clicks should have been 100 milliseconds; the estimated duration should match the actual light duration. The results show the time difference between the two clicks to be longer than the actual light duration at the short stimulus intervals and to become more accurate as the duration of the light increases. Since the subjects aligned the clicks to their perception of the light onset or offset, for short durations the time difference between clicks must have been based on the actual exposure of the light and its iconic trace. For longer light durations, subjects could accurately align the clicks; apparently there was no iconic trace, and their perception of the light matched its actual onset and offset.

The difference between perfect performance and the observed performance in Figure 2.1 provides a direct estimate of the duration of iconic memory. The results show that viewers thought that the light was on longer than it really was when this stimulus was shown for short durations of 10–400 milliseconds. Furthermore, this viewer error was greater under dark-adapted than light-adapted conditions. Both of these results are shown in Figure 2.1 by the discrepancy between the function for the observers' actual performance and the main diagonal of each graph, which represents theoretically perfect performance. The discrepancy for each pair of functions is larger for short light durations than long durations and for dark-adapted than light-adapted conditions. These results indicate that iconic traces are found only for very brief visual exposures, and last from one-quarter to one-half of a second under the conditions employed. For stimulus durations of longer than a half-second exposure, little or no iconic memory is available. Second, and perhaps equally important, the fact that the experimental lighting conditions had an effect on iconic memory duration suggests that the iconic trace is visual in form. A visual factor such as light adaptation might not be expected to affect the memory trace of objects briefly stored in some nonvisual form.

Afterimages and the Locus of Iconic Traces

Afterimages are visual phenomena which share similarities with iconic traces. A color afterimage can be obtained by staring at a bright color for 10 to 15 seconds and then looking at a plain white field. The experience is one of perceiving the complementary color. If you stare at red, you will see green. Motion aftereffects of a complementary nature are also possible. If you stare at a waterfall

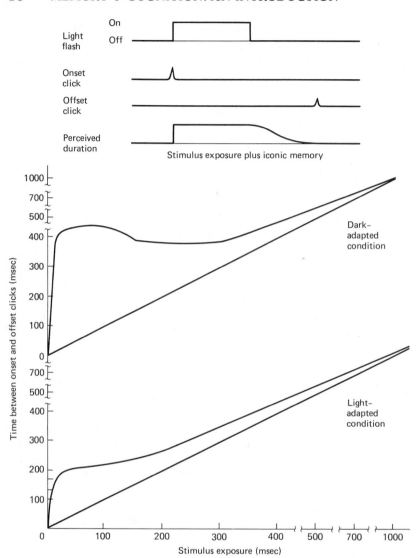

FIGURE 2.1. The duration of a light flash, estimated by clicks that have been aligned to its perceived onset and offset (top). The average time between light onset and offset clicks for dark-adapted and light-adapted subjects as a function of the exposure duration of the light (bottom). Perfect performance is indicated by the main diagonal in each graph; observed performance is indicated by the connected points. (Adapted from Haber and Standing, 1970)

for a fixed period of time and then look at a stationary scene, everything will appear to move upward. These afterimages and aftereffects are the result of prolonged stimulation of the sensory receptors which, when fatigued, give rise to the illusion of color or movement along a complementary dimension. These phenomena, called *negative afterimages* or *aftereffects*, differ from iconic traces in that they result from prolonged stimulation and last for extended periods of time. Iconic traces, by contrast, are found with very brief stimuli and last for only a short period of time. These differences, and others based on subjective experience, were reported as long ago as 1860 by Fechner in his *Elements of Psychophysics* (1860).

Afterimages, however, can be found with brief, intense visual stimulation. Shooting a photographic flashbulb in a dark room will give rise to a positive afterimage which appears to be a ghostlike image of what was seen during the flash (Massaro, 1975). At present there is little experimental evidence to distinguish positive afterimages from iconic traces, as both seem to result from a continuation of neural activity. For the purposes of this book, we will label the visual persistence arising from brief visual stimulation as *iconic memory*, even though it is realized that the distinction between iconic traces and afterimages is difficult to make.

While current research has not differentiated positive afterimages and iconic memory, headway has been made in determining the locus of these traces in the visual processing system. In attempting to locate the source of a particular phenomenon, we might try to distinguish between peripheral and central processes. A *peripheral process* has its locus in a sensory receptor, while a *central process* involves the brain or central nervous system. We could hypothesize, for example, that iconic traces are peripherally produced in the retina of the eye or centrally determined farther back in the visual track of the brain.

There is now strong evidence that iconic memory can be peripherally based in the light-sensitive retina of the eye. The retina, which is composed of rod and cone cells, serves as the light receptor for normal vision. The rods function mainly at low levels of illumination found at night, while the cones function at higher levels of brightness which occur during the day. In rare instances, people are born with rods and no cones. These individuals, called *rod monochromats*, are completely color blind and unable to see under conditions of bright lighting. Sakitt (1975) made use of the latter deficiency in a rod monochromatic person to determine the locus of iconic memory. Since a rod monochromat cannot see during periods of bright illumination, Sakitt persented her subject with a bright visual field containing an even brighter array of visual letters for 50 milliseconds. Both the background and the letters were white. Sakitt reports that no matter how bright the letters were made, the subject could not see them. However, if the subject closed her eyes after the letters were shown, she saw an iconic trace of the visual display and could readily report the letters which now stood out. What was invisible with the eyes open became visible with the eyes closed.

This paradoxical result may be explained in terms of the neural activity of the retina of the eye. According to Sakitt, when the subject closed her eyes, retinal illumination was eliminated, but retinal stimulation was not. Retinal activity takes an appreciable period of time to recover from earlier stimulation. The fact that the rod monochromat could "iconically" see the bright letters from the surrounding field may mean that the retinal area stimulated by the letters received more light energy and hence sent out stronger neural signals than the remaining areas of the retina, which were stimulated less strongly by the dimmer surrounding area of the visual display. Sakitt believes that it is this neural activity in the rods of the retina that is largely responsible for iconic memory. For this reason, we hold that iconic traces are localized in the retina of the eye and can therefore be considered to be a peripheral phenomenon.

The conclusion that iconic memory is entirely a peripheral pheonomenon is not warranted on the basis of the above data. Sakitt's work definitively demonstrates that icons can have a retinal locus; it does not rule out the possibility of central factors affecting iconic memory as well. A study by Haber and Standing (1969) seems to provide evidence that iconic memory can, under different circumstances, have a central locus. Their task involved repeatedly presenting subjects with a visual form on a white background for 10 milliseconds, interspersed with periods of only a white background. They sought to determine how much time could elapse between repeated presentations of the form before the subjects realized that the form was actually being presented intermittently and not continuously. The maximum blank duration turned out to be approximately 250 milliseconds, or a quarter of a second. Since the form was presented intermittently the subjects' experience of a continuous presence over the blank intervals of a quarter of a second or less must have been based on iconic traces. So far, this is simply another demonstration of the existence of iconic memory and an estimate of its duration, which is consistent with the previously cited research.

In an interesting twist, however, Haber and Standing decided to observe what would happen if the recurring visual form was not viewed binocularly with both eyes, but was viewed dioptically instead. Now each brief presentation of the form was directed to an alternate eye of the viewer; the two eyes were never simultaneously stimulated. If the iconic trace of the form observed previously is only a retinal phenomenon, then subjects should now report that the form is going on and off if the blank period between presentation of the form is 250 milliseconds. Remember, if each blank period is 250 milliseconds in length, the time between stimulation for a given eye is doubled to 500 milliseconds because form presentation alternates between eyes. To keep the time interval between presentation to the same eye under 250 milliseconds, a blank interval of less than 125 milliseconds would have to be used.

The results of this experiment indicate that subjects perceived the form as being continuously present with blank intervals of up to 250 milliseconds, even though each eye was stimulated individually on an alternating basis. These data suggest that iconic traces are a central phenomenon located beyond the eyes, where information from the two receptive surfaces is integrated. The findings of Haber and Standing (1969) and Sakitt (1975) need not be viewed as necessarily contradictory. Iconic memory, like other visual phenomena—such as masking, to be discussed later—may have both peripheral and central components (see Turvey, 1973); the particular circumstances may determine which is evidenced. The possibility of multiple loci has been noted previously (Crowder, 1976).

ICONS AND INFORMATION PROCESSING

Constructing a Model

Documented research on the topic of iconic memory began in 1871 with the publication of Baxt's study of the number of stimuli that could be read following a single, brief exposure (Murray, 1976). While research continued along these lines through the end of the nineteenth and the beginning of the twentieth centuries, interest waned until recent times with the publication of a monograph by Sperling in 1960. Like Baxt before him, Sperling was interested in the amount of information that could be perceived in a single, brief presentation. Unlike earlier investigators, Sperling devised specific experimental techniques which enabled him to

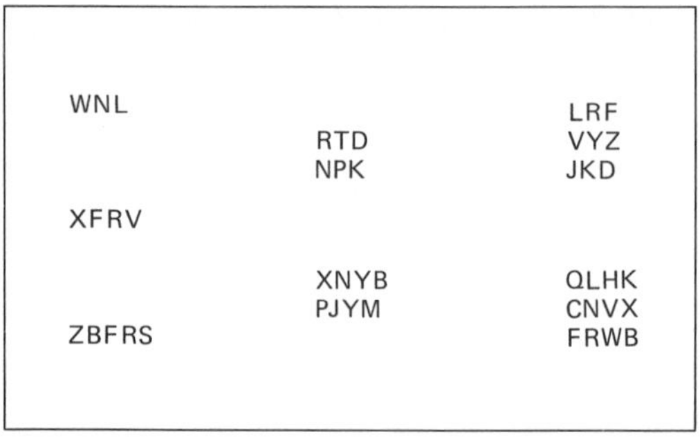

```
WNL                                    LRF
                    RTD                VYZ
                    NPK                JKD

XFRV

                    XNYB               QLHK
                    PJYM               CNVX
ZBFRS                                  FRWB
```

FIGURE 2.2. A sample of consonant letter arrays of various sizes, of the type used by Sperling (1960).

answer the questions he posed. To conduct his experiments, Sperling used a machine called a *tachistoscope*. This is a device which allows an experimenter to present visual stimuli at precisely controlled exposure durations and brightness levels. The subjects were presented with arrays of up to twelve letters, such as those shown in Figure 2.2, for 50 milliseconds. After the letters were flashed, the subjects had to write down all the letters they could remember. The experimental results are shown in Figure 2.3, which presents the number of letters reported as a function of the number of letters displayed. Theoretically perfect performance is shown by the dotted main diagonal line. If subjects reported everything that was shown, their performance would fall along this line. The actual results, shown by the *whole report* function—which represents the attempts to report each array size in its entirety—indicate that the subjects were perfect only with very small arrays of three or four letters. With larger array sizes, ths subjects' whole report output did not match the stimulus input. Even though the subjects were trying to report the entire array, they could never recall more than four or five letters correctly.

Why is there a discrepancy between stimulus input and whole report output? To answer this question, it is necessary to understand what is happening between the brief presentation of the visual array and a subject's limited recall. Some idea of the cognitive operations that mediate between stimulus input and response output is found in the model of visual identification shown in Figure 2.4. This highly simplified model has been derived from the more complex processing models proposed by Sperling (1967; 1970).

As shown in Figure 2.4, a briefly exposed letter array gives rise

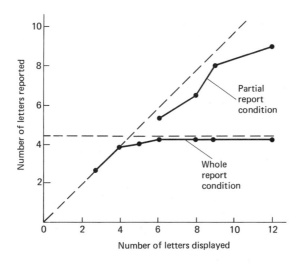

FIGURE 2.3. The number of letters reported for whole report or available for partial report in the Sperling task as a function of the number of letters in the stimulus array. The observed data for each condition are indicated by the connected points and may be compared with the maximum possible performance shown by the main diagonal. (Adapted from Sperling, 1960)

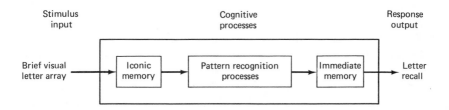

FIGURE 2.4. A simplified model of letter identification for brief tachistoscopic exposures.

to an iconic trace which contains information about the visual experience that has not yet been identified. There is no conscious control over this process. It is simply the initial registration of the information which is performed automatically as an inherent operation of the visual system. As information is registered by the eyes and brain, it is categorized and identified on the basis of what is known. Neural mechanisms in the eyes are sensitive to low-level physical qualities such as color or spatial position, while higher-level operations involved in the identification of pattern or form must be performed more centrally in the brain (Haber & Hershenson, 1973). Stimulus identification of familiar visual forms such as letters is achieved automatically without the need of conscious attention based on skills acquired developmentally through learning (LaBerge & Samuels, 1974). This process of stimulus identification is more generally referred to as the process of pattern recognition.

For familiar stimuli such as letters, the pattern recognition process can identify the forms, which may then be maintained in a state of awareness by mental rehearsal (Waugh & Norman, 1965). Rehearsing identified patterns is a way of preserving the effects of immediate past stimulation. For this reason, we may label this means of preserving the most recent past as *immediate memory* in Figure 2.4. Other names that have been used for this type of memory include *primary memory* (James, 1890; Waugh & Norman, 1965) and *short-term memory* (Atkinson & Shiffrin, 1968; Glanzer & Cunitz, 1966). For the present, we can distinguish iconic memory from immediate memory on the basis of the identifiability of the visual stimuli: Visual forms held in iconic storage have not yet been identified, while those held in immediate memory have been recognized.

The model in Figure 2.4 presents the letter identification operations as a series of stages in order to simulate a time-extended process. By necessity, however, this view may erroneously represent a continuous set of operations in a discrete, artificially separated manner. The value of a model such as that depicted in Figure 2.4 is that it may help us understand the processes which appear to be logically necessary for a task of this type. The danger, as noted by Crowder (1976) and many others, is that a model may suggest strict temporal sequencing when, in reality, such fine lines may not be drawn. Processes could be performed sequentially in a nonoverlapping temporal fashion, sequentially in a partially overlapping manner, or simultaneously. Most models are not precise on this matter, and in this sense, their diagramatic representations are misleading, as they imply more than is generally known.

In light of the model of visual identification shown in Figure 2.4, and with the above caution in mind, it is possible to formulate the problem of limited recall in the Sperling task in terms of definite, testable hypotheses. Three general possibilities suggest themselves. First, it may be that only four or five letters can be perceived and held in iconic memory after a brief 50 millisecond exposure. This hypothesis suggests that initial iconic storage is limited in its capacity; only four or five letters can be recalled because only four or five letters are initially seen. Second, perhaps iconic storage is not severely limited in its capacity, but pattern recognition processes, because they take time to perform, have sufficient time in a brief exposure to recognize only four or five letters. Third, response output may not match stimulus input because of a limit on the capacity of immediate memory. More than four or five letters may be initially seen and recognized, but only this number can be maintained by mental rehearsal in immediate memory.

To determine if initial iconic storage is limited to only a few items, Sperling (1960) devised a partial report procedure. In the new procedure, a tone was presented immediately after a brief, twelve-letter visual array was shown. The tone acted as a cue and told the subject to recall either the top, middle, or bottom row of four letters, depending upon whether the tone was of high, medium, or low frequency. Under these conditions, subjects had to recall a maximum of only four letters, something they had already demonstrated they could do. If the subjects could use the tone cue and recall all of the letters in a row correctly, it must be that all of the stimuli in the entire visual array were initially perceived in iconic memory. The proportion of letters recalled correctly for any row must match the proportion of letters initially available in the whole display, since the tone cue comes on after the display is gone and all of the rows are equally likely to be probed. This same reasoning is used in grading student course work. A student is examined on only a portion of the material covered in the course. If the test is fair and the student does not know the questions in advance, then test performance is an accurate indicator of overall course performance (Sperling, 1960).

The results obtained by Sperling with the partial report procedure are shown in Figure 2.3. The number of letters in the visual display is plotted as a function of the estimated number of letters available in iconic memory. The observed performance approximated perfect performance over all but the largest array size used. Subjects could certainly see at least nine letters, and very likely many more. A related study by Averbach and Sperling (1961) used the partial report procedure with dark-adapted subjects and high-intensity stimulus displays. They estimated that seventeen letters could be held briefly in iconic memory. Clearly, the limit on recall of four or five letters with the whole report task does not appear to be based on a limit of iconic memory capacity; much more can be seen than can be immediately recalled.

How many letters can be seen in a single brief exposure? This is a difficult question to answer precisely for a number of reasons. First, the tone cue that is used in the partial report task must itself be interpreted before the correct row in a letter array can be identified. The process of tone identification takes time (Eriksen & Rohrbaugh, 1970), and performance on letter identification may suffer when large arrays are displayed. The partial report procedure might thus underestimate the true capacity of iconic memory. Second, it is well known that our ability to see fine detail decreases dramatically as stimuli are moved from the point of visual fixation toward the periphery of the visual field (Alpern, 1962). Use of large visual arrays requires coverage of more of the visual field—and, in particular, more of the periphery of the visual field, where acuity is lower. If the quality of the iconic representation is a function of the level of visual acuity, then a large array is hampered in a way that does not affect a small array, and measures of iconic capacity will again be underestimated. In light of these considerations, it would appear that the capacity of iconic memory under ideal experimental conditions would be limited by the resolving power of the eye. To date, we do not know exactly how many letters can be seen in a brief exposure, but the number is greater than four or five and is probably quite large.

Given that iconic storage is not limited, recall in the whole report procedure must be limited due to either pattern recognition processes or immediate memory. The means of distinguishing between these two hypotheses is to present the initial visual display for a longer period of time. If the limit is due to a small capacity of immediate memory, then providing more time for pattern recognition processes should not produce a greater response output. Alternatively, if immediate memory is not limited, then performance on the whole report task should improve. Sperling (1960) performed this manipulation with the whole report procedure by presenting some letter arrays for 50 milliseconds and some for 500 milliseconds. He found that subjects recalled no more than four or five letters under either condition. These data suggest that the recall limit is a function of immediate memory. Time available for processing can affect the number of letters to be recalled up to a maximum of four or five letters, suggesting that pattern recognition processes do take appreciable periods of time (Mackworth, 1963). But extra processing time will not produce additional letters for recall; performance is limited by immediate memory.

These results may be summarized in terms of the visual identification model in Figure 2.4. When a brief visual array is presented, it gives rise to a representation in iconic memory. The information can be maintained as long as the stimulus is present and as long as its representation exists in iconic form. It is only because the brief visual stimulus produces an iconic trace that a subject can use a tone cue in the partial report procedure to select the top, middle, or bottom row of an array for further processing. The selected forms are identified by the pattern recognizers and made available to immediate memory for either rehearsal or recall. Recall is limited to only four or five items because of a limit in immediate memory. The importance of the work of Sperling and others is that it demonstrates that iconic memory exists and that we are capable of processing information from the iconic store when such information is no longer externally available.

Validating the Model

If the visual identification model has validity, it should make predictions in accord with what is known in sensory psychology and perception. Recent research has shown that the retina of the eye is sensitive to information about color, edges, lines, orientation, and motion (see Haber & Hershenson, 1973). The complex pattern recognition operations discussed previously do not have to decide if the stimuli are arranged in the top row or the bottom row, or if they are red or green. Instead of concentrating on the gross, physical aspects of the array, the pattern recognizers can concentrate on identification of the visual forms. This is why, in the Sperling task, subjects could use the tone cue to decide which row of visual forms should receive additional processing. Even though the iconic trace contains only uninterpreted visual forms, information about spatial location is available to permit subjects to use the cue. A similar prediction would be made in the event that the visual array contained a mixture of red letters and green letters. Since color information is available at a very low level and does not require the operation of the pattern analyzers, it should be possible for subjects to perform the Sperling task with a color cue given immediately after a display of red and green letters. This seems to be the case. Subjects can report letters of either color just as accurately as with a tone cue for spatial location (von Wright, 1972).

If the stimuli are changed, however, so that half of the stimuli are letters and half are digits, and subjects are given a letter or digit recall cue immediately after a mixed array is shown, what should happen? Remember, iconic storage contains unanalyzed information about visual forms. Information about the spatial arrangement of the forms and their color may be available, but the forms have not yet been identified. There are no receptors in the eyes for distinguishing numbers from letters. Complex pattern recognition processes must do this job. A recall cue for letters or numbers given after the brief visual presentation can be of no use to the subject because the information has not yet been identified. This is exactly what has been found. Under these conditions, partial report is no better than whole report (Sperling, 1960; von Wright, 1972).

Another condition in which partial report is no better than whole report is found when the partial report cue has been delayed beyond the life of the iconic trace. In terms of the model, if the partial report cue immediately follows the brief exposure of the stimulus, we know that subjects can use the cue and selectively continue the processing of the specific item or items for recall. However, as the partial report cue is delayed, the iconic trace suffers decay and the superiority of the partial report procedure over the whole report condition disappears. With increasing delays, partial report performance approximates that of whole report (Averbach & Coriell, 1961; Sperling, 1960). Subjects will always recall four or five letters as they process as many items as they can from the fading display while waiting for the partial report cue. Depending upon experimental conditions, cue delays of 250 milliseconds (Averbach & Coriell, 1961) to 1 second (Sperling, 1960) completely eliminate the partial report superiority. These studies, like those cited previously with light pulses and moving slits, show iconic memory to be a short-lived, rapidly decaying experience.

Additional support for the visual identification model is available from studies of visual masking where two visual stimuli are presented closely in time. A brief four-letter array could be presented and followed by a second visual stimulus called a *masking field*, which is composed of many bits and fragments of letters all randomly arranged. In terms of the model, the time between the letter array and the mask will be of major importance. If the masking stimulus is presented after the four letters have already been identified and are being actively rehearsed in immediate memory, the mask should not affect performance since the subject has the letter names available. Generally speaking, a subsequent visual stimulus should not affect the processing of an earlier visual stimulus if the first stimulus has already been identified. But if the visual mask is presented just after the letter array such that the letters

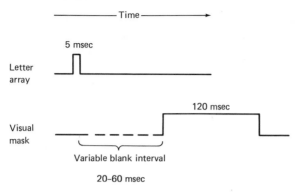

FIGURE 2.5. The masking conditions used by Sperling (1963).

have not yet been identified and still exist only as unidentified visual forms, then the arrival of the visual mask should disrupt performance. An experiment by Sperling (1963) manipulated the time between the brief exposure of a four-letter array and the presentation of a visual mask. A schematic outline of the temporal parameters is presented in Figure 2.5. When the letter array was shown for 5 milliseconds and the mask for 120 milliseconds, 60 milliseconds between the two stimuli were needed by subjects to recall all four letters correctly. For each 10 millisecond reduction in the time between the array and the mask, one less letter was reported. Apparently, what was happening was that the mask was coming on while the letters were being identified. The letters that were recognized before the mask came on were reported, while those that had not yet been identified became obliterated by the second visual input.

Presenting a mask between 10 and 20 milliseconds after the letter array produced a subjective experience of having seen letters, although none of the letters could be specifically identified (Haber & Standing, 1968). This finding suggests that pattern recognition may entail a general classification followed by a specific identification of the actual instances. In the first classification, the pattern recognizers determine the general category of the visual input (e.g., letters, faces). After the visual input has been classified in terms of general category membership, a specific identification of the visual form is undertaken (e.g., A, B, C). In Haber and Standing's (1968) experiment, subjects apparently had enough time to perform a general classification of the visual information so as to identify the forms as letters, but they did not have enough time to identify any of the specific instances. Of course, if the mask is presented even closer in time to the first stimulus, it completely disrupts performance as the first letters get absorbed into the mask. Under these conditions, even a general classification is impossible, and subjects report seeing only the mask. The situation involving masking may be directly analogous to the earlier discussion of successive color mixture. If enough time is available for processing, each color is seen individually; without enough time, the two colors fuse, making separate identification impossible. A similar phenomenon can be found in masking (Eriksen & Hoffman, 1963), although as Turvey (1973) notes, there are probably many ways in which a masking stimulus can affect the perception of a preceding stimulus.

The preceding studies were concerned with *backward masking,* the effect of a second visual stimulus on the processing of the first stimulus. It is possible to reverse conditions and examine forward masking. A study by Guthrie and Wiener (1966) was performed along these lines and provides an additional bit of evidence in support of the visual identification model. The stimuli used in this study are shown in Figure 2.6. Subjects saw one of the A stimuli (A_1, A_2, A_3, or A_4) followed immediately by the B stimulus for 500 milliseconds. The A stimuli, which were presented too briefly to be identified, differed in terms of whether they were drawn with angles or curves and whether a gun was present in the man's right hand. The B stimulus was devoid of angles and curves, and no gun was present. The subject's task was to make mood and character judgments of the B stimulus. In light of what has been presented so far, the results should come as no surprise; stimulus B was judged to be more hostile and aggressive when it was preceded by stimulus A_2 or A_4 than when preceded by A_1 or A_3. The presence of the gun was completely irrelevant. The only things that mattered were the visual cues of angles and curves. Sharp angles produced more feelings of hostility and aggressiveness than did smooth curves. In accord with the model, the first stimulus may have been available in iconic storage only long enough for low-level physical features like edges and contours to be analyzed. There was certainly not enough time available for the complex pattern recognizers to identify a gun if one were present. Consequently, subjects never reported perceiving a gun, and its presence did not have an effect upon performance. What they saw were contours, and this information colored their mood for the second stimulus. Taken together, the data from cue selectivity, delay of cue, and forward and backward masking are in agreement with the simple model of visual identification shown in Figure 2.4.

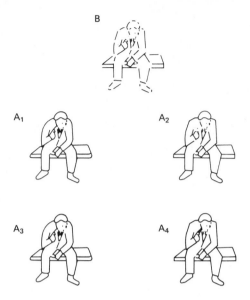

FIGURE 2.6. The stimuli used by Guthrie and Wiener (1966). Sub-jects saw one of the A stimuli, followed by the B stimulus. (From Guthrie and Wiener, 1966)

ICONIC MEMORY AND NORMAL "SEEING"

Continuous Information Processing

Of what importance are iconic traces for everyday visual expe-rience if such traces are found only with brief visual exposures? This question is formulated, in part, on the intuitive belief that normal visual perception is based on prolonged fixations and not on brief visual experience. Under many circumstances, however, brief fixations of approximately a quarter of a second are common (Haber & Herschenson, 1973), and some theorists have argued that our normal mode of looking greatly resembles a sequence of very brief exposures (e.g., Sperling, 1960). This may be true of looking at pictures, visual scenes, or reading text. Consider the picture in Figure 2.7 and the tracings of eye movements made by an eye camera while a person was viewing the picture for time periods of 2 and 30 minutes each (Yarbus, 1967). When looking at a picture the experience is one of seeing it in its entirety (Hochberg, 1970a). Concentration on details is possible, of course, but mainly there is a

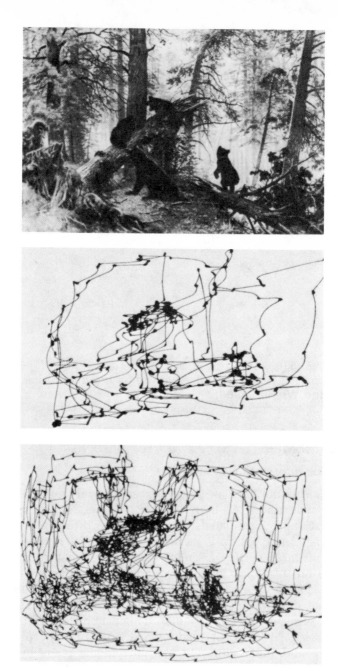

FIGURE 2.7. Shishkin's picture "Morning in the Pine Forest" (top) and records of eye movements made over the picture for 2 (middle) and 30 minutes (bottom) of free viewing. (From Yarbus, 1967)

feeling that the eyes move smoothly and continuously over the surface to form an impression of the scene. This smoothness, this continuity, is an illusion. The eye movement recordings show this to be so. The eyes are actually jumping back and forth across the picture as new details are brought into focus. Again and again the viewer comes back to the areas in the picture of high informational value (Mackworth & Morandi, 1967). Trees are vertically scanned to determine the general layout of the scene, but repeatedly the viewer focuses on the bears in an attempt, perhaps, to understand the experience that is captured in the picture.

The same illusion of smooth, continuous eye movement is found in reading. Once more, however, the eyes actually move in an irregular, stop-and-go pattern (Judd & Buswell, 1922; Kolers, 1973). Recordings made during reading demonstrate that as the eyes scan in a left-to-right direction, they pause several times and fixate at various points within the line. The duration of these fixations may last approximately a quarter of a second, although the times are variable; some fixations are shorter and some are slightly longer. During a pause, the eyes may fixate on large words or small words, and at the beginning, middle, or end of a word. For a given line of eleven to fifteen words, the eyes may fixate eight times in their visual scan of the text (Judd & Buswell, 1922). This irregular, stop-and-go pattern of fixations is easy to demonstrate outside of the laboratory by placing a mirror next to a page of text. Ask someone to read and observe the eyes through the mirror. The above findings should be readily observable.

A careful examination of eye movements reveals that there are actually several different types. The first type is a fine tremor which results from the pull of the six eye muscles upon each eye in an attempt to maintain the eyes in a particular position (Barlow, 1952; Riggs et al., 1953). Aside from the fine tremor when the eyes are fixating, there is also an involuntary slow drift which serves to stimulate new cells in the retina of each eye as previously stimulated cells become fatigued (Riggs et al., 1953). Artificially inhibiting these movements results in a rapid cessation of normal visual perception (Pritchard, 1961). The third type of eye movement is called saccadic movement. These eye movements, which occur no more than four to five times per second, are the movements that are observed during reading or viewing a scene. Figure 2.7 is a record of these saccadic movements.

An understanding of eye movements is important because during viewing, external information can be processed only when the eyes are fixating. Little external information can be processed just before, during, or just after a saccadic eye movement due to a suppression in visual acuity (Latour, 1962; Volkman, 1962). Why, then, does the act of reading or picture viewing appear to be a smooth, continuous process when, in many instances, it is more like a sequence of brief visual exposures? One possibility is that a brief exposure gives rise to an iconic trace, which persists during a saccadic eye movement while the processing of new external information is temporarily suppressed. As the eyes move during a saccade, the iconic trace moves with them (Davison, Fox & Dick, 1973). Although visual activity for external signals is suppressed during an eye movement, such movement does not appear to affect iconic memory (Doerflein & Dick, 1974). This could imply that information can be processed continuously on the basis of what is abstracted from the external stimulus and its iconic trace. Information from successive fixations and iconic traces would be similar in terms of gross physical qualities and could be integrated into a single sense of the object being perceived. While it is clear that information from successive glances is integrated (Hochberg, 1970a), the manner in which this is accomplished is not yet known.

If iconic memory has a role in normal viewing conditions, it follows that aberrations or abnormalities in iconic storage may produce serious problems in tasks which give rise to iconic traces. Reading, for example, would be greatly hampered if each fixation gave rise to an iconic trace and that iconic trace did not decay by the next fixation. The result would be analogous to a forward masking situation, where two visual inputs appear to overlap in time. There is some evidence that this may happen under some circumstances for reasons that are yet undetermined. Stanley (1975) obtained a sample of school children classified as dyslexics (i.e., children with reading problems) by their teachers and compared them on an iconic memory task with a group of children who did not have any reading difficulties. The results showed the duration of iconic memory to be longer for the dyslexia group than the comparison group. Stanley (1975) has argued that some of the problems that dyslexic children have may be due to interference produced by iconic traces which last too long. While this may be so, iconic difficulties cannot account for all of the problems of dyslexia. At present, dyslexia is no more than a global label that is applied to children who have many different types of reading problems, but who are otherwise normal in their studies (Keeney, 1971). A general review of dyslexia is beyond the scope of this book, and no attempt to explain this complex problem in terms of iconic abnormality alone is intended. Among other things, dyslexia can entail problems in visual acuity, eye movement patterns, letter reversals, and poor memory for what has been read (Ingram, 1970; Shapiro, 1972; Vernon, 1958).

Perhaps a more direct example of the use of iconic memory to make discrete inputs seem continuous is found when viewing a movie. A motion picture film is a sequence of discrete frames which, if shown at the optimum speed, gives rise to the illusions of continuity and movement. Continuity is believed to result from iconic memory, which bridges the gap from one frame to the next so that a gap or dark screen is never seen between frames (Arnheim, 1974; Gregory, 1973; Rock, 1975). The perception of movement is more complex, and may involve integrating information over time in a manner analogous to that found during multiple fixations of a fixed display. Rock (1975), for example, believes that perceived movement in movies is a cognitive construction that is inferred from nonmoving, static displays. Similarly, Arnheim (1974) holds that continuous movement is based on the integration of momentary, static stimulation. As evidence, he cites a report from Teuber of a brain-damaged person who was apparently incapable of visual integration. This person saw a moving motorcycle as a series of overlapping, nonmoving circles (Arnheim, 1974, p. 387). These data lend some support to the contention of Sperling (1960) that our normal mode of seeing greatly resembles a sequence of very brief exposures and that iconic memory may serve a function in this process.

Alternative Conceptions

Not all psychologists would agree with the above views. At one extreme, Dick (1974) has argued that the iconic trace is the sole basis of information processing; the physical stimulus per se is redundant. Alternatively, Gibson (1966) has proposed that perception consists of picking up invariant information from a changing environment; it is not based on brief, static displays. Most recently, Neisser (1976) has written that iconic memory cannot play a major role in normal perception since it is not present during a visual fixation and must be destroyed by each new fixation. While not denying the existence of iconic memory or mental processes such as those outlined earlier in Figure 2.4, Neisser has proposed a different view of perception based on constructing anticipations of environmental events (Neisser, 1976). According to Neisser, schemata are anticipations based on past experience which direct our exploration of an object in the environment. The visual exploration, in turn, may change the anticipatory schema so that the whole perceptual process is capable of operating in a cyclic fashion. Accounting for expectancy or perceptual anticipations is, of course, possible within the general framework of the information processing approach shown in Figure 2.4. In subsequent chapters we will review how this may be accomplished. For the present, there is debate over the view that perception is based on static visual information obtained from brief visual fixations and that iconic memory plays a major role in normal perception.

A different view, which has yet to be mentioned, has been noted by Turvey (1977). Iconic memory may serve as a maintenance system between environmental stimulation and immediate memory such that it can hold information until the limit of immediate memory has been reached. This notion is consistent with earlier cited findings, which show the duration of iconic memory to be inversely related to the length of stimulus exposure (i.e, when stimulus exposures are brief, iconic traces are long; when stimulus exposures are long, iconic traces are brief). If iconic memory can serve as a maintenance system for processing information into immediate memory, then little maintenance would be needed for long exposures, as the external information would already have been processed and iconic storage would be superfluous. In this sense, iconic memory would serve as a means for producing maximal information processing within the limit of the immediate memory system.

SUMMARY

1. Following visual stimulation, there may be a brief visual memory trace called an icon.

2. The perceptual phenomenon of color mixture is obtained if two different colored lights are shown simultaneously or successively at a rapid rate. Successive color mixture is evidence for iconic memory.

3. A stationary object can be seen in its entirety from behind a rapidly moving slit which shows only a narrow band of the object at any specific moment in time. Object perception through a moving slit is additional evidence of iconic memory.

4. Iconic memory can last for 250 to 500 milliseconds or more for very brief stimulus exposures of 50 milliseconds, but have little or no duration for longer exposures of 500 milliseconds.

5. Under conditions of equivalent stimulus exposures, longer-lasting iconic traces are found with dark-adapted than with light-adapted viewers. This suggests that iconic traces are visual in nature.

6. Afterimages can be positive or negative. Positive afterimages and iconic traces cannot be easily discriminated.

7. There is some evidence that iconic memory has a peripheral locus in the retina of the eye. Other evidence suggests a more central locus. Both views may be correct.

8. Subjects can generally recall no more than four or five letters from a visual display shown for 50 milliseconds. This limit on performance was reviewed in terms of a limit on the capacity of iconic memory, the time for pattern recognition, and the capacity of immediate memory.

9. Use of the partial report procedure and a variable length exposure duration indicate that performance is limited because of immediate memory.

10. Viewers may selectively process information in iconic memory on the basis of physical cues such as color or location, but not categorical cues such as form or meaning.

11. Iconic memory can be disrupted by the presentation of a second visual stimulus, a mask, closely in time. The closer in time the mask is presented to the first stimulus, the poorer the performance.

12. There is evidence from reading and picture viewing that normal perception consists of many brief fixations over time. While firm conclusions cannot yet be drawn, iconic memory may serve to bridge the gap between successive, brief fixations. Iconic memory, however, cannot provide a means of integrating successive fixations into a single experience.

13. Differing conceptions of the role of iconic memory have been offered, but still await experimental verification.

CHAPTER THREE

Echoic Memory &
Auditory Experience

OBJECTIVES

1. To demonstrate the existence of a brief sensory memory in the auditory modality which corresponds to that found in the visual modality.
2. To specify the selected echoic memory properties of duration and locus.
3. To relate echoic memory to an information processing model of immediate memory recall.
4. To speculate on the possible function of echoic memory in speech perception.

INTRODUCTION

In the preceding chapter, we viewed visual perception as a time-extended process that could be facilitated by the presence of iconic memory. The nonimmediacy of perception can perhaps be more directly demonstrated in the case of audition, where stimuli are presented sequentially over time. Speech perception, for example, is based on a more or less continuous flow of information as words are spoken one after another. There is no sense of listening to a sentence and hearing it in its entirety at any moment in time. For this reason, a number of theorists have argued for the necessity of a brief memory trace in audition that corresponds to the iconic trace found in vision (e.g., Crowder, 1976; Massaro, 1975; Neisser, 1967). This trace, termed an *echo* by Neisser (1967), could extend the perceived duration of brief auditory stimuli so as to facilitate the recognition of sound patterns. In this chapter, we will review evidence on the existence of echoic memory, define some of its important properties, and speculate on its role in speech perception.

DEMONSTRATIONS OF ECHOIC MEMORY

The Modality Effect

As with iconic memory, the evidence for echoic memory is indirect, as the echo is inferred on the basis of performance differences in simple tasks. One such task involves a test of immediate memory; subjects are presented with a series of verbal stimuli and asked to recall as many of the items as possible in their correct serial order. The stimuli may be digits, letters, or words and are presented one after another at a rapid rate. The results typically show that when lists of up to nine itmes are used, subjects fairly accurately recall the first few items in their correct positions, but then they make frequent errors of order or omission, sometimes mixing up the order of items and sometimes forgetting one or more of the items.

The immediate recall task is relevant to sensory memory because different results are obtained when the stimuli are presented visually or auditorily. Figure 3.1 shows the results of an experiment by Corballis (1966) which compared the immediate recall of visually or auditorily presented stimuli. Each stimulus was a digit presented for 300 milliseconds with .5 to 1.9 seconds between stimuli. After the last digit in the nine-item series, the subjects were asked to recall the items orally in their correct order. Following trials for both modes of presentation, the number of errors was obtained for visually and auditorily presented items as a function of their serial position in each list. *Serial position* refers to an item's sequential location in a list of to-be-recalled items; the first item in the list occurred in Serial Position 1, and so on.

Corballis (1966) found that items which were presented earliest in the list were recalled accurately regardless of their mode of presentation. This high level of performance for the initial items is called a *primacy effect*; in later chapters, we will examine possible reasons for its occurrence. Similarly unaffected by presentation mo-

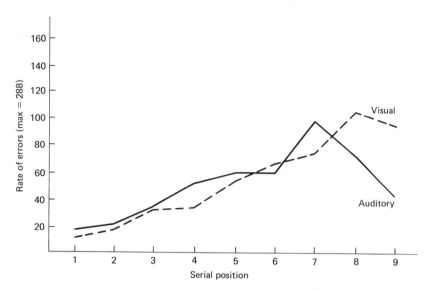

FIGURE 3.1. The number of errors in immediate recall for visually or auditorily presented digits as a function of their serial position in a nine-item list. An error was defined as a failure to recall a particular item. (Adapted from Corballis, 1966)

dality was the recall of items from the middle of the list. Although performance was much poorer on these items than on those preceding them in the list, Figure 3.1 shows that there was no effect of type of presentation. Effects of presentation modality were found only on the recall of items from the end of the list—in particular, the last item. While recall for both modes of presentation improved for the last item, the improvement was greater for the auditory mode. The overall improvement in performance for terminal items is called a *recency effect*, and the difference in recall between visual and auditory presentations is called a *modality effect*.

The results shown in Figure 3.1 may be viewed as evidence for echoic memory if each stimulus presentation gives rise to either an echoic or iconic memory trace, and echoic traces are more beneficial to item recall than iconic traces. Following Crowder and Morton (1969), each stimulus presentation is capable of producing a sensory memory while it is being interpreted. Recall performance varies across item serial positions because of forgetting, but the recall of the last item is superior following auditory presentation because its echoic trace either lasts longer (Crowder & Morton,

1969) or is more beneficial to performance than the corresponding iconic trace following visual presentation. Even though all of the list items are presumably identified, the subjects may selectively rehearse the last one or two items before they begin their ordered recall of the entire list (Crowder, 1976). This rehearsal of the terminal items may somehow strengthen those items for the recall that follows. If an echoic trace occurs just after the last item has been presented, it is likely that the subject will rehearse that item correctly and recall it correctly at the end of the list. By way of contrast, lists presented visually may produce an iconic trace of the last item, but the trace may be masked by succeeding visual experience or too brief in its duration to provide an increment in recall performance.

Assuming that the modality difference is based on the availability of echoic memory, it follows that the same pattern of results should be obtained for visually presented stimuli that are spoken orally by the subjects during list presentation. Differences between oral and silent rehearsal of visually presented items should affect only the recency portion of the list, and oral rehearsal should be superior to silent rehearsal. This is exactly what has been found by Murray (1966) and Conrad and Hull (1968). According to Crowder (1970), the crucial feature is that the subject's ears must be stimulated; it makes no difference whether the source of the auditory stimulation is the subject's voice or that of someone else reading the list during presentation. Regardless of the source, auditory stimulation is capable of producing an echoic memory which can facilitate recall.

The Suffix Effect

Another source of evidence for echoic memory in the immediate recall task is provided by studies of the suffix effect (Crowder, 1971a; Crowder & Morton, 1969). If we assume that the superior recall of the last item in an auditory list is due to the presence of an echoic memory trace, then the addition of a superfluous auditory stimulus, a suffix, at the end of the sequential list should disrupt the echoic trace and attenuate recall performance on the last item. This is a simple experiment to perform. Crowder (1971a) presented subjects with a sequential list of nine auditory digits at a rate of four digits per second. After the last item, subjects heard either an auditory tone or the digit "zero" spoken at the same rate as the preceding items. The function of the tone or zero was to inform the

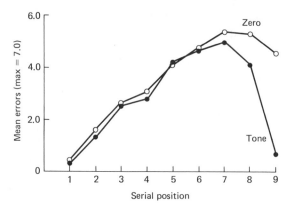

FIGURE 3.2. The average number of errors in immediate recall for auditorily presented digits for each serial position for lists followed by an auditory "zero" or tone suffix. An error was defined as a failure to recall a particular item in its correct location. (Adapted from Crowder, 1971a)

subjects to begin recalling the preceding nine items in their correct order; the subjects knew in advance that they did not have to recall the tone or zero suffix. Yet, as the results in Figure 3.2 demonstrate, a zero suffix had a deleterious effect upon recall performance for the last item, while the tone had little or no effect (Crowder, 1971a).

The disruption produced by the zero in Crowder's study, termed the *suffix effect*, has been examined in detail by Morton, Crowder, and Prussin (1971) and Crowder (1972). Among their findings are the following observations: (1) the closer in time the suffix is presented to the last item in the list, the greater the disruption in recall performance for that item; (2) the physical similarity between the suffix and the list items is of paramount importance; the greater the similarity, the greater the disruption; (3) the meaning of the verbal suffix is largely irrelevant; equivalent effects are found with digit, letter, or word suffixes provided they are spoken in the same voice as that used for the list. We may better understand the relationship between the suffix effect and echoic memory by considering each of the above findings in more detail.

First, the finding that the magnitude of the suffix effect is dependent upon its temporal proximity to the last list item closely resembles the finding in vision that iconic memory can be disrupted by visual masking. A similar interpretation can be offered for the suffix effect; the suffix item acts as an auditory masking stimulus and disrupts the echoic trace of the preceding item. Without the echoic trace, the recency effect is lost and the suffix effect is produced. As in visual masking, the effects of auditory masking are time-dependent; if sufficient time elapses between the presentation of the last list item and the suffix, no disruption occurs. Unlike visual processing, suffix disruption can be found over relatively long intervals of between 2 and 5 seconds (Crowder, 1976).

Second, according to Crowder and Morton (1969), information in echoic memory exists as a form of "precategorical auditory storage"; such information has not yet been categorized in terms beyond the physical qualities of sound. As with iconic traces in vision, echoic traces are sensitive to the physical aspects of subsequent stimulation. Suffixes which are physically similar in acoustic properties, although very different in terms of underlying meaning, should and do have comparable disruptive effects on the recall of the last list item.

Finally, for the reason just outlined, physically dissimilar suffixes which share the same meaning have diminished effects on recall performance. A list of items spoken by a male voice followed by a suffix spoken by a female voice will not show the degree of disruption on last item recall as the same list and suffix spoken by the same voice throughout. Subjects are apparently better able to segregate the list items from the suffix when physical cues such as sex of voice are present. Similar results of selectivity achieved on the basis of physical cues were reported previously for iconic memory.

The above findings are in accord with the assumption that an echoic trace is present in the auditory modality, which corresponds in many respects to the iconic trace found in the visual modality. Both can be considered as forms of sensory memory.

PROPERTIES OF ECHOIC MEMORY

Echoic Trace Duration

Although there is no compelling reason to expect the sensory memories from different modalities to correspond exactly in their temporal durations, if echoic memory is truly a sensory memory, we would expect it to be brief. How long does echoic memory last? We observed in the last chapter that questions of this type are difficult to answer directly. The duration of iconic memory is a function of many variables; echoic memory is no different. Estimates of echoic trace duration vary with the procedures adopted for testing. In this section, we will review four different tests of echoic memory. We will consider, in turn, the procedures of partial report, sampling, recognition masking, and simultaneity judgment.

PARTIAL REPORT PROCEDURE. The partial report procedure, used to test for the presence of echoic memory, is similar to the procedure used by Sperling (1960) to study iconic memory. In the visual task, subjects were presented with an array of letters and cued to recall a particular row of items after the brief display had terminated. The partial report cue was defined along a spatial dimension of top, middle, or bottom row in the letter array. A similar procedure has been adopted in tests of echoic memory with slight variations, owing to the auditory nature of the stimulus input and its necessarily sequential mode of presentation.

Moray, Bates, and Barnett (1965) simultaneously presented subjects with a series of up to four letters on each of four different loudspeakers placed in different spatial locations. In the whole report condition, the subjects attempted to recall as many of the sixteen different letters as possible. In the partial report condition, one of four different lights was shown to the subject one second after the last letter had been presented on each loudspeaker. The light served as a cue to indicate which loudspeaker input should be reported. In this manner, the different loudspeaker inputs corresponded to the letter array rows in the Sperling task, and the poststimulus light cue was analogous to Sperling's tone cue. To get an estimate of the total number of letters available one second after the last item on each loudspeaker had been presented, the number of letters reported under partial report was multiplied by four. The results showed the number of letters available for partial report to be greater than the number of letters recalled by whole report. These results are similar to those found by Sperling (1960) in his study of iconic memory, and they have been considered as evidence for echoic memory.

How long does the partial report advantage last? Moray et al. (1965) used only a one second partial report cue delay. To answer the question of echoic trace duration, it is necessary to vary the interval between the auditory stimulus and the partial report cue. In addition, it would be desirable to have evidence on the sensory basis of the hypothesized echoic trace. The studies of Sperling (1960) and von Wright (1972) showed that poststimulus cuing on a physical dimension such as stimulus location was far superior to cuing on the basis of a nonphysical dimension such as digit or letter stimulus categorization. These same findings should be obtained with the partial report procedure in tests of echoic memory.

Darwin, Turvey, and Crowder (1972) performed two experiments to determine the duration of echoic memory and whether poststimulus cuing differences would be evident between location and stimulus category cues. In the first experiment, Darwin et al. used a procedure similar to that used by Moray et al. (1965); they simultaneously presented subjects with a series of three auditory stimuli on three different loudspeakers placed in separate locations. The stimuli consisted of letters and digits, and both were presented in mixed fashion on each loudspeaker. All stimulus sequences were presented within a one second interval on each loudspeaker so that, over all loudspeakers, nine stimuli were presented within one second. Depending upon experimental conditions, the subjects were asked for either whole report of all of the items they could remember or partial report from just one loudspeaker based on a light cue which appeared 0, 1, 2 or 4 seconds after the last auditory stimulus on each loudspeaker. A different light cue corresponded to each of the different loudspeakers used for stimulus input.

The results of Darwin et al.'s first experiment are shown in Figure 3.3. The estimated number of items available for partial report was superior over all delays to the number of items recalled by whole report. This superiority was greatest immediately after stimulus presentation and markedly reduced with longer and longer delays. By four seconds, the magnitude of the difference between partial report and whole report was very small. These findings have been viewed as evidence for the presence of echoic memory, which lasts for approximately two seconds (Darwin et al., 1972).

In their second experiment, Darwin et al. used the same stimuli and temporal conditions as before, but now they compared whole report with partial report based on a poststimulus cue which corresponded to stimulus category. One of two lights was presented 0, 1, 2, or 4 seconds after stimulus presentation and indicated that subjects were to report either digit or letter stimuli exclusively. As in the first experiment, both types of stimuli were presented in mixed fashion on each of the three loudspeakers. If the previously observed partial report advantage was based on echoic memory, this advantage should be lost in the present experiment because the subjects were asked to select information on the basis of a nonphysical dimension. Although selection of nonphysical, categorical information from echoic memory should not be possible, the results showed

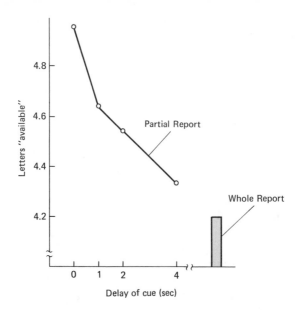

FIGURE 3.3. A comparison of the number of letters reported for whole report immediately after hearing nine items or available for partial report after a 0 to 4-second delay. (Adapted from Darwin, Turvey, and Crowder, 1972)

an advantage of partial report over whole report at each of the delay conditions tested. The positive outcome is contrary to expectations and implies that either echoic memory may contain some categorical information—a view that is inconsistent with the notion of echoic memory as precategorical acoustic storage (Crowder & Morton, 1969)—or the partial report advantage in this task is based on something besides echoic memory.

A similar finding was obtained by Massaro (1972b) in an experiment in which he presented subjects with two lists of four items at a rate of four items per second. The tests were composed of digits and letters, and they were simultaneously presented to the subjects' ears separately by means of earphones. In one condition, the subjects were cued by a poststimulus auditory tone to report all items from a particular ear, while in another condition they were cued to report only a particular stimulus type. Although there was no comparison of partial report to whole report, and no delay in the partial report cue, the results did show that partial report based on the stimulus category of digits or letters was slightly better than that based on the stimulus location of left or right ear. Once again, the advantage of a physical poststimulus cue over a nonphysical cue found with a partial report in studies of iconic memory was not observed in this auditory task.

If echoic memory is defined as a mode of precategorical acoustic storage that contains information which has not yet been identified, then clearly, the finding of a partial report advantage based on a nonphysical, categorical cue is inconsistent with this definition. Because of this conflicting result, the partial report studies do not seem capable of providing conclusive evidence of either the existence or the duration of echoic memory. It may be that all items are identified in this task even for the rapid presentation rates employed. A partial report advantage may be found simply because there are fewer items to recall for partial report than for whole report, and this advantage may decline over time due to forgetting in immediate memory (Massaro, 1975).

SAMPLING PROCEDURE. Another procedure in which echoic memory has been inferred can be found in studies which sample the subject's knowledge of presumably nonattended information. Erickson and Johnson (1964) had subjects read prose over a two-hour interval and presented a faint tone at randomly determined points during the reading. At intervals of 0 to 10 seconds after the tone, the reading light was turned off and the subjects were asked if they had recently heard a tone. On half of the occasions in which the light was turned off, no tone had been presented. The results showed that tone detection was better at short delays than at long delays. If the subjects were fully attending to the reading each time the tone was presented, these findings could be viewed as evidence for a tonal echoic memory, which is rapidly lost over a period of several seconds.

Glucksberg and Cowan (1970) also used the sampling procedure, but they employed tighter constraints on attention to try to ensure that the subjects were attending to the appropriate input. In this experiment, the subjects heard two continuous prose passages played separately in each ear at the same time. This technique, called dichotic stimulation, permitted attention to be directed to a single ear by requiring the subjects to shadow the message arriving at one ear by repeating it orally as it was heard. The message arriving at the other ear, which was to be ignored, had single digits inserted into it at irregular points in time. Thus, while the subjects were actively shadowing the message in one ear, a digit could be presented in the other ear. Glucksberg and Cowan interrupted the subjects at various intervals after a digit presentation and asked for digit recall. As evidence for echoic memory, they found that digit recall was approximately 25 percent if the subjects were interrupted less than one second after digit presentation and that performance declined quickly over 3 to 5 seconds.

Although a precise measure of echoic trace duration is not possible by this procedure, it is clear that the usefulness of the echoic trace does not exceed several seconds. One problem with studies which employ the sampling procedure is that they present a continuous flow of auditory information while simultaneously trying to measure the duration of an echoic trace from a nonattended source. This procedure appears to complicate the job of providing an estimate of echoic memory duration. A simpler task can be more direct.

RECOGNITION MASKING. One task which offers a simpler and more direct measure of echoic memory involves recognition masking. Massaro (1970; 1972a) has employed a masking procedure which appears to approximate closely Sperling's masking studies of iconic memory. Sperling found that if a visual mask followed a brief visual letter array very closely in time, subjects could not report any letters from the array. With increasing temporal intervals between the letter array and the mask, however, the number of letters reported increased up to the limit of immediate memory. The same general procedure was adopted by Massaro to observe effects of echoic memory. In one study, subjects were presented with one of two possible vowel sounds for twenty milliseconds followed by an auditory masking stimulus of the same loudness after an interval of 0 to 500 milliseconds. The subjects' task was to identify which of the two vowels had been presented.

The results of the Massaro vowel-identification study are shown in Figure 3.4. Vowel identification was a direct function of the length of the interval between the vowel and the mask; correct performance was near chance (50 percent) for very short intervals but improved to better than 95 percent for intervals of about 250 milliseconds. Massaro has argued that the improvement in performance must be based on the presence of an echoic memory produced by the initial vowel stimulus. This echoic trace apparently lasts for 250 milliseconds as vowel identification improves over this interval. The basis for the inference of echoic memory is the same as that used previously by Sperling: A brief stimulus which was not sufficient for

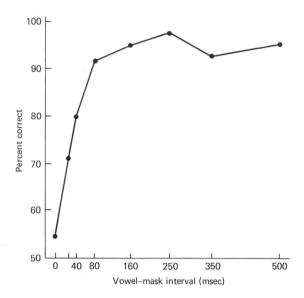

FIGURE 3.4. The percentage of correct vowel identifications as a function of the length of the blank interval between the brief vowel and auditory mask. (Adapted from Massaro, 1972a)

identification when followed directly by a mask became sufficient if a blank interval preceded the mask. These findings make sense if it is assumed that vowel identification continued over the blank interval on the basis of an echoic trace which lasted for at least a quarter of a second. The present data cannot determine whether echoic memory is available beyond this time span because vowel identification is near 100 percent and longer stimulus-mask intervals are not capable of showing any additional improvement. Nevertheless, other data from Massaro (1970; 1972a) show that performance did not improve for intervals longer than 250 milliseconds even though additional improvement was possible. These data suggest that the duration of echoic memory is approximately a quarter of a second, an estimate very similar to that observed under some conditions for iconic memory.

    In related studies, Massaro observed that stimulus recognition data like those shown in Figure 3.4 were found only if the stimulus and the mask were both presented auditorily. If a visual mask followed an auditory stimulus, no disruption occurred and auditory recognition of the first stimulus was maximally effective over all stimulus-mask intervals (Massaro & Kahn, 1973). This finding is reminiscent of the effects of stimulus similarity on the suffix effect noted previously by Morton et al. (1971) and Crowder (1972). Since the suffix effect has been viewed as a form of auditory masking (Crowder, 1976), this outcome is not surprising. Subsequent auditory inputs, if presented closely to those preceding them in time, may serve as masking stimuli and disrupt any available echoic traces.

SIMULTANEITY JUDGMENT. The last procedure to be considered is similar to that used by Haber and Standing (1970) to study the duration of iconic memory. Efron (1970) used the *simultaneity judgment* procedure to provide a measure of echoic trace duration. In this task, the subjects were presented with a tone for 10 to 500 milliseconds followed by a light flash for 5 milliseconds. Efron varied the time interval between the offset of the tone and the onset of the light flash; the subjects' task was to decide when the offset of the tone and the onset of the light occurred simultaneously. The results, shown in Figure 3.5, indicate that for brief tones, considerable time could elapse between tone offset and light onset and both occurrences could still be judged as simultaneous. For tone durations of 130 milliseconds or more, however, no time could occur between tone offset and light onset for a simultaneity judgment. These results indicate that tones presented for less than 130 milliseconds had a perceived duration which was longer than their actual duration. This difference is a measure of echoic memory duration, as simultaneity judgments were made on the basis of echoic trace offset and light onset. Tone durations of more than 130 milliseconds produced no echoic memory, as the simultaneity judgments were accurate; the perceived duration and actual duration of these tones were the same.

The relationship observed by Efron between tone length and echoic memory duration may be easily seen in Figure 3.6. The perceived duration of a tone of 130 milliseconds or less was always 130 milliseconds. This constant was based on the actual tone length and its echoic trace; the shorter the tone, the longer the echoic trace. This same relationship was found by Haber and Standing (1970) and can be seen in Figure 2.1; for dark-adapted subjects, the perceived duration of a light of 500 milliseconds or less always approximated 500 milliseconds. Although the duration of iconic memory is different from that reported for echoic memory

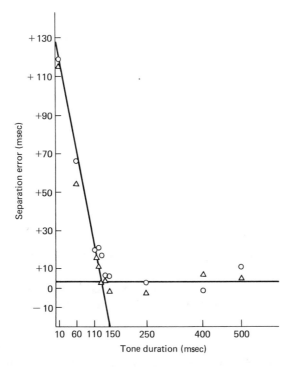

FIGURE 3.5. The degree of separation error that subjects made in simultaneity judgments between the offset of the auditory stimulus and the onset of the visual stimulus as a function of auditory stimulus duration. (Adapted from Efron, 1970)

by Efron (1970), the relationship between stimulus length and sensory memory is the same. For this reason, Efron's study provides compelling evidence for the existence of echoic memory and, once more, demonstrates that questions about duration are not answered simply. What was found for iconic memory has also been found for echoic memory: Both are brief, both vary inversely in their duration with the length of the actual stimulus, and both are capable of yielding different duration estimates under different conditions and procedures. As more is learned about the factors which affect sensory memory duration, greater specification will be obtained. The studies of Haber and Standing (1970) and Efron (1970) are important because they show that the duration of sensory memory, whether iconic or echoic, is not a constant unit of time.

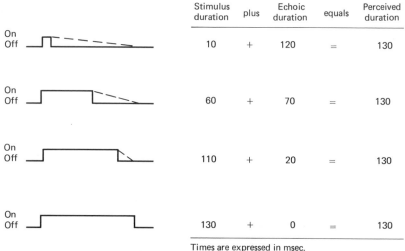

Times are expressed in msec.

FIGURE 3.6. The relationship between auditory stimulus duration and echoic trace duration observed by Efron (1970).

Locus of Echoic Memory

The locus of echoic memory is another area of potential convergence between echoic and iconic memory. Although peripheral and central components have been demonstrated for iconic memory, the limited research done on echoic memory (Hawkins, 1974; Massaro, 1970; Pisoni, 1973) suggests only that echoic memory has a central locus. Because tests of a peripheral locus of echoic memory have not been devised, the existence of a peripheral component in the cochlea of the ear remains a matter for speculation.

The evidence for a central locus of echoic memory is based on the finding that dichotic and binaural masking produce similar results. In his recognition masking studies, Massaro (1970) sometimes presented the brief auditory stimulus and subsequent masking noise to separate ears instead of presenting each input to both ears. When the stimulus and mask are presented to separate ears, the presentation is called *dichotic;* when the same items are presented to both ears, the presentation is termed *binaural.* Massaro found the same pattern of results for both dichotic and binaural presentations: Stimulus identification increased as the blank interval between the first stimulus and mask increased over 250 milliseconds. This suggests that the echoic trace was affected by the mask centrally where the auditory input from each ear was integrated. If echoic memory were only a peripheral phenomenon, a mask presented to a different peripheral receptor should have no effect upon performance at any of the stimulus-mask intervals. Since this was not observed, an explanation of echoic memory as a peripheral phenomenon is incorrect. Whether echoic memory is exclusively a central phenomenon remains to be determined.

ECHOIC MEMORY AND INFORMATION PROCESSING

Crowder and Morton (1969) have outlined a theoretical description of echoic memory in their model of precategorized acoustic storage. The model, which is shown in Figure 3.7, is drawn as an incomplete diagram of information processing in an immediate memory task. According to this model, incoming information may be presented to either the visual or auditory modalities. Pattern recognition processes, which attempt to identify each stimulus as it is presented, can proceed as long as the stimulus is physically present or persists on the basis of a sensory trace. For Crowder and Morton, a stimulus held in sensory memory prior to its identification exists in a precategorical state. This means that the subject does not yet know what has been seen or heard; the stimulus has not been identified. After a stimulus is identified in terms of its linguistic content, it can be articulated and maintained for recall by silent or vocal rehearsal. In Figure 3.7, silent rehearsal is shown as a small feedback loop between articulation and categorization; after each item is categorized, it can be articulated and then categorized and rearticulated again and again. The categorization-articulation loop corresponds to immediate memory and serves to maintain a limited amount of information until a response can be made.

A much larger feedback loop is shown in Figure 3.7 for categorized items that are articulated and then vocalized. An item, once vocalized, functions as a stimulus repetition; the subject reexperiences the same stimulus once more, but now in the subject's own voice. The effect is to restimulate the information processing sequence from the initial auditory registration of the information. Consequently, a regenerated echoic memory is possible for vocal rehearsal, but not for silent rehearsal. This assumption is based on the modality effect studies cited previously, which showed that auditory and visual presentations yielded comparable results if the stimuli were vocalized. More importantly, the vocal rehearsal feed-

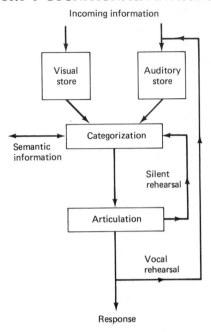

FIGURE 3.7. Crowder and Morton's model of information flow in immediate memory tasks. (Adapted from Crowder and Morton, 1969).

back loop suggests one major difference between echoic and iconic memory: Only echoic memory can be self-generated. There is no way for self-generation to occur in the visual modality; iconic memory can be produced only by external light sources. With this important exception noted, the Crowder and Morton model shown in Figure 3.7 may be seen as a more general model of information processing than that shown previously for iconic memory in Figure 2.4.

ECHOIC MEMORY AND SPEECH PERCEPTION

Each of the studies of immediate memory discussed at the beginning of the chapter have used the concept of echoic memory in considering the recency, modality, and suffix effects. One additional factor about these immediate memory effects must be considered because it has important consequences for the possible role of echoic memory in speech perception. The recency, modality, and suffix effects are found only for stimuli that differ in vowel sounds; if the stimuli share the same vowel sound, these effects are not found. This observation was made by Crowder (1971b) in a comparison of immediate memory for stimuli which differed in terms of vowel sounds such as *bah* and *bih* or stop consonant sounds such as *bah* and *dah*. The lists of speech sounds were presented visually, and the subjects were asked to read each stimulus either silently or orally as it appeared. The results showed that a modality effect was produced between the silent and overt rehearsal conditions only for the list composed of different vowel sounds; no modality effect was found between the two rehearsal conditions for the lists composed of different consonant sounds. In subsequent studies, Crowder (1971b) demonstrated that for same vowel, different consonant lists, there is no recency effect, no suffix effect for lists presented auditorily, and no modality effect for comparisons of auditory and visual presentation. If echoic memory is the basis for these effects in lists that differ in vowel sounds, Crowder's results imply that there is no echoic memory for stop consonant sounds. Echoic memory acts selectively on different speech signals (Crowder, 1971b; 1975).

Crowder's findings are relevant to speech perception because categorical differences between vowels and stop consonants have been found in speech perception research (e.g., Liberman, 1967; Pisoni & Tash, 1974; Studdert-Kennedy, 1970). Liberman et al., for example, presented subjects with a consonant-vowel syllable such as *du* and asked them to report what they heard as the duration of the vowel in the syllable was progressively shortened. Liberman et al. found that subjects continued to report hearing the complete syllable until the vowel was almost entirely eliminated. At that point, a nonspeech whistle rather than an isolated consonant was heard; the consonant could not be heard alone. In a different approach, Massaro (1974) has demonstrated that vowels and consonant-vowel or vowel-consonant syllables each take approximately 250 milliseconds for identification in studies of recognition masking. According to Massaro, these items may serve as the perceptual units in speech perception.

The studies which show that vowel sounds are important for both echoic memory and speech perception suggest that these two phenomena are closely related. What function might echoic memory serve in normal speech perception? Some theorists, such as Massaro (1975), assume that continuous speech is processed into an echoic or preperceptual auditory storage mode and that recognition processes operate on this sensory memory. For Massaro, speech perception involves a process of continuously identifying sound patterns on the basis of their acoustic features while they are briefly held in echoic memory. From his studies of recognition masking, Massaro has estimated that the duration of successive speech signals in echoic memory is approximately a quarter of a second. This duration corresponds closely with the time needed for accurate vowel, consonant-vowel, or vowel-consonant syllable recognition in the masking studies and the duration of syllables emitted in normal speech (Massaro, 1975).

As in the study of iconic memory, positions other than that advocated by Massaro are possible. It may be that echoic memory is not a necessary aspect of speech perception except in those instances where the speech signal is presented very briefly. The fact that echoic traces are found only with brief auditory stimuli (Efron, 1970) and that long-lasting echoic traces would be disruptive in any medium of continuous information input could be viewed as support for this view. Whether echoic memory can serve as a source of information about other speech qualities, such as pitch, stress, and intonation, remains a possibility. These qualities, Crowder (1976) notes, are conveyed by vowel sounds.

SUMMARY

1. Echoic memory can extend the perceived duration of brief auditory stimuli to facilitate the recognition of sound patterns.

2. The recall of the last item in an immediate recall test is greater following auditory presentation than visual presentation. This modality effect can also be found for visually presented items that are orally rehearsed.

3. Recall performance for the last item is reduced when it is followed by a redundant stimulus. This suffix effect is dependent upon the physical similarity of the suffix to the list items.

4. The presence of echoic memory is presumed to be responsible for the modality effect; the absence of echoic memory is presumed to be responsible for the suffix effect.

5. Measurement of echoic trace duration has been attempted by partial report, sampling, recognition masking, and simultaneity judgment procedures.

6. The partial report studies have not provided conclusive evidence for echoic memory because poststimulus cuing on a nonphysical categorical basis has been as good as cuing on a physical basis. This finding is contrary to the view of echoic memory as a mode of precategorical acoustic storage.

7. Although sampling nonattended auditory messages has provided evidence for the existence of echoic memory, this procedure is not well suited for measuring its duration.

8. Recognition masking studies have provided unambiguous evidence for an echoic trace that can serve as a basis for stimulus identification for approximately a quarter of a second.

9. The study of simultaneity judgment has found that the duration of echoic memory is inversely related to the length of the physical stimulus.

10. Echoic memory is similar to iconic memory in that both are brief, both vary inversely with stimulus length, and both yield different estimates of their duration with different procedures.

11. Evidence from dichotic masking studies implies that echoic memory has a central locus. Whether echoic memory may also have a peripheral locus has not been determined.

12. An information processing model of immediate recall has used echoic memory as a mode of precategorical acoustic storage which can maintain auditory information long enough to be categorized in terms of its linguistic content. Once information has been categorized, it can be articulated and rehearsed either silently or vocally.

13. Only vocal rehearsal can serve to regenerate echoic traces. The inability to regenerate iconic traces constitutes a major difference between echoic and iconic memory.

14. The modality and suffix effects are found only for lists composed of different vowel sounds. Comparable effects are not found if the stimuli differ only in stop consonant sounds.

15. Categorical differences between vowels and stop consonants have also been found in speech perception research.

16. Since vowel sounds are important for echoic memory and speech perception, theorists have speculated on the possible function of echoic memory in speech perception.

17. One possibility is that continuous speech is processed into

echoic memory, and speech perception is based on the recognition of sound patterns held in echoic memory.

18. Another possibility is that echoic memory serves as a means of maintaining information about qualities such as pitch, stress, and intonation as these qualities are conveyed in vowel sounds.

CHAPTER FOUR

Selective Attention & Immediate Memory

OBJECTIVES

1. To review the origin, necessity, and bases of selective attention.
2. To consider several examples of selectivity failure.
3. To examine the attentional demands of encoding, rehearsal, and recall processes and to consider the effects of practice.
4. To consider immediate memory as a selective attention process.
5. To discuss forgetting in terms of limited attentional capacity.

INTRODUCTION

The issue of information selectivity seems so obvious that we generally take it for granted. Consider the common example of the cocktail party, first noted by Cherry (1953). At a typical party, a large number of people are gathered in a room, standing and talking to one another in small groups. Many conversations are going on at the same time. Yet, while we may hear bits and pieces of many of these conversations, generally we have little trouble following and participating in a particular conversation. This simple example illustrates the selective quality of attention. At times, however, we can be distracted by something we overhear in another conversation; perhaps we have heard our name mentioned or that of someone important to us, and we turn to hear what is being said. Attention, although selective, is often subject to distraction. The principles of selective attention and the causes of distraction are the subjects of the first part of this chapter.

SELECTIVE ATTENTION

Origins of Selectivity

A consideration of the origins of selectivity is a good place to begin a discussion of attention. Neonate research has sought to determine if selectivity is an innate or an acquired process. The studies to be reviewed indicate that shortly after birth, infants are capable of demonstrating stimulus preferences based on complexity or novelty; the more complex or novel the stimulus, the more frequently it is selected as the object of attention.

Fantz (1963) simultaneously presented infants who ranged in age from ten hours to five days with an array of visual stimuli and recorded the amount of time the infants looked at each stimulus. The stimuli consisted of a white disc, a yellow disc, a disc composed of newsprint, a disc composed of concentric circles, and a disc which contained a schematic face. This set of stimuli was shown several times, and each time the ordering of the stimuli was varied from left to right so that a particular stimulus was never repeated in the same location. Fantz found that the viewing time for each stimulus varied directly with its complexity; the blank white disc was viewed least often, while the face was viewed most often. Visual selectivity, when measured by viewing time, was present in these infants shortly after birth.

Viewing time has also been used by Weizmann, Cohen, and Pratt (1971) as an index of selectivity in a test of novelty preference. They presented neonates with a floral arrangement suspended above a crib for 30 minutes each day for one month. After one month, Weizmann et al. presented the flowers and a second stimulus object which the infants had not seen before. They found that the infants selected the novel stimulus for more viewing than the familiar stimulus.

A similar preference for novelty was found in the auditory

modality by Eimas, Siqueland, Jusczyk, and Vigorito (1971) in a study which demonstrated that one-month-old infants could distinguish between different consonant sounds. Using the sucking response, which all infants could perform, Eimas et al. presented a *buh* sound whenever an infant sucked on a dry nipple. They found that over a period of several minutes, the rate of sucking on the dry nipple increased when it was followed by the sound. After several minutes of sucking and hearing the same sound, the response habituated and the rate of sucking dropped back to its previous level; the infants may have reduced sucking because they were tired of hearing *buhs*. Eimas et al. tested this possibility by dividing the infants into two groups; one group continued to hear a *buh* sound whenever it sucked on the nipple, while the other group heard a *puh* sound. The results showed that sucking decreased for those infants still presented with *buhs* but increased for those infants hearing *puhs*. A high rate of response returned when a novel stimulus—a *puh*—was introduced.

Collectively, the neonate research indicates that infants can demonstrate selective attention on the basis of different stimulus dimensions in different sensory modalities. These findings suggest that the ability to act selectively is an innate process of mind.

Necessity of Selectivity

The fact that selectivity is manifest across different sensory modalities indicates that there is a limit to attentional capacity. Informally, we make this observation every day. There are some activities that can be done simultaneously and others that can only be done alone. Driving and talking can usually be done at the same time, but typing and talking can be extremely difficult. Since typing and talking involve different sensory modalities and response modes, the interference between the two activities implies that there is a limit to attentional capacity and that the limit is central rather than peripheral. Posner and Keele (1970) discuss attentional capacity as a limitation of space. Since typing and talking interfere with each other, some aspect of each may be thought of as demanding processing space. For driving and talking, there is no interference because one of the tasks makes little demand on space. Situations may change, however; driving on an open highway may require minimal processing space, but driving in heavy traffic may require considerable space and thereby inhibit conversation. For this reason, we may think of attention as a limited resource; attention is selective so that we may function as efficiently as possible within its limits.

Experimental evidence on the central locus of limited attentional capacity is available in studies of stimulus detection. In one study, Shiffrin, Craig, and Cohen (1973) compared simultaneous detection of a tactile stimulus from three possible locations with sequential detection of a stimulus in each location separately. Simply comparing detection in three locations with one location might show poorer performance in the multilocation condition because three decisions are harder to make than one. Shiffrin et al.'s procedure equates the number of decisions that must be made in each condition. Vibrators were attached to the palm of the right hand, the tip of the left index finger, and the left forearm. If attentional capacity is limited in the peripheral receptors, then simultaneously monitoring three areas for a faint vibration should be more demanding and less accurate than sequentially monitoring one area at a time. Alternatively, if attentional capacity is limited centrally, performance should be equivalent for both conditions since each requires the detection of a single event. Shiffrin et al. found that the subjects were equally good at vibration detection under both conditions.

In a second study, Shiffrin and Grantham (1974) compared stimulus detection performance in different sensory modalities to determine if subjects could simultaneously monitor three modalities for a stimulus as effectively as they could monitor only one modality at a time. The results showed that the subjects could detect the occurrence of a visual, auditory, or tactile stimulus while simultaneously monitoring each of these three modalities as readily as when they were sequentially monitoring each modality in turn. Once again, there was no evidence of a peripheral limit in attentional capacity. Selectivity is necessary because attentional capacity is limited, but selectivity is not achieved at the level of the sensory receptors. Central processes are responsible for selective attention.

Bases of Selectivity

DEVELOPMENT OF THE FILTER MODEL. Research on the bases of selectivity began with the publication of Cherry's (1953) studies of dichotic speech perception. Cherry simultaneously presented different messages to each ear and required subjects to shadow one of the messages by repeating it orally as it was heard. After the messages were completed, the subjects were asked questions about the information presented to the nonattended ear. The subjects could tell whether a voice was present, whether the voice changed from a male to a female speaker, and whether nonspeech signals such as whistles were present in the nonshadowed material. They could not report the contents of the nonshadowed message, the language, whether the language changed during the message, or whether the nonshadowed message contained grammatically correct speech or nonsense speech. These results indicate that the subjects were aware of gross physical aspects for both the shadowed and non-shadowed messages, but they were aware of meaningful aspects for only the shadowed material. Selectivity appears to have been based on the physical characteristics of the stimuli. All input was attended to at a low level of physical analysis; that which conformed to the constraints of the shadowed message was fully recognized, while other material was rejected as irrelevant.

Essentially the same conclusion was reached by Broadbent (1958). He presented digit strings dichotically at a fast rate and found that subjects reported the digits by ear rather than by their temporal order of arrival. If the subjects simultaneously heard the sequence 6-9-3 in one ear and 4-2-5 in the other ear, the subjects organized their recall by recalling all the digits from one ear first, then one or two digits from the other ear; they did not report the digits in pairs as they were heard. Broadbent formulated an early model of attention which held that the limited capacity system for processing environmental stimulation is protected by a selective filter which serves to screen irrelevant information on the basis of physical qualities. Physical qualities that could be used for selecting information include the intensity, pitch, and spatial localization of sounds (Broadbent, 1958). Information is analyzed in terms of these physical dimensions and selected if it conforms in the desired respects. Subjects have information about the physical qualities of nonshadowed messages in Cherry's research because these differences provide the basis for information selection.

Gray and Wedderburn (1960), however, forced a modification of this position; they showed that information could be selected on the basis of meaning. Using a procedure similar to that used by Broadbent, they presented words and digits dichotically across the two ears. The subjects may have heard the stimulus sequence MICE-2-CHEESE in one ear and 6-EAT-9 in the other ear. When asked to recall what they had heard, the subjects frequently recalled the stimuli in meaningful units (e.g., MICE EAT CHEESE). If selectivity is based entirely on physical cues, such as sound localization, the subjects might have been expected to report the digit-word sequences by ear, as Broadbent had found with digits. The fact that integrated sequences were recalled indicates that selectivity can be based on the meaning of the information.

Treisman (1964) extended Broadbent's model of attention to include selection based on physical and meaningful features. Instead of the single selective filter proposed by Broadbent, Treisman proposed a hierarchy of filters to examine incoming information. All stimuli are first analyzed on a physical basis; those stimuli which have the appropriate physical dimensions receive further processing and are analyzed for meaning, while all others are simply attenuated. When selection cannot be made in terms of physical differences, as in the case of two people speaking in the same voice and intensity from the same location, selection between the messages is possible by analyzing the content of each message in terms of meaning. According to Treisman, selection is made during the analysis of the competing messages; one gets selected as relevant, the other gets attenuated as irrelevant or less relevant. In the case of speech, the grammatical structure of the language facilitates this ongoing process, as it limits the type of words that may occur at different points in a sentence. Similar views, which stress the importance of meaning for selective attention, have been offered by Deutsch and Deutsch (1963) and Norman (1968).

A discussion of the filter approach to selecive attention is not complete without noting that selection on the basis of physical or meaningful relevance to previous stimulus input is not the only means available. Moray (1959) found that subjects occasionally stopped shadowing in a dichotic listening task when their names were presented in the nonshadowed material. This result suggests that selection based on personal meaningfulness is possible. Similarly, the waking of a parent to the cry of a newborn child, but not to the sound of a passing vehicle, suggests the importance of personal meaningfulness. Obviously, a baby's cry could not be considered to be relevant to the previous activity of the sleeping parent; allowance must be made for selection based on personally meaningful stimuli, as they may have survival value for the person or the species. How this form of selectivity is accomplished is not known.

AN ALTERNATIVE TO FILTERING. Hochberg (1970b) and Neisser (1967; 1976) have presented an alternative to the filter models of Broadbent and Treisman. Instead of viewing selective attention as a negative process of rejecting unwanted information, they see selective attention as a postive choice. The object of attention is not that which remains after all else has been removed; it is that which is selected from all else which remains. In a study of selective looking, Neisser and Becklen (1975) presented subjects with two visual displays that were superimposed. One display consisted of a ball toss game and the other of a hand slap game. In a situation analogous to that of looking out of a window at dusk, when one can see either the reflection of the room or the outdoor scene, Neisser and Becklen found that subjects could attend to either visual display at will. These results have been used to argue against a filter model of selective attention because long practice should be necessary to develop a filter for eliminating undesired signals. Since superimposed visual displays are rarely encountered, the opportunity for prior practice is negligible, and subjects should have experienced difficulty in selectively attending to one display over the other if the filter model were correct (Neisser & Becklen, 1975).

Neisser and Becklen hold that selective attention is based on picking up certain information and leaving the rest unused. In the superimposed displays, the ball toss and hand slap games were differentiated by their own intrinsic rules. Subjects could visually follow either game by picking up its continuous and coherent motion, which could then guide further information pickup. Unusual events, which were occasionally inserted into the nonattended game, generally passed unnoticed. One might argue that these events went unnoticed not because the subjects failed to pick them up but because they were seen with less distinct peripheral vision; sharp foveal vision was used for viewing the attended game. The eye movement data of Yarbus (1967) do demonstrate that the eyes focus on different aspects of a scene when different information is requested. But eye movements cannot be the basis for selective looking; eye movements are a consequence of attention, not a cause. Without a plan for guidance, the eye movement records would show a haphazard pattern and selective looking would not be possible. Eye movements are attempts to pick up information that has been determined by the structure of the information being examined. That structure is used to formulate new expectancies and to guide the pickup of new information (Neisser & Becklen, 1975). This position, outlined in greater detail by Neisser (1976), is similar to Hochberg's view of selective attention in speech perception and reading (Hochberg, 1970b). Selective attention is seen as an intrinsic part of the perceptual process, not an additional aspect requiring filtering mechanisms for a satisfactory explanation.

Failures of Selectivity

The example of hearing your name in a nonshadowed message (Moray, 1959) illustrates a failure of selectivity, as the task required subjects to attend to the shadowed message. The name was a distracting stimulus which directed attention away from the primary message. Distractability is an essential part of the attentional system; it allows the limited capacity to be redirected to new sources of stimulation as the need arises. A loud, unexpected noise, for example, will always be distracting and command attention. A loud noise might imply danger, and it would be important for signals of this type to be noted quickly so that appropriate action might be taken.

RESPONSE COMPETITION. Not all types of distraction can be viewed in terms of survival value; some forms are acquired through experience. Stroop (1935) devised a color naming task in which subjects were shown an array of 100 color stimuli. The array could contain 100 color names printed in black ink, 100 color names printed in interfering colors—such as the word RED printed in blue ink—or simply 100 color chips. In some conditions, the subjects were required to read the names of the 100 words as quickly as possible. In other conditions, the subjects were asked to ignore the words and name the 100 colors as quickly as possible. In each array, the 100 stimulus items were obtained by using a sample of colors or their names several times. Response times for the different arrays and instructions are shown in Figure 4.1. Reading 100 color names printed in interfering colors was just as fast as reading the same names printed in black ink. Interfering colors did not slow down the reading rate. In the other comparisons, significant impairments were found. Naming 100 color chips took longer than reading the equivalent number of color names, as the subjects had to determine the name for each chip before they could report it. Most disruptive, however, was the task of naming the colors when they spelled interfering color words. The average time for this task was almost double that of color naming based on color chips, and nearly three times that based on simply reading the colored words.

Why is an array of color names printed in interfering colors so easy to process when subjects are required to read the words, but so difficult to process when they are required to name the colors? Reading color names printed in black ink is faster than naming color chips, so it is clear that reading is faster than naming. This

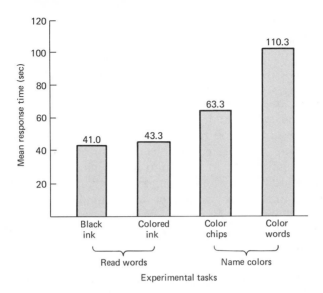

FIGURE 4.1. *Mean response times for reading or naming 100 words or colors. (Adapted from Stroop, 1935)*

explains why reading color names when they are printed in interfering colors is not distracting; before the ink color has been recognized, the word has already been identified. In the disruptive condition, subjects must name the ink color and try not to read the word. But because it is easier to read words than name color chips (Gholson & Hohle, 1968; Hock & Egeth, 1970), the subjects have two relevant responses in each instance by the time they have determined the name of a color: the name of the word and the name of the ink color. The result is distraction through response competition (Egeth, Blecker, & Kamlet, 1969). The subjects must continually remember to name the color and not the word. Selectivity is difficult in this task because past experience has made both aspects of the colored stimulus seem relevant. Even though subjects may wish to attend only to the color of the ink, after a lifetime of reading, they cannot ignore other meaningful attributes of an attended object or message (Kahneman, 1973). When both sources provide color name information, response competition is produced.

EPILEPSY. An extreme form of selectivity failure is found in cases of grand mal and petit mal epilepsy (Gastaut & Fischer-Williams,

1959; Goldensohn, 1965). These disorders are produced by distur-bances in the electrical activity of the brain. Grand mal epilepsy, which is the most common type, is characterized by a severe attack which renders the person unconscious and produces convulsive muscular activity. These attacks may last a minute or more and occur several times a year or several times a day. Because grand mal seizures can be controlled by medication, they are rarely seen today.

More directly related to the problem of selective attention is petit mal epilepsy. Unlike grand mal seizures, petit mal attacks consist of a relatively short reduction in consciousness, rather than a complete loss. The person appears to be daydreaming, but unlike a daydream, the person cannot be interrupted. The person may speak, but such speech is usually repetitious and unrelated to what is currently happening. Petit mal attacks may last from 10 to 40 seconds and may occur several times per week or more than 100 times per day. For reasons as yet unknown, this form of epilepsy, which is found primarily in children and is controllable by medica-tion, is outgrown as children approach adulthood. Obviously, this failure of selective attention is not the result of motivational factors, as is the case with daydreaming; this failure is physiologically de-termined. The petit mal attack represents a complete breakdown of the selective attention system since the child is impervious to events in the environment. Communication is not acknowledged, and there is no memory of any event that occurs during the trance-like state.

ATTENTIONAL DEMANDS OF COGNITIVE PROCESSES

If selective attention is a consequence of a limited-capacity attentional system, it is important to know what aspects of a task make demands upon such a system. Following Kerr (1973), we will consider the attentional demands of encoding, rehearsal, and recall processes and examine the effects of practice.

Encoding Processes

Encoding may be defined as the process of interpreting a stimulus and storing a representation of that interpretation in mem-ory. The act of reading, for example, requires the interpretation of visual forms as the eyes move across a page. A number of studies have suggested that simple stimuli such as letters may be encoded automatically with no demands on attentional capacity (e.g., Eriksen & Spenser, 1969; LaBerge & Samuels, 1974; Posner & Boies, 1971; Shiffrin & Gardner, 1972). As an example, the research of Posner and Boies will be reviewed as representative of studies of the attentional demands of stimulus encoding.

Posner and Boies (1971) used a letter-matching task in which subjects were shown two letters sequentially and asked to decide if they were the same (e.g., A-A) or different (e.g., A-B). During a trial, the subjects were given a brief warning signal followed a half second later by the first letter, which remained on the display screen for one second. After this interval, the first letter was removed and a second letter was shown. The subjects pressed one button with their right index finger if the two letters were the same or another button with their right middle finger if the letters were different. Since the task was a simple perceptual comparison task, speed of response was the primary performance measure.

On half of the trials the subjects had an additional task to perform. A noise could be presented to the left ear at any one of eight possible locations during a particular trial. The noise could occur before the trial warning signal, after the warning signal, at four possible times after the first letter was shown, or at two possible times after the second letter was shown. Whenever the noise was presented, the subjects had to press a third button with their left index finger. The subjects were told that the letter-matching task was primary, but responses to the noise, as well as to the letter stimuli, should be made as quickly as possible.

Figure 4.2 shows response times on the secondary task of noise detection for each of the eight possible locations within a trial. Noise detection times decreased over the first five locations, then sharply increased over the next two locations, and finally dropped again on the last location. Posner and Boies attributed the drop in noise detection time following the warning signal to an increase in the subjects' preparation. This preparation was general, and the processing of all stimuli, including the noise, was facilitated. Most important for the study of attentional demands of letter encoding are the detection times for noises presented immediately after the presentation of the first letter. Noise detection times did not increase over these locations, demonstrating that the encoding of the first letter did not interfere with the processing of the noise. According to Posner and Boies, this finding suggests that letter encoding does not require attentional capacity. The increase in noise detection times for later locations just before or after the presenta-

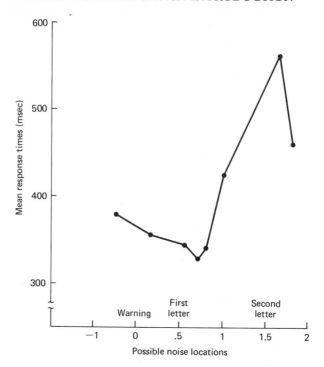

FIGURE 4.2. Mean response times for the secondary task of noise detection as a function of the location of the noise during trials of perceptual letter matching. (Adapted from Posner and Boies, 1971)

tion of the second letter was attributed, in part, to maintaining the first stimulus and then comparing it to the second stimulus. These activities, since they demand attentional capacity, leave less for the noise-detection task, so its response times become longer.

Rehearsal Processes

Essentially the same secondary task procedure used by Posner and Boies (1971) to study the attentional demands of encoding was used by Stanners, Meunier, and Headley (1969) to study the demands of rehearsal. Subjects were given three sets of either easy-to-pronounce (e.g., *bal, fus, tiv*) or difficult-to-pronounce (e.g., *abl, drs, quw*) letter triads to remember. The triads were followed by a 7-second rehearsal interval and a recall cue. The delayed recall task was distinguished by the presence of a secondary buzzer-detection task which occurred during the rehearsal interval. At 1, 2, 4, or 6 seconds after the letters were shown, a buzzer was sounded and the subjects had to make a speeded manual response to note its occurrence.

If attentional demands of rehearsal are indexed by the degree of interference produced on a secondary response, the following conclusions may be drawn from the buzzer-detection times in Figure 4.3: Attempting to remember letter triads interfered substantially with buzzer detection when compared to a control condition of only buzzer detection; the interference was greater for difficult-to-pronounce triads than for easy-to-pronounce triads; and the amount of interference decreased as the interval between the presentation of the letter triads and the buzzer increased. These results suggest that interference was produced when subjects were trying to remember the letter triads; rehearsal processes demand attentional capacity and less capacity is left for buzzer detection. Difficult-to-pronounce letter triads require more attention than easy-to-pronounce triads, and the attentional demands for both stimulus forms decrease as the amount of rehearsal increases. Although attentional capacity may not be needed for the encoding of letter stimuli, the results of Stanners et al. strongly indicate that attention is needed for letter rehearsal. A similar conclusion was reached by Shulman and Greenberg (1971), who found that retaining information for delayed recall was an active, attention-consuming process.

Recall Processes

Of the several processes considered, recall seems to require the most attention; it produces the largest amount of interference on a secondary detection task (e.g., Johnston, Wagstaff, & Griffith, 1972; Trumbo & Milone, 1971). Johnston et al. (1972) read subjects a list of six words followed by a cued recall test of one word. The category name SPORT, for example, might be used as a recall cue for the list word GOLF. Either during the presentation of the list words or after the recall cue, a light could change in brightness. When this occurred, the subjects were required to press a button as quickly as possible. Compared to a control condition in which subjects responded only to brightness changes, the results showed that the memory task produced significant interference in response times for brightness change detection. The interference effect was greater during item recall than during list presentation, and it de-

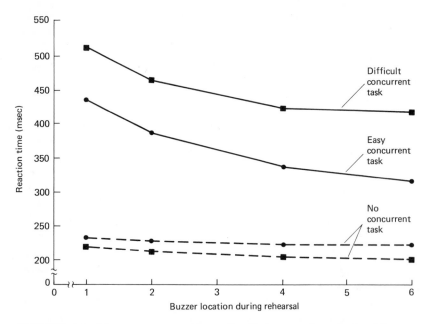

FIGURE 4.3. Mean response times for the secondary task of buzzer detection as a function of buzzer location during the rehearsal interval and the pronunciation difficulty of the concurrently held letter stimuli. (Adapted from Stanners, Meunier, and Headley, 1969)

creased over successive trials. These data indicate that recall initially requires considerable attentional capacity, but, with practice, the demands on capacity are reduced.

Practice and Automaticity

We noted earlier that many people find it difficult to type and talk simultaneously. According to Shaffer (1975), this is not true of skilled typists. Shaffer found that secretaries could type while simultaneously shadowing different verbal material or reciting nursery rhymes from memory. Many hours of typing practice permit this skill to be performed with reduced demands upon attention. How does practice reduce attentional demands? LaBerge and Samuels (1974) discuss human performance in terms of accuracy and automaticity. For LaBerge and Samuels, accuracy and automaticity represent different levels of performance. At the level of accuracy, performance may be perfect, but it may still make demands upon attentional capacity. At the level of automaticity, performance no longer requires attention. Continued practice serves to produce performance automaticity.

Bachrach's (1970) study of SCUBA-diving accidents reveals that tragic consequences are possible when lifesaving routines are not automatized. One routine regularly taught is that the weight belt worn by divers should be discarded in the event of trouble underwater. A weight belt can be an additional hindrance to reaching either safety or fresh air at the surface. Yet, in a number of diving accidents, divers were found still wearing their weight belt. In their panic to reach the surface, they apparently did not think of removing it.

The problem faced by SCUBA divers and all other people in potentially dangerous situations is that under conditions of stress, responses must be made automatically; other factors will make strong demands upon attention so that simpler things, such as removing a weight belt, will not be considered. These lifesaving responses will be made only if they have been practiced to the point where they are overlearned and can be performed automatically. The use of fire drills in grammer schools is a step in this direction. Children are given practice in exiting a building in a quiet and orderly manner to avoid the effects of panic which could negate the previously learned escape routines. We may conclude, from the LaBerge and Samuels study, that although children may function perfectly during a fire drill, unless the activity is practiced to the point of being overlearned, automaticity is not likely and a panic might still occur during a fire. Given the limited fire drill practice that most children receive, the practice may be of little value in an emergency. By most accounts, many hours of practice are necessary to reduce the attentional demands of different responses.

IMMEDIATE MEMORY

Attention as a Limited Resource

We found earlier that the attentional demands of different cognitive processes vary when measured in terms of performance on a secondary task. Letter encoding produced no measurable demands upon attention, while rehearsal and recall produced sizable demands. These findings led to the view that perceptual analyses may be performed automatically, while higher-level operations may require considerable attention. An early caution against this interpre-

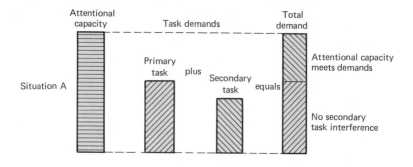

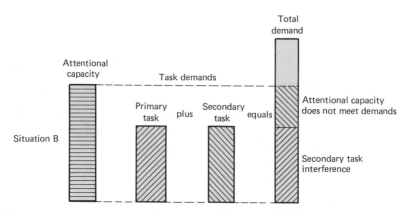

FIGURE 4.4. A hypothetical outline of attentional capacity and the processing demands of various tasks. Secondary task interference is produced whenever the limited attentional resources are exceeded.

tation was raised by Kerr (1973) and later by Norman and Bobrow (1975). They reported that the lack of measurable interference effects on a secondary task is not sufficient evidence to conclude that the primary task could be performed without attention. Assuming a limited attentional capacity, enough capacity may remain for maximal processing of a secondary task even though a primary task is performed simultaneously. Figure 4.4 shows how encoding and rehearsal might both require attentional capacity—yet, since rehearsal requires more capacity, only the rehearsal condition would show secondary task interference.

The view which holds that all processing makes attentional demands on limited resources (Norman & Bobrow, 1975) is very different from the earlier view of attention-free processing. How performance is affected depends upon which process is viewed as primary and which as secondary, and how much of the limited resources are demanded by each task. In general, performance on a secondary task depends on the available resources after the capacity needed for a primary task has been allocated. Automaticity would reduce the attentional demands of either a primary or secondary task through practice so that less attention would be required and less secondary task interference produced. All cognitive processes would thus require attention, but the amount would vary with the priorities of the moment and the degree of performer practice.

If we think of attention as a limited resource, what is the relationship between selective attention and immediate memory? One possibility is that selective attention determines the contents and duration of immediate memory. This view assumes that selective attention and immediate memory are different; *selective attention is a process which puts information into an immediate memory structure*.

An alternative possibility is that selective attention and immediate memory are the same process. Selective attention does not put information into immediate memory; selective attention, by determining the objects of attention, *is* immediate memory. Mental rehearsal, for example, could be seen as selectively attending to a series of stimuli in a cyclic pattern. Unless necessary, we do not want to postulate a separate limited-capacity attentional system which produces selective attention and another limited-capacity immediate memory structure which produces limited recall. One limited attentional process may be capable of determining performance on tasks done simultaneously and tests of immediate memory. If this view of selective attention and immediate memory is correct, both the capacity and the duration of immediate memory should vary directly with the demands made upon the limited attentional resources. For this reason, we will review immediate memory in terms of capacity, duration, and forgetting.

Capacity

Is the capacity of immediate memory a fixed quantity, as the structural position would hold, or is the capacity determined by the demands of the task up to the limit of the attentional resources? Data collected over many years suggest that the view of immediate memory as a fixed capacity structure is incorrect. Jacobs (1887) studied immediate memory by determining the maximum number of stimuli that could be recalled in perfect order by school children of different ages. Jacobs found that the span for immediate recall was higher for digits than letters, increased with student age, and was highest for the best students in the class.

Guilford and Dallenbach (1925) extended the research on memory span by defining the span as the maximum length of a stimulus series that could be perfectly recalled 50 percent of the time. Guilford and Dallenbach found that the span of immediate recall varied with the type of stimuli used. A memory span of 7.58 was obtained for digits, 7.21 for letter consonants, and 5.86 for words. While these estimates will vary with the cutoff point used to determine the span, the finding of a fixed capacity limit has not been strictly observed for different classes of stimuli.

Miller (1956), however, argued that the span of immediate memory was fixed within a limit of seven plus or minus two chunks. Although a number of investigators have attempted to define a chunk in terms of stimulus learning rates (Simon, 1974) or forgetting rates (Melton, 1963), an exact definition has never been provided. For our purposes, we note that a chunk functions as a single stimulus; seven letter consonants and seven words are both seven chunks. In a test of immediate recall, the number of letters reported would be greater if seven words were used as stimuli than if seven letter consonants were used. But we would not conclude that the memory span was greater for word stimuli than for letter stimuli since the subjects treat words as whole units. The appropriate unit of analysis in immediate memory is in the number of chunks, and this number is slightly smaller for words than for letters.

The importance of information chunking is readily seen in De-Groot's (1965; 1966) studies of immediate memory in chess players. In one task, DeGroot compared the memory spans of novice and master chess players by allowing each to look at a chess game in progress for 5 seconds and then asking each to attempt to reproduce all of the pieces on a blank chess board. The masters could reproduce an entire chess board almost perfectly, while the novices seldom got more than half of the pieces in their correct location. When the same task was repeated with a chess board composed of randomly arranged pieces, the number of pieces accurately reproduced by the masters deteriorated to the level of the novices. These data indicate that the difference between the masters and the novices when reproducing actual chess games is not due to a difference in the immediate memory span. It appears to be based on a difference in the manner of observing the board. With an actual game, chess masters see the board in terms of clusters of action; there are relationships among specific pieces that enable the entire collection to be grouped into meaningful units or chunks. Novices, however, do not have the backlog of experience to see these relationships quickly; they experience the board as a collection of many unrelated pieces. According to Chase and Simon (1973), the difference between masters and novices is the size of the immediate memory chunk. With the same number of chunks, masters can reproduce more pieces because their chunks contain more information.

The studies of memory span and chunking may be viewed as attempts to measure immediate memory capacity under optimal conditions. The various estimates of capacity reflect an upper limit because there were no competing demands upon attention. If immediate memory is a selective attention process, measures of memory span should vary with attentional demands. The data of Baddeley, Thomson, and Buchanon (1975) offer support for this position. In a test of immediate recall, Baddeley et al. read lists composed of five words and manipulated the number of syllables per word in different lists over a range of one to five syllables per word. Contrary to the fixed capacity view, they found that memory span decreased from approximately four and a half words for one-syllable word lists to two and a half words for five-syllable word lists. In other conditions, immediate recall was tested on trials where the subjects had to count from 1 to 8 during the visual presentation of the word lists. The addition of this distractor task decreased immediate recall performance. Since counting required attentional capacity, we may assume that less capacity was available for the immediate memory task, and performance suffered accordingly. This relationship between the task demands and the memory span suggests that the span is not a fixed, independent quantity, as the structural view would hold. Instead, immediate memory capacity varies with available attentional resources.

Duration

The same relationship between attentional capacity and performance is found in studies of the duration of immediate memory (e.g., Brown, 1958; Peterson & Peterson, 1959; Watkins, Watkins, Craik, & Mazuryk, 1973). Peterson and Peterson (1959) studied immediate memory duration by presenting subjects with three consonant letters followed by a distractor task lasting 3 to 18 seconds prior to letter recall. The original three letters were presented auditorily, followed by a three-digit number. After hearing the letters and number, the subjects had to count backward by threes from that number until a recall cue was given (e.g., 309, 306, 303, and so forth). Counting backward, which served to prevent the subjects from actively rehearsing the letters over the retention intervals, had a considerable effect upon recall. Letter recall decreased from 80 percent to approximately 10 percent as the period of distraction increased form 3 to 18 seconds. These data might suggest that the duration of immediate memory does not extend beyond 18 seconds.

Murdock (1961), however, showed that the duration of immediate memory is a function of the number of stimuli the subject is trying to retain while counting backward. In general, the lighter the memory load, the longer the duration. Murdock examined immediate memory duration for three letters, three words, and one word. Recall performance after 0 to 18 seconds of counting backward is shown in Figure 4.5 for each of the three stimulus conditions. Consistent with the view that three letters and three words are both three chunks, the effect of the distractor task was the same on both stimulus conditions; recall declined from approximately 94 to 20 percent over 18 seconds of counting backward. Much less affected by the same distractor task was the recall of a single word, which varied from 98 to only 84 percent over the identical retention intervals. In terms of attentional capacity, when concurrent demands of counting and remembering are made upon limited resources, three-chunk memory loads may not receive sufficient capacity. The result is a shorter estimate of immediate memory duration for heavier memory loads than lighter memory loads (see also Melton, 1963).

The suggestion that immediate memory duration is a function of the available attentional resources is strongly supported by the results of Posner and Rossman (1965). They presented subjects with a sequence of five digits followed by one of several interpolated distractor tasks for 5 to 30 seconds prior to digit recall. The interpolated tasks varied in difficulty and consisted of writing digit pairs, adding digit pairs, counting backward by threes from a digit pair, or classifying digit pairs in terms of whether they were high or low and odd or even. Digit recall decreased over the retention intervals as a function of the difficulty of the interpolted tasks (i.e., writing, adding, counting, and classifying). Posner and Rossman viewed these data in terms of competing demands for limited attentional resources. When the demands of a concurrent task were relatively

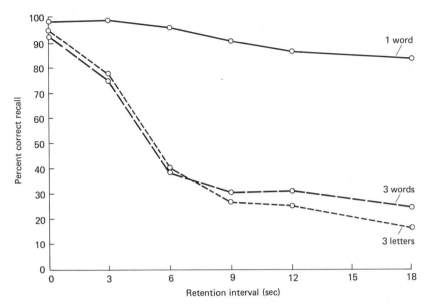

FIGURE 4.5. Immediate memory recall as a function of the length of the intervening distractor task and the number and type of stimuli to be recalled. (Adapted from Murdock, 1961)

low, some attentional capacity could still be allocated to the original stimulus items, and those items showed good retention. When interpolated task demands were high, coexistence became increasingly difficult and the initial items were lost.

The selective attention view of immediate memory sees duration as a function of the available attentional capacity. When other stimuli are presented which have higher priorities, these new stimuli make demands upon the limited resources and capacity may be withdrawn from previously attended objects. Immediate memory is simply another name for the object or objects of attention. Its duration varies directly with information-processing priorities which, because they can change from moment to moment, affect the amount of attentional capacity available. Drawing boxes around labels such as immediate memory, as we did in an earlier chapter (Figure 2.4), can serve a useful purpose in facilitating thinking about underlying cognitive processes. But a danger exists when the boxes come to be thought of as structures rather than as processes. The position presented in this chapter is that immediate memory is best thought of in terms of a selective attention process.

Forgetting

Forgetting in immediate memory has traditionally been attributed to interference or decay processes. We will review evidence for each factor and then consider if these same findings may be explained in terms of limited attentional capacity.

FORGETTING DUE TO INTERFERENCE. Most interference accounts of forgetting have assumed that immediate memory is a structure of limited and fixed capacity. The *interference-as-displacement* position holds that incoming information is deposited in immediate memory in the order of its arrival. So long as space remains available in the immediate memory container, new information can be accommodated and previously deposited information can remain. Once the capacity is filled, however, something must give; either new information cannot be processed or previously deposited information must be discarded. If previously stored information is displaced by new information, the displaced information may be forgotten (e.g., Atkinson & Shiffrin, 1968; Waugh & Norman, 1965). The running memory experiment of Atkinson and Shiffrin (1968) has been interpreted as consistent with this interference-as-displacement position. When subjects are presented with a continuous series of stimuli and asked for recall of a particular item after a number of items have intervened, recall performance is good only if the number of intervening items is small.

An alternative approach to forgetting is the *interference-by-similarity* position. While immediate memory is still viewed as a limited capacity structure, information can be lost by means other than displacement. Item similarity can have negative effects on immediate memory tasks so that forgetting can occur even though the capacity of immediate memory has not been reached. This position holds that as the similarity of the information in immediate memory increases, the subject's ability to differentiate the information decreases; forgetting is produced by confusion as subjects become less accurate in their recall.

Of the two interference approaches, the displacement position is easier to dismiss. The previously cited results of Peterson and Peterson (1959) and Murdock (1961), showing that a sequence of three chunks is rapidly forgotten over a period of 18 seconds of counting backward, does not seem in accord with the displacement position. The subjects were not storing more and more information as they counted backward; they were engaging in a mental arithmetic task which made a more or less constant demand upon processing. The interference-by-similarity position does not have trouble accounting for these data because it is known that the amount of forgetting that occurs over a retention interval depends upon the amount of practice the subjects have had with the same class of stimuli (Keppel & Underwood, 1962; Wickens, 1970). Keppel and Underwood (1962) found that the amount of forgetting in the Peterson task over 18 seconds increased over trials; performance was perfect on the first trial but dropped to 60 percent by the third trial. Wickens, Born, and Allen (1963) found that this negative effect of previous trials could be avoided by changing the class of stimuli that the subjects were trying to remember. The negative effect of previous trials on the same class of stimuli is called *proactive interference*, and the resulting improvement in retention produced by a change in stimulus class is called a *release from proactive interference*. Stimulus similarity is implicated as a cause of forgetting because retention varies inversely with the amount of exposure to a particular class of stimuli. Forgetting in the Peterson task may thus be attributable to both proactive and retroactive sources of interference. Item retention is affected by interference produced by stimulus similarity from previous trials (proactive) and counting backward on the current trial (retroactive). We have encountered these processes before in our discussion of forward and backward masking. Forward masking is a type of proactive interference, and backward masking is a type of retroactive interference.

FORGETTING DUE TO DECAY. The *decay hypothesis* holds that information in immediate memory will be forgotten over time if it is not rehearsed; interference by other stimuli is not necessary to produce forgetting. The strongest evidence for this position comes from research by Reitman (1974) and Shiffrin (1975). Reitman (1974) presented subjects with five words and asked for either immediate recall or delayed recall over an interval of 15 seconds. During the 15-second delay period, Reitman required subjects to listen for faint auditory tones. If a tone was detected, the subjects were required to press a response key as quickly a possible. On some trials no tones were presented, while on other trials from one to fourteen tones were presented. The purpose of the tone-detection task was to prevent rehearsal of the five words in immediate memory. To test the decay hypothesis, Reitman compared the performance of words recalled immediately after presentation with those recalled after 15 seconds of tone detection. Only trials in which no tones had been presented were analyzed since these trials were assumed to be interference-free. Consistent with the decay hypothesis, Reitman found that recall performance declined over time in the absence of specific interference. These findings are in sharp contrast to the earlier reports of Reitman (1971) and Shiffrin (1973), who failed to find evidence for decay over time. Reitman (1974) has attributed her most recent findings to better experimental procedures, which controlled for previously undetected rehearsal.

FORGETTING AND ATTENTIONAL CAPACITY. Evidence has been presented to indicate that forgetting in immediate memory can be produced by either interference or decay processes. Our attempt should not be to choose between these approaches but to see if forgetting can be explained in terms of a more general factor which is responsible for interference and decaylike effects. The view presented in a previous section has argued for immediate memory as a selective attention process. Information is processed and retained as a function of the amount of attentional capacity that has been allocated. Interference need not be viewed as a process of displacing information from a limited-capacity immediate memory; it can be seen in terms of competing demands for a limited resource. Immediate memory is limited because attentional capacity is limited; when additional tasks make excessive demands upon attentional capacity, performance suffers; we can label this effect forgetting. This approach would account for the retroactive interference effect found in the Peterson task (Murdock, 1961; Peterson & Peterson, 1959; Posner & Rossman, 1965) in terms of competing demands on attention. The same idea can be extended to the results of Reitman (1971; 1974) and Shiffrin (1973; 1975) by attributing the forgetting due to decay to an increase in the number of items to remember. Reitman found no forgetting for three words in her 1971 study but significant forgetting for five words in her 1974 study. Shiffrin (1975) varied the number of letters to remember and found that forgetting varied with the memory load. Since tone detection can be assumed to make some demands upon attention, even when no tone is presented, the recent findings suggesting forgetting due to decay may actually reflect interference as larger memory loads make heavier demands on the limited attentional resources. Of course, if we assume that the tone-detection task consumed all of a subject's attentional resources, we have a maximum interference situation and all processing of the memory stimuli is stopped. When attentional capacity is withdrawn, information no longer has any means of support and is quickly lost.

Forgetting can therefore be described as a process of withdrawing attentional resources.

While this view of forgetting provides a basis for understanding a number of findings in immediate memory research, it does not explain the proactive interference findings of Wickens et al. (1963) or the release from proactive interference data of Wickens (1970). Attributing these effects to stimulus similarity only begs the question of how similarity produces forgetting. It may be that an examination of the qualitative effects of different attentional analyses will be helpful in understanding performance differences in memory tasks. We will examine the role of attention in memory in the chapters which follow.

SUMMARY

1. *Selective attention is the process of allocating attentional resources to one object or event over another.*

2. *Research with neonates indicates that infants can demonstrate stimulus preferences. These findings suggest that the ability to act selectively is an innate mental process.*

3. *Attention is selective because it has a limited capacity. Studies within and across different sensory modalities indicate that attentional capacity is limited centrally.*

4. *Early research suggested that selective attention was based on physical stimulus dimensions. A selective filter was assumed to screen information on the basis of physical qualities.*

5. *Later research proposed a hierarchy of filters to analyze incoming information. Attention was viewed as a process of selecting relevant information; all other information was attenuated.*

6. *Alternatives to filtering as a basis for selective attention have been proposed. Selective attention can be seen as an intrinsic part of the perceptual process in which the observer picks up certain information and leaves the rest unused.*

7. *Distractability is an essential feature of the attentional system because it allows the limited capacity to be redirected to new sources of stimulation. Some forms of distractability appear to be innate, as in the case of loud, unexpected stimuli, while other forms are acquired, as in the example*

of response competition. Epileptic seizures are examples of attentional failures that are physiologically determined.

8. *The process of interpreting a stimulus and storing a representation of that interpretation in memory is called encoding. Early research suggested that encoding of simple stimuli, such as letters, required no attentional capacity.*

9. *A more cautious view would hold that the attentional demands of encoding are so small that a second task can be performed simultaneously with no interference.*

10. *When interference on a secondary task is used as an index of attentional demands, both rehearsal and recall processes make measurable demands on the limited attentional resources.*

11. *Long hours of practice enable a task to be performed with reduced attentional demands. Highly learned, automatized routines are especially important in potentially dangerous situations where there may be no time for rational thought.*

12. *One view of the relationship between selective attention and immediate memory is that selective attention determines the contents and duration of information in immediate memory. Selective attention is a process and immediate memory is a structure.*

13. *The alternative position adopted in this chapter is that selective attention, by determining the objects of attention, is immediate memory.*

14. *Consistent with the view of immediate memory as a selective attention process, both the capacity and the duration of immediate memory have been shown to vary with the attentional demands of different tasks.*

15. *Forgetting in immediate memory has traditionally been attributed to interference or decay processes. The position presented here holds that forgetting depends directly on available attentional resources. Immediate memory is limited because attentional capacity is limited. When additional tasks make excessive demands upon attentional capacity, performance suffers; we label this effect forgetting.*

CHAPTER FIVE

Pattern Recognition Processes

OBJECTIVES

1. *To review the different approaches to pattern recognition, including template matching, feature analysis, and data driven and conceptually driven processing.*

2. *To review the evidence for feature analysis and consider its shortcomings.*

3. *To review the evidence for conceptual guidance and show how it can supplement feature analysis.*

4. *To examine pattern recognition in terms of abstraction and generation.*

INTRODUCTION

Like selective attention, pattern recognition is an enormously complex topic that is typically taken for granted. Consider the fact that by the time a child has learned to read, he or she can recognize letter stimuli in an endless variety of forms. By way of contrast, sophisticated machines designed to recognize visual stimuli are quite restricted in their tolerance of variation in form. Machines used by banks to record the number code printed on bank checks, for example, will permit no variation in form, size, orientation, or position of the visual characters. The human processing system is not so restricted. We can recognize numbers or words displayed in different typefaces or handwriting scripts; we can recognize a melody, whether played by an orchestra or whistled by a single person; and we can recognize an animal as a dog even though we may have never seen the particular animal or its breed before. In short, we have the ability to recognize seemingly different things as the same.

In this chapter, we will examine the pattern recognition processes which permit us to read words on a printed page or to see objects in a visual scene. We will find that pattern recognition consists not only of abstractive processes which classify information from particular to more general categories but also generative processes which construct specific information on the basis of previous abstractions. Seeing objects in cloud formations is just as much a part of pattern recognition as recognizing friends or identifying objects.

TEMPLATE MATCHING

Restricted Pattern Recognition

The pattern recognition machines used by banks to read the number code on bank checks illustrate the process of recognition based on template matching. The bank's computer identifies the special numbers by scanning each character and comparing it to the list of digit representations stored in its memory. The digit representations in the computer's memory function as templates in much the same way that drawings or objects can be reproduced from the same pattern or mold; a character is said to be identified when it matches one of the stored digit templates.

Problems with Template Matching

While the template idea can be extended to human pattern recognition by assuming that we have templates stored in memory of all of the things we are able to recognize, there are a number of problems with this approach. If we draw an analogy to the bank check example, what happens if the form, size, orientation, or position of a stimulus is changed so that it no longer matches any template? Recognition should fail, yet we know it frequently does not. Stimuli such as Ⓐ and ⓨ are still identified correctly as the first letter of the alphabet. We could add more templates to

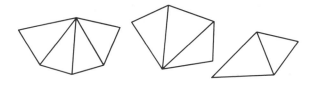

FIGURE 5.1. A sample of irregular polygons.

cover many more stimulus possibilities, but this is not a realistic solution since we could not prepare for all of the different stimulus variations that could be presented. A more promising alternative would be to incorporte normalizing operations, as suggested by Selfridge and Neisser (1960). One such operation could involve rotating unidentified stimuli on a preset basis to adjust for height and width so that the long axis is always vertical and the short axis is always horizontal (e.g., ⊘ through normalization becomes Ⓐ).

Normalizing procedures, although helpful, are still not powerful enough to salvage the template approach. Many recognizable stimuli vary so widely from instance to instance that recognition by template matching seems all but impossible. Consider the fact that we can readily identify irregular polygons (Calfee, 1975), as shown in Figure 5.1; no single template or collection of templates could serve to provide recognition of all of the possible irregular polygons that could occur. Similarly, the normalizing operations that could readily be applied to letter or number stimuli to alter their orientation or size to some predetermined value would not help in identifying the polygons. These types of observations suggest that the template approach to pattern recognition should be abandoned; it lacks sufficient power to account for human performance.

A more promising approach would seem to entail an examination of the components or features of a stimulus in an attempt to construct a representation of that stimulus out of its component parts. Each of the objects in Figure 5.1, for example, could be recognized as an irregular polygon, not because each object matched a stored template but because each drawing, by the arrangement of its features, satisfied the definition of an irregular polygon. This approach differs from the template approach in that a representation of the stimulus is not compared with templates in memory in order for recognition to occur. Instead, the features which are extracted from the stimulus are compared as a set to lists of defining features in memory. Pattern recognition may still be based on a

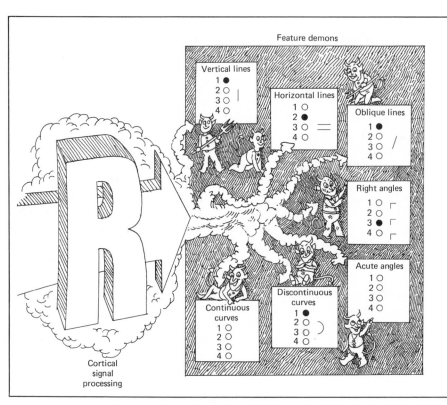

FIGURE 5.2. Selfridge's (1959) Pandemonium model.

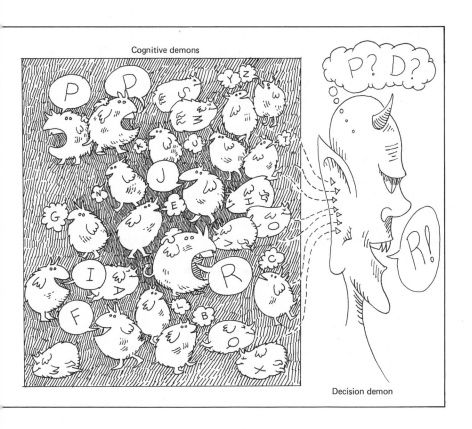

Cognitive demons

Decision demon

matching process, but matching based on feature analysis permits much greater variation in the identification of stimulus patterns.

FEATURE ANALYSIS

Pandemonium: Feature Extraction and Interpretation

As a result of the limitations of the template approach, a number of theorists have turned to feature analysis as a viable recognition alternative (e.g., Gibson, 1969; Selfridge, 1959). The Pandemonium model of Selfridge (1959) is shown in Figure 5.2. Using letter stimuli as an example, it provides a demonstration of pattern recognition by feature analysis.

Selfridge proposed that pattern recognition consists of a series of stages of feature analysis carried out by "demons" who work at different levels in the pattern recognition hierarchy (Selfridge, 1959; Selfridge & Neisser, 1960). Demons are simply a convenient way of representing a physiological or psychological process without specifying in detail how the process actually works. As shown in Figure 5.2, the letter R is an external stimulus which has been received by the visual system and sent to the visual cortex for additional processing. Feature demons examine the newly received information in terms of the number and types of distinct visual features. At this point, the visual stimulus has been identified only in terms of its component features. The feature demons then pass their information on to the cognitive demons, which serve as stored representations for letter stimuli. These cognitive demons become active to the extent that the features passed on to them match the list of features which define each letter. The model derives its name of "Pandemonium" from the assumption that the cognitive demons scream for the attention of the decision demon to the degree that the processed features match the stored feature lists. In the example shown in Figure 5.2, the cognitive demons for P, D, and R are screaming for the decision demon, while most of the other cognitive demons cannot be heard. The job of the decision demon is to decide what letter has been shown; this is done by listening to the cognitive demon that is yelling the loudest.

We may summarize the essential points of the feature analysis approach shown in the Pandemonium model by noting several things. First, pattern recognition is based on a general set of features (e.g., vertical lines, horizontal lines, and so forth) that are applicable to all letters. The template approach required a unique match between a stimulus and a stored template; the feature analysis approach permits greater flexibility as a set of features are abstracted from a stimulus and the abstracted set is then compared to character representations in memory. Second, feature analysis is viewed as consisting of a sequence of feature extraction and feature interpretation. Feature extraction involves noting the different features in the displayed letter, while feature interpretation consists of matching the extracted features to the stored letter representations and then deciding on a final categorization of the stimulus (Smith & Spoehr, 1974). This conceptualization of pattern recognition fits neatly into the information processing scheme outlined in Figure 2.4, but we will see that pattern recognition need not always work according to this simple formulation.

Evidence for Feature Analysis

NEUROLOGICAL EVIDENCE. The Pandemonium model of Selfridge (1959) rests on the assumption that pattern recognition is based on feature analysis. One line of evidence which supports this position is the neurological data of Hubel and Wiesel (1962, 1963, 1965). They recorded the firing of specific cells in the visual cortex of an immobile cat while visual stimuli of various types were shown. Hubel and Wiesel found that certain cells responded only when specific visual stimuli, such as a line of a particular length and orientation, were presented. Other cells responded to lines moving in a given direction or angles of a particular size. These cells in the brain of the cat functioned as detectors for specific visual features, thereby lending credibility to the assumption of feature analysis in man. Dodwell (1970) presents a more complete review of this line of research.

PERCEPTUAL CONFUSIONS. According to the Pandemonium model, if we respond to letter stimuli in terms of their visual features, letters which share visual features are more likely to be erroneously identified than letters which have few features in common. This is indicated in Figure 5.2 by the decision demon choosing among P, D, and R, rather than S, X, and R. Experimental confirmation of perceptual confusions based on visual feature similarity is available in Gibson's (1969) analysis of letter features and Kinney, Marsetta, and Showman's (1966) study of letter identification.

Gibson (1969) classified each letter of the alphabet in terms of such features as straight or curved lines, intersections, symmetry, and discontinuity. The letter F, for example, is composed of horizontal and vertical straight lines which intersect and are discontinuous. The letter V, by contrast, is composed of diagonal lines and is symmetrical. We would not expect people to confuse the letters F and V on a perceptual identification task. The letters C and G, however, appear very similar since both are defined, in part, by a curved line with an opening on the right side. C and G, since they share a predominant visual feature, might be expected to generate identification errors. Kinney et al. (1966) recorded verbal identification errors for briefly presented letter or digit stimuli. Consistent with expectations based on feature analysis, errors occurred among characters that were visually similar (e.g., G for C, B for 8) but not among those that were dissimilar (e.g., F for V, A for S). These findings provide additional support for the existence of visual features and their use in pattern recognition.

VISUAL SEARCH STUDIES. The last evidence to be considered for feature analysis comes from the visual search studies of Neisser (1964). Similar to the search processes used to find an object on a cluttered desk or locate a friend in a crowded room, the visual search task requires subjects to locate a particular item in a long sequence of stimuli. As an example, consider List 1 in Figure 5.3. Find the letter K in List 1 by starting at the top and scanning down the list one row of letters at a time. The subjective impression is one of passing over irrelevant letters so quickly that they seem blurred and not really seen at all. Yet as Neisser (1964) points out, since we can successfully locate the K, we must extract information from each row of letters. One possibility is that we extract visual features and these features are sufficient to allow the search to proceed without fully identifying each letter along the way.

Idealized results of a visual search study in which subjects had to find a particular letter in a list of fifty rows of letters are shown in Figure 5.4. These functions, which are based on results reported by Neisser (1964), represent the average performance of subjects after one and ten sessions of practice. In each session, the subjects were given numerous lists and asked to locate a different letter each time. The position of the critical letter was systematically varied so that it could occur anywhere in the list. Figure 5.4 presents the time to find the critical letter as a function of its position in a list and the amount of practice given to the subjects. Although highly practiced subjects searched faster than less practiced subjects, the results show that the time to locate a critical element was

List 1	List 2	List 3	List 4
EHYP	UDUGQR	IVMXEW	JEWELS
SWIQ	QCDUGO	EWVMIX	ACTUAL
UFCJ	CQOGRD	EXWMVI	OWN
WBYH	QUGCDR	IXEMWV	TUNICS
OGTX	URDGQO	VXWEMI	CLUES
GWVX	GRUQDO	MXVEWI	WILES
TWLN	DUZGRO	XVWMEI	PORTS
KJBU	UCGROD	MWXVIE	RAGED
UDXI	DQRCGU	VIMEXW	SOON
HSFP	QDOCGU	EXVWIM	PHOTOS
XSCQ	CGUROQ	VWMIEX	GATES
SDJU	OCDURQ	VMWIEX	SOURED
PODC	UOCGQD	XVWMEI	PORTLY
ZVBP	RGQCOU	WXVEMI	AERIAL
PEVZ	GRUDQO	XMEWIV	QUITS
SLRA	GODUCQ	MXIVEW	UNDUE
JCEN	QCURDO	VEWMIX	COMA
ZLRD	DUCOQG	EMVXWI	DRAWL
XBOD	CGRDQU	IVWMEX	NASTY
PHMU	UDRCOQ	IEVMWX	DOPE
ZHFK	GQCORU	WVZMXE	CREEPS
PNJW	GOQUCD	XEMIWV	SODA
CQXT	GDQUOC	WXIMEV	SNEEZE
GHNR	URDCGO	EMWIVX	LAMB
IXYD	GODRQC	IVEMXW	PUTS
QSVB			MIMIC
GUCH			SURETY
OWBN			FIGS
BVQN			SANG
FOAS			CHERUB
ITZN			ENTRY
VYLD			VEERED
LRYZ			RIFLED
IJXE			THE
RBOE			SAND
DVUS			LISTEN
BIAJ			TREAD
ESGF			SIZES
QGZI			SCION
ZWNE			TUG

FIGURE 5.3. Selected examples of different visual search tasks used by Neisser, 1964. See text for details.

a direct function of its location in the list. Straight lines closely approximate the data obtained by Neisser and suggest that visual search consists of a rapid sequential scan from the top of the list to the row containing the critical item. On the first day of practice, letter location time increased by approximately one second for each additional row of letters that the subjects were required to scan. By the tenth day of practice, the rate of increase was only 100 milliseconds for each additional row. From these data, we can infer that subjects increased their rate of scanning from one row of letters per second to ten rows of letters per second over the course of the experiment.

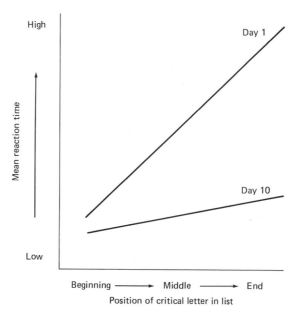

FIGURE 5.4. Idealized search time to locate a critical letter as a function of its position in a list and the degree of practice of the viewer.

Differences in the rate of search as a function of list content provide direct evidence for feature analysis. In Lists 2 and 3 of Figure 5.3, find the letter Z. Most people find Z more quickly in List 2 than List 3 because the letters in List 2 were chosen to have few visual features in common with the letter Z, while the letters in List 3 were selected to be as visually similar as possible. A rudimentary analysis of the visual features of each letter is sufficient to find the Z in List 2 but is not sufficient in List 3. For List 3, the letters must be examined in more detail to determine which row contains the Z. These data provide additional evidence for feature analysis and suggest that pattern recognition operations may vary with the demands of the task.

    This latter possibility can be seen by varying the instructions for searching the word list in Figure 5.3. First, find the word SAND by scanning from the top of the list. After locating SAND, stop; rescan the list for the name of an animal. People are much faster at finding SAND than the animal name—which, incidentally, was scanned on the first search for SAND. To find SAND, a scan on the basis of visual features is sufficient. To find the animal name, each word must be identified; this involves analyzing its meaning to determine if the word is an animal name. Analyzing visual features is much faster than analyzing meaning, so differences in visual search are found. This observation indicates that pattern recognition can entail a relatively simple feature analysis or a more complex analysis of stimulus meaning or category (e.g., Jonides & Gleitman, 1972; Reicher, Snyder, & Richards, 1976). These different types of analysis will be examined in more detail in the section on abstraction and generation.

Finally, pattern recognition operations can be affected by practice in ways other than simply increasing the rate of search. After a year or more of training, professional newspaper scanners are reported to be able to scan a newspaper at rates in excess of 1,000 words per second while looking for citations of 100 or more critical references (Neisser, 1964). Laboratory studies have only begun to examine the effects of extended practice on visual search. Neisser, Novick, and Lazar (1963) found that if the critical items were held constant over a one-month period, subjects could search for ten items in a visual list as quickly as they could search for one item. Extended practice not only increased the rate of search, it permitted the search to be conducted on a number of stimuli simultaneously. Subsequent research suggests a note of caution in interpreting these results. Kaplan and Carvellas (1965) and Wattenbarger (1967) found that subjects could search for multiple items as quickly as one item only if the subjects were permitted to sacrifice accuracy for speed. When accuracy was stressed, searching for multiple items was always slower than searching for a single item. This inverse relationship between speed and accuracy has been called a *speed-accuracy tradeoff* (Pachella, 1974; Wickelgren, 1974). Generally, when errors are held to a minimum, the data indicate that items are scanned one at a time (e.g., Atkinson, Holmgren, & Juola, 1969; Kaplan & Carvellas, 1965), although Egeth and others have found some conditions where, with practice and distinctive critical items, subjects appear to be able to scan for several items simultaneously (Egeth, Atkinson, Gilmore, & Marcus, 1973; Egeth, Jonides, & Wall, 1972).

Problems with Feature Analysis

As attractive as feature analysis is, there are several problems with this approach which render it deficient as a general model of pattern recognition. Sutherland (1972) has noted that features may be defined in at least three different ways. There are local features such as the presence of an oblique line or acute angle; global features such as character symmetry which are not based on any particular local feature; and concatenations of local features which together are more complex than any of the individual local features. Although pattern recognition requires feature analysis, a listing of the local features will not always be sufficient (e.g., b, d, p, q); in some manner the relationship among the features must be noted (Sutherland, 1972).

The visual search studies of Neisser (1964) provide another indication of how feature analysis is limited and hint at the manner in which this approach could be augmented. Studies of scanning for words such as SAND in Figure 5.3 show that unpracticed subjects scan at the rate of approximately five words per second (Neisser, 1964). If this figure is multiplied by 60 seconds, a scanning rate of 300 words per minute is obtained. Depending upon the level of difficulty of the material, however, the college students who served as subjects in these experiments normally read at rates of 300–600 words per minute. Given the relative simplicity of the words used in the visual search lists, we might wonder why reading is faster than scanning. One possibility is that reading provides a grammatical and meaningful context for the words which subjects can use to facilitate the ongoing pattern recognition process. Word lists lack contextual support, so each word must be recognized as a unique entity. The possibility that context can facilitiate pattern recognition suggests that recognition is not based only on the information currently being extracted; the perceiver's knowledge of the immediate past and the more remote past may be used to generate expectancies and influence recognition processes as well. We will examine this issue in greater detail in the next section.

DATA DRIVEN AND CONCEPTUALLY DRIVEN PROCESSING

Two Kinds of Processing

Norman (1976) distinguishes between data driven and conceptually driven processing in pattern recognition. *Data driven processing* is typified by the sequence of operations shown in the Pandemonium model in Figure 5.2; features are the data examined by the perceptual system in an attempt to arrive at a correct identification of the stimulus. From the encoding of the features to the identification of the stimulus, the output of each stage serves as the input for the next stage to drive the processing sequence. *Conceptually driven processing* differs from data driven processing in that a prior conceptualization or expectancy can drive the recognition process. Instead of viewing pattern recognition as beginning with feature analysis and ending with stimulus identification, it is possible to view recognition as beginning with an idea of what may be present and then seeking supportive evidence by means of a limited feature analysis. Since we have already reviewed the case for data driven processing in the section on feature analysis, this section will present the evidence for conceptual driven processing. We should keep in mind, however, that under normal circumstances, both data driven and conceptually driven processing are necessary to describe pattern recognition (Norman, 1976; see also Palmer, 1975).

Evidence for Conceptual Guidance

CONTEXT EFFECTS. The strongest evidence for conceptual guidance comes from studies which manipulate stimulus context. As Biederman (1972) notes, objects are always perceived in an environmental context; they are never seen in isolation. Biederman studied the effects of context on object recognition by briefly presenting subjects with a picture of a common scene, such as a street or a kitchen. The scene was shown in either a normal, coherent manner or in a jumbled fashion by sectioning the picture and rearranging the pieces. Although objects were always shown in their correct orientation, the normal arrangement of the objects was destroyed in the jumbled pictures. By this manipulation, Biederman hoped to determine the effect of a coherent background on object recognition. The results showed that subjects recognized objects better following a brief viewing of a coherent scene than a jumbled scene. Moreover, this difference was found even when the subjects were told where to look within each scene before the scene was shown (Biederman, 1972). These data provide clear evidence of a facilitative effect of context on pattern recognition.

In subsequent research, Biederman has sought to determine how context affects pattern recognition. Biederman, Glass, and Stacy (1973) measured the effect of context on object recognition time by showing subjects a picture of an object followed by a coherent or jumbled scene. The subjects' task was to search the scene and indicate whether the critical object was present by making a positive or negative response. The effect of context was studied in two ways: first, context was varied by presenting scenes in a coherent or jumbled fashion; second, in those instances when the object was not present in a scene, context was varied by presenting conceptually related or unrelated scenes. If the subjects were looking for a fire hydrant, a picture of a street would be a related scene, while a picture of a kitchen would be an unrelated scene. Biederman et al. found strong effects of context on both variables. Subjects searched coherent scenes faster than jumbled scenes; when the object was not present, subjects searched unrelated scenes faster than related scenes.

Biederman's data indicate that context may function by providing the viewer with an overall characterization or schema (Bartlett, 1932) of the scene. While the subjects search a scene for a critical item, they simultaneously develop an overall idea of what the scene represents (e.g., the top of a desk, a view of a lake, and so forth). This schema, which is constructed on the basis of the objects that have been recognized, can be used in searching for the critical object if it has not yet been found (Biederman, Rabinowitz, Glass, & Stacy, 1974). After looking at a scene and determining that it is a kitchen, we can quickly respond negatively if we are searching for a fire hydrant because we know that fire hydrants are not found in kitchens. However, if we are searching for a toaster, we would take longer to search because a kitchen is a logical place to find a toaster. In this manner, we can see both data driven and conceptually driven processing at work. Abstracting information from the scene to formulate an overall schema would be evidence for data driven processing; using the schema based on past experience to make decisions about either terminating or continuing the search would be evidence for conceptually driven processing. Context facilitates pattern recognition by suggesting reasonable possibilities to the perceiver. Similar effects have been found in studies of letter recognition (e.g., Aderman & Smith, 1971; Reicher, 1969; Wheeler, 1970), word identification (e.g., Tulving & Gold, 1963), and sentence identification (e.g., Miller & Isard, 1963). Through context, conceptually driven processing can supplement data driven processing.

READING. The finding that contextual information facilitates sentence identification has important implications for reading. According to Hochberg (1970b), the act of reading shares characteristics with other forms of looking. Since we have already seen evidence of data driven and conceptually driven processing in studies of object recognition, we might expect to find evidence for these modes of processing in reading. Hochberg (1970) and Neisser (1976) view skilled reading as a process of sampling the meaning of a passage by generating expectancies of a word or phrase. The expectancies are based on what has already been read and what is about to be read, as seen by peripheral vision. As expectancies are generated, they are checked by looking at a few features by direct foveal vision. If the features confirm the expectancies, the eyes move along; new expectancies are generated and additional information is sampled (Hochberg, 1970b). Evidence supporting this interpretation has been provided by Malt and Seamon (1978).

How data driven and conceptually driven processing may interact in reading is shown in Figure 5.5 After reading the first few words in the example, attention is drawn to the first letter of the word FATHER and a feature analysis is performed. Simultaneous with this data driven processing, powerful conceptually driven processing is employed to generate a reasonable, but limited, set of possible interpretations of the features that have been abstracted. These expectancies are based on contextual information from what has already been read and what the reader knows about the subject matter and the language. As in the studies of object recognition, where we did not find fire hydrants in kitchens, grammatical rules dictate that we do not find adverbs or verbs after the word HIS. We read the word FATHER because it matches our expectancies and the data we have abstracted. Kolers (1970) has provided data which are consistent with this position by observing that reading errors, when they occurred, were largely determined by grammatical considerations. When subjects misread a noun or a verb, they overwhelmingly substituted an incorrect noun or verb in its place; grammatical errors were relatively rare. These contextual effects found in reading provide additional support for conceptually driven processing.

Features and Knowledge

One of the problems of looking at pattern recognition in terms of feature analysis is that it is difficult to know what features have been extracted in any given context. Features can vary between sensory modalities and within sensory modalities. For visual pattern recognition, the features may be simple line segments, more complex relationships, or higher-order aspects such as texture or shadow. This complication suggests that the Pandemonium model

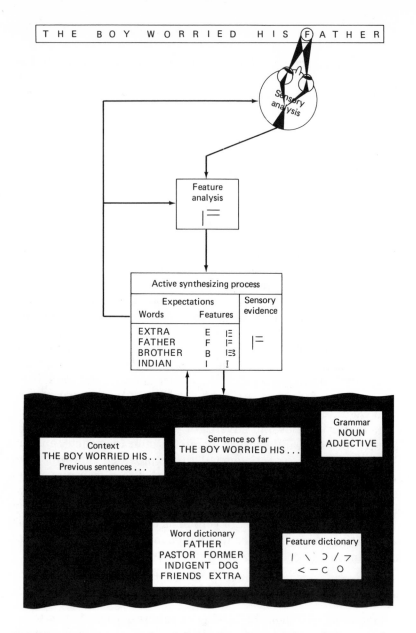

FIGURE 5.5. An example of the interaction of data driven and conceptually driven processing in reading (from Lindsay and Norman, 1972). Although the present example shows reading to be a letter-by-letter process (see Gough & Cosky, 1977), this is not a necessary assumption for our purposes. Others (see Theios & Muise, 1977) have argued against this view.

in Figure 5.2 which extracts and interprets local features for letter recognition should be viewed as a special case of a general class of feature analysis models. We may define this approach to pattern recognition as one which is based on feature extraction and interpretation without specification of the features involved.

We have seen that the initial picture of pattern recognition as a series of stages entailing feature extraction and interpretation is insufficient; conceptually driven processing is needed to supplement data driven processing. Stimuli occur in a context and pattern recognition processes make use of it. Through context, our knowledge of the world suggests which things are plausible and which things are implausible. In the absence of an external context, such as when viewing inkblots or looking at clouds, we may still recognize objects through a combination of data driven and conceptually driven processing. In these instances, conceptual guidance could be based on personal or motivational contexts. The view of pattern recognition as consisting of data driven and conceptually driven processing is still the same; we have simply broadened the definition of context to include the environment of the stimulus and the environment of the perceiver.

ABSTRACTION AND GENERATION

Abstraction and the Isolation of Memory Codes

In the discussion of data driven and conceptually driven processing, we argued that pattern recognition is accomplished by feature analysis and expectancy operating together. In this section, we will examine these processes in more detail to determine the type of memory codes (i.e., traces or representations) that are established during pattern recognition and to show how these codes can be used to affect subsequent recognition.

Abstraction can be defined as a process of recoding information into a reduced or condensed form. By *recoding*, we mean the substitution of one type of representation for another. In reading or looking at an object, different types of information can be abstracted. We can concentrate on an item's appearance, its name, or its meaning. How we might abstract these differnt types of information can be seen in Figure 5.6, which shows a simplified version of the LaBerge and Samuels (1974) model of reading. According to this model, reading is a process of abstracting printed information and recoding it through visual, phonological, and semantic memory systems. In

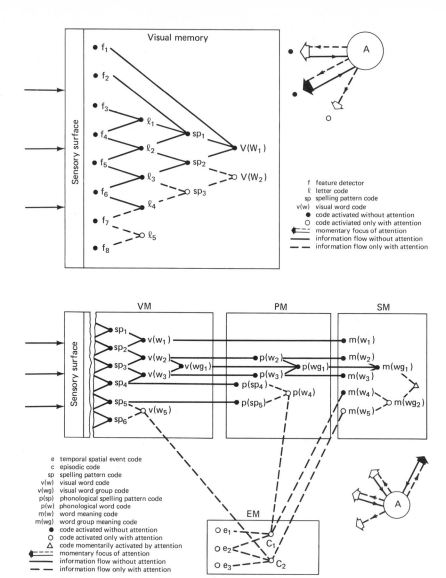

FIGURE 5.6. The LaBerge and Samuels (1974) model of reading. The top half shows how visual representations for words are constructed initially on the basis of abstracted visual features. The bottom half shows the associative network connecting the visual, phonological, and semantic memory codes. A solid line represents an automatic association of visual, phonological, and semantic codes for a given stimulus, while a dashed line shows associations at an early stage of learning. These nonautomatic associations are mediated by past experience represented by episodic memory. (Adapted from LaBerge and Samuels, 1974)

many respects, this model is similar to the Pandemonium model discussed earlier. The visual memory system shown in the top half of Figure 5.6 indicates that incoming stimuli activate feature detectors, which in turn can activate specific letter codes. Just as a particular combination of features can activate a specific letter, so too can a particular combination of letters activate specific spelling patterns—which, in turn, can feed into specific word codes. The same principle used in the Pandemonium model to construct letters from features has been extended in the present example to construct visual representations for words.

How the name and meaning of a visual word might be abstracted is shown in the bottom half of Figure 5.6. LaBerge and Samuels suggest that the memory codes for letters, spelling patterns, and words can be represented by a richly interconnected network of associations which tie together the visual, phonological (i.e., sound patterns), and semantic memory systems. When dealing with highly familiar stimuli, the abstraction of a visual word code can activate its corresponding phonological and semantic word codes so that the name and meaning of the word are also abstracted. LaBerge and Samuels discuss how these systems and their associative networks could develop so that reading with comprehension can occur. For our purposes, we should note that the model outline so far is entirely a data driven processing system.

Experimental evidence in support of the abstraction of isolable memory codes for visually presented stimuli is available in the studies of Posner and others (e.g., Ingalls, 1974; Parks & Kroll, 1975; Posner, Boies, Eichelman, & Taylor, 1969; Posner & Mitchell, 1967). Posner demonstrated that the process of recognizing a stimulus such as the letter A can entail the abstraction of different memory codes depending upon the demands of the task. In different studies, subjects were presented with a pair of letters either simultaneously or sequentially and asked to determine if the letters were the same or different. Letter pairs could be the same in terms of physical appearance (e.g., A-A) or name (e.g., A-a), or they could differ (e.g., A-B or A-b). The results showed that same letters were classified faster than different letters and physically identical letters were classified faster than letters which were only nominally the same (Posner et al., 1969; Posner & Mitchell, 1967). These results cannot be attributed to a speed-accuracy tradeoff since other studies have shown errors to be lower on physical identity trials than on name identity trials (e.g., Blake, Fox, & Lappin, 1970; Taylor & Reilly, 1970).

Posner and Mitchell (1967) interpreted their data as a measure of the depth of stimulus abstraction required to classify letter stimuli. Stimulus pairs such as *A-A* required only a visual match to determine that they were the same, and for these decisions a visual level of abstraction was sufficient. For other letter pairs, such as *A-a*, abstraction to the name code for each stimulus was necessary to classify the stimuli as the same. This approach may explain why it took longer to search the word list in Figure 5.3 for the animal name than for the word SAND. To find SAND, we needed only to abstract a visual code for the letters or words in the list; to find the animal name, we had to abstract the meaning of each word. In these examples, visual abstraction precedes phonological or semantic abstraction, but this need not always be true. In the case of listening, phonological abstraction would precede all other types.

Generation and Formation of Expectancies

In the LaBerge and Samuels (1974) model shown in Figure 5.6, stimulus abstraction is represented by the activation of visual, phonological, or semantic memory codes for a particular stimulus. But stimulus abstraction is not the only way these memory codes can be activated. LaBerge and Samuels hold that attention is capable of activating memory codes in the absence of external stimulation. Thinking of a familiar stimulus such as the word TREE or imagining a tree could be sufficient to stimulate the memory codes for that stimulus. This aspect of the model is important, for it allows the system to be influenced by conceptually driven processing.

Many studies have shown that the encoding time for a visual stimulus can be reduced if it is preceded by an identical visual stimulus (e.g., Eichelman, 1970; Kirsner, 1972; Posner & Boies, 1971). Still other studies (e.g., Meyer, Schvaneveldt, & Ruddy, 1974; Rosch, 1975; Seamon, 1973) have shown that stimulus processing can be facilitated by the presentation of semantically related stimuli prior to the current stimuli. These findings have been interpreted by Posner and Boies (1971) as examples of pathway activation. If stimuli are processed in the same or similar fashion, the processing pathway (i.e., neurological network) may still be activated from the first occurrence of a stimulus and may therefore process the second occurrence more rapidly. For our purposes, the processing pathway for a given stimulus may be defined as the set of memory codes that are capable of being activated by the presentation of that stimulus or attention to (i.e., thinking about) that stimulus. Schematic examples of processing pathways can be seen in the lower half of Figure 5.6 as links between memory codes for the same stimulus.

Since a stimulus is processed faster if it is preceded by an identical stimulus and attention is capable of activating memory codes in the absence of external stimulation (LaBerge & Samuels, 1974), it follows that the processing of external stimuli should be influenced by attention. Thinking of a stimulus in terms of its appearance or name should facilitate the processing of that stimulus. Studies by Hinrichs and Krainz (1970), Peterson and Graham (1974), Posner et al. (1969), Seamon (1976; 1978), and Tversky (1969) support this view; subjects are able to influence the processing of a stimulus by activating specific memory codes prior to its appearance. This activation by attention is an example of generation and evidence for conceptually driven processing. The fact that subjects can activate specific memory codes by attention implies that expectancies can be generated which can influence pattern recognition. This lends support to the models of LaBerge and Samuels (1974) and Hochberg (1970b), which assume an important role for attention and expectancy in reading. It also lends support to the major tenet of this chapter: Pattern recognition is accomplished through the interaction of data driven and conceptually driven processing.

SUMMARY

1. *Unlike machine recognition, human pattern recognition is not restricted to stimuli of a particular form, size, orientation, or position.*

2. *Template matching is an elementary approach to pattern recognition, which assumes that recognition is accomplished by matching an external stimulus with an internal representation.*

3. *Even allowing for normalizing operations, the template approach is an unrealistic way of describing pattern recognition. For many kinds of stimuli, no single template or collection of templates could serve to provide recognition of all the various stimuli that could occur.*

4. *Feature analysis offers more generality than template matching in that a set of features which have been extracted from a stimulus is matched with a list of defining features in memory.*

5. Feature analysis is viewed as consisting of feature extraction and feature interpretation.

6. Support for feature analysis is available from neurological studies which show evidence of feature detectors; character identification studies which show evidence of visual confusion; and visual search studies which show evidence of visual interference and levels of perceptual analysis.

7. Studies of visual search demonstrate that pattern recognition processes can vary with the demands of the task and the degree of practice of the perceiver.

8. Although feature analysis is an improvement over template matching, it does not account for the perceiver's expectancy of what is likely to occur.

9. A more complete account is provided by viewing pattern recognition as a combination of data driven and conceptually driven processing.

10. The use of features to identify a stimulus would be an example of data driven processing, while the use of expectancy to sample selected features would be an example of conceptually driven processing.

11. Stimulus context effects in reading and identifying objects provide strong support for the reality of conceptually driven processing. Context serves to indicate which interpretations are plausible and which are implausible.

12. Different kinds of information can be abstracted from a stimulus during pattern recognition. These different types of information can be represented as memory codes for visual, phonological, or semantic information.

13. Memory codes can be activated not only by the presentation of an external stimulus but by the focus of attention in the absence of external stimulation.

14. Expectancy can be viewed as the attentional activation of visual, phonological, or semantic memory codes.

CHAPTER SIX

Conceptual Approaches to Memory Formation

OBJECTIVES

1. *To distinguish between memory structures and control processes.*
2. *To outline an approach to memory performance based on short-term and long-term storage and to examine the evidence which supports this position.*
3. *To examine the effects of rehearsal on memory formation*
4. *To outline an approach to memory performance based on levels or depth of information processing.*
5. *To outline a unified account of memory performance which incorporates ideas from both short-term and long-term storage and levels of processing.*

INTRODUCTION

In previous chapters we discussed concepts such as sensory memory, immediate memory, and pattern recognition. Although each of these topics is important in its own right, we have not discussed the more permanent aspects of memory and how such memories are formed. To do so requires an understanding of the different conceptual approaches available. One approach, typified by William James's (1890) distinction between primary and secondary memory, views memory as a dichotomy. Information that is currently held in consciousness is readily available and said to reside in *primary memory*; information not in consciousness, but capable of being retrieved, is said to exist in *secondary memory*. The limited primary memory corresponds in a general manner to our earlier use of immediate memory (see Chapter Four), while the unlimited secondary memory is seen as a more or less permanent repository of all the things we know.

For some researchers, the lines of demarcation are not so obvious. A continuum of retention may be possible whereby information may exist in more than simply short-term (i.e., brief) or long-term (i.e., permanent) fashion. In this chapter, we will examine these different conceptual approaches and pay close attention to the hypothesized processes responsible for memory formation.

SHORT-TERM AND LONG-TERM STORAGE

Memory Structures and Control Processes

Early models of the memory system which employed James's primary and secondary memory dichotomy were outlined by Hebb (1949) and Waugh and Norman (1965). Waugh and Norman held that information which is perceived enters a limited-capacity primary memory, where it can be maintained by rehearsal or else forgotten. While information is being rehearsed in primary memory, it may be transferred to secondary memory. Secondary memory is viewed as a storage space of unlimited capacity which is dependent upon rehearsal for information transfer but not information maintenance.

A more detailed description of the memory system has since been put forth by Atkinson and Shiffrin (1968). In their trichotomous system, Atkinson and Shiffrin distinguish between memory structures and control processes. A *memory structure* is defined as one of the permanent features of memory. These include the sensory register (i.e., sensory memory systems), the short-term and long-term stores, and the component processes which remain constant from one situation to another. Control processes, on the other hand, are those operations that a person may use to interact with the information in a memory structure. These processes vary widely across situations and individuals.

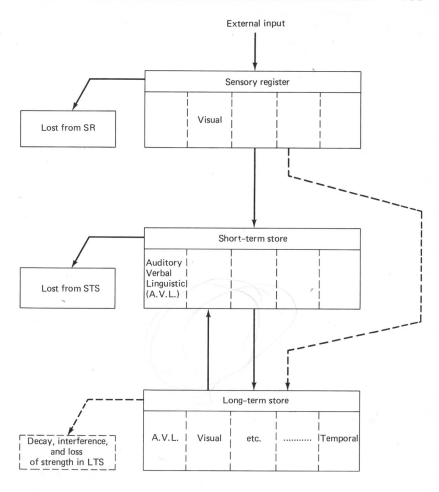

FIGURE 6.1. The Atkinson and Shiffrin memory system. (Adapted from Atkinson & Shiffrin, 1968)

The Atkinson and Shiffrin memory system is presented in Figure 6.1. The *sensory register* is simply another name for sensory memory. Atkinson and Shiffrin assume that each modality may have its own corresponding sensory memory. Visual sensory memory or iconic memory (see Chapter Two) is shown in the figure as one example. Information can be held in the sensory register for a brief period of time before it decays and is lost. The short-term store, like Waugh and Norman's (1965) primary memory, is a limited-capacity working memory. It receives information from the sensory register and from the long-term store—which, like Waugh and Norman's secondary memory, is a relatively permanent information store of unlimited capacity.

Many of the control processes which operate on the structural components have already been described. We noted previously that subjects are able to select information in iconic or echoic memory for further processing on the basis of low-level physical cues (see Chapters Two and Three). While subjects cannot produce an iconic representation, they can selectively operate on that representation under specific conditions. We have also seen that subjects are able to maintain information in immediate memory by engaging in a cyclic process of mental rehearsal. By rehearsing the names of a set of stimuli, a limited number of stimuli can be remembered until a recall signal is provided. The rehearsal of stimulus names implies that subjects have available specific auditory, verbal, or linguistic components of each stimulus in short-term storage. These memory representations are shown in Figure 6.1 as one of several different types of information codes that subjects may have available in short-term storage. Also discussed previously are the means by which information can be lost from the short-term store (see Chapter Four). What has not been discussed are the different types of permanent memory representations in the long-term store and the various control processes involved in memory formation. In large measure, the long-term store is the subject matter for the remainder of this book.

Of foremost importance is the manner in which the memory system acquires permanent information. The formation of long-term memory is a way of defining learning. For Atkinson and Shiffrin, *learning* is the transfer of information from short-term to long-term storage. According to this model, information enters the short-term directly from the long-term store and only indirectly from the sensory register. A word, for example, cannot be entered into the short-term store as a verbal unit until it has been identified in the long-term store. This identification is assumed to be fast and automatic for familiar stimuli. Once a limited set of stimuli have been identified, they can be maintained indefinitely in the short-term store by means of mental rehearsal. Atkinson and Shiffrin assume that as the information is held in short-term storage, it is automatically transferred to long-term storage. This transfer takes the form of copying the information in both stores.

Two independent control processes are responsible for information transfer. The first is *rehearsal*, which is a form of stimulus repetition. Aside from maintaining information in short-term storage, rehearsal is sufficient for establishing weak memory traces in long-term storage. Coding, the second control process, is defined by Atkinson and Shiffrin as an alteration or addition to the information in the short-term store which restricts the amount of information but enhances the strength of the traces produced in the long-term store. Forming associations between stimuli would constitute one type of coding process. Of the two control processes, rehearsal is more beneficial to the short-term store because it allows for more information to be maintained. Coding, on the other hand, is more beneficial to the long-term store because it allows for the establishment of stronger or more retrievable memory traces. We will have much to say about these control processes and the assumptions made by Atkinson and Shiffrin in later portions of this chapter. Before doing so, however, we should see how Atkinson and Shiffrin have modified their views since their system was first presented in 1968.

Revisions of a Conceptual Model

Atkinson (Atkinson, Herrmann, & Wescourt, 1974) has altered his views only slightly over the years. The basic model, although fitted with more boxes to represent such things as control processes and response generators, is still readily identifiable. No fundamental changes in any of the underlying assumptions regarding the memory structures and associated control processes have been made. Atkinson does indicate that the three memory stores need not represent different neurological systems; they may simply represent different phases in the activation of the same neurological system.

For Shiffrin (1975), the model has undergone substantial change as the three memory stores have become more unified. Stimulation from the sensory register goes directly to the long-term store, where it activates its permanent trace. This activation of information in the long-term store is equivalent to placing information in the short-term. Shiffrin now holds that the short-term store is not separate from the long-term store, as the earlier version had suggested (see Figure 6.1). Instead, the long-term store can be likened to a collection of electrical wires, and the short-term store can be represented by those wires that are presently carrying current. Like Atkinson, Shiffrin still maintains that rehearsal and coding are involved in the maintenance and transfer of information from short-term to long-term storage. But since Shiffrin has unified the memory stores, the conception of information transfer must be modified. Transfer is now defined as the establishment of a connection between information not previously associated in long-term storage. In contrast to Atkinson, while the terminology has remained the same, some of the assumptions and definitions have changed for Shiffrin. Although the structural metaphor is probably more applicable today for Atkinson than for Shiffrin, both theorists still view memory in the general manner seen by James (1890) nearly a century ago.

Evidence for Separate Short-Term and Long-Term Storage

In this section, we will review selected behavioral and neurological evidence which supports the separation of short-term and long-term storage. Rather than attempt an exhaustive review (see Wickelgren, 1973), we will examine several different types of data to obtain a sample of current thinking. The types of data we will review concern the recall ability of college students, retardates, patients suffering from a type of amnesia known as Korsakoff's syndrome, and neurological patients who have had portions of their brains damaged or removed.

We should note that at one time it was believed that short-term and long-term storage could be differentiated on the basis of different information codes. The view that short-term storage is based on phonetically coded information and long-term storage is based on semantically coded information is no longer seriously held. There is ample evidence that short-term storage can contain semantic information (e.g., Shulman, 1970) and long-term storage can contain phonetic information (e.g.,Bruce & Crowley, 1970; Gruneberg, Colwill, Winfrow, & Woods, 1970). As Wickelgren (1973) notes, the recognition and articulation of speech require that phonetic and semantic information be available in both short-term and long-term storage.

FREE RECALL PERFORMANCE. In a free recall task, subjects are presented with a stimulus sequence that is greater than the memory span. The task derives its name from the fact that following the presentation of the stimuli, the subjects are asked to recall all of the stimuli in any order that they can remember. When the recall of each stimulus is examined as a function of its presentation position (e.g., first, second, third, and so forth), the result is invariably the same: There is fair-to-good recall of the initial list items, generally

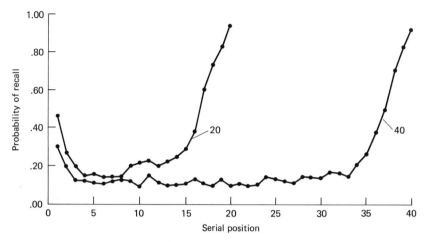

FIGURE 6.2. Mean serial position curves for free recall from lists of twenty and forty words presented at a rate of 1 second per stimulus. (Adapted from Murdock, 1962)

poor recall of the middle items, and superior recall of the terminal items (Murdock, 1962). Figure 6.2 shows mean serial position functions for lists of twenty and forty words when each word was presented for 1 second. The high recall for the initial items is called a *primacy effect* and is felt to reflect the output of long-term storage; the high recall of the terminal items is called a *recency effect* and is felt to reflect the output of short-term storage.

If primacy and recency reflect long-term and short-term storage, each memory store should be sensitive to specific experimental manipulations. Glanzer and Cunitz (1966) tested this possibility in two experiments. The first experiment was based on the assumption that the primacy effect reflects the contribution of long-term storage. Allowing that rehearsal maintains information in the short-term store and transfers it to the long-term store, it follows that initial items, since they have more opportunity for rehearsal, should show good long-term storage. Alternatively, the recency effect is assumed to reflect the output of short-term storage because these stimuli were presented just prior to the time for recall. As such, these items have a high probability of still being maintained by rehearsal in short-term storage at the start of recall. The items from the middle of the list suffer poor recall because they have neither sufficient rehearsal for transfer into long-term storage nor continued rehearsal for maintenance in short-term storage.

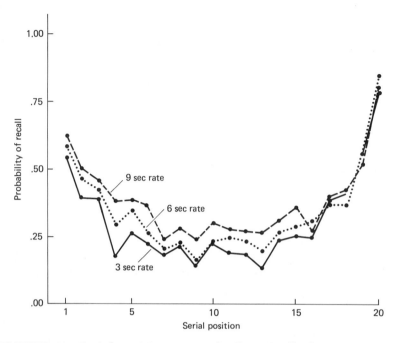

FIGURE 6.3. *Serial position curves for free recall of a twenty-word list presented at rates of 3, 6, or 9 seconds per item. (Adapted from Glanzer & Cunitz, 1966)*

If primacy is a function of increased rehearsal for initial list items, it follows that if the stimulus presentation rate is varied, the degree of primacy should vary also. More specifically, the slower the presentation rate, the greater the amount of rehearsal and transfer to long-term storage and the larger the primacy effect. Rate of presentation should not, however, have any effect on the recency portion of the serial position curve since these items are assumed to be recalled from the short-term store. Figure 6.3 shows the results obtained with lists of twenty words presented at rates of 3, 6, or 9 seconds per word. The serial position functions show recall to vary directly with presentation rate over all but the most recently presented items. Primacy was affected by the stimulus presentation rate; recency was not. Under special circumstances (see Bernbach, 1975), the presentation rate can have a small effect on recency, but these conditions do not obviate the present interpretation of primacy and recency in free recall.

In a second experiment, Glanzer and Cunitz (1966) attempted

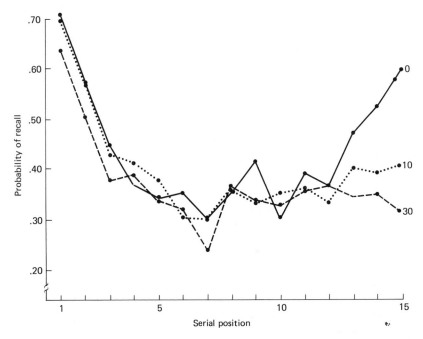

FIGURE 6.4. Serial position curves for free recall of a fifteen-word list with 0, 10, or 30 seconds of distraction between list presentation and recall. (Adapted from Glanzer & Cunitz, 1966)

to manipulate the recency portion of the serial position function while leaving the rest of the function intact. Assuming that the recency effect reflects the contribution of the short-term store, the rehearsal of these most recently presented items should be disrupted by a distractor task presented between list presentation and recall. To test this hypothesis, Glanzer and Cunitz presented subjects with a fifteen-word list followed by 0, 10, or 30 seconds of counting interpolated between list presentation and free recall. These data, shown in Figure 6.4, support the hypothesis. The interpolated activity of counting numbers had a negative effect on only those items recalled from the end of the list (see also Postman & Phillips, 1965); following 30 seconds of distraction, the recency effect was eliminated. As before, there are special circumstances that provide exceptions to this rule. If stimuli are made more distinctive, a small recency effect can be obtained even after a distractor task is employed (Bjork & Whitten, 1974). This special recency effect would seem to reflect long-term rather than short-term storage in the same sense that our high recall of the names of recent past presidents would be based on long-term storage. These observations do not refute the evidence for short-term storage in free recall. They simply indicate that recency effects can be obtained from long-term as well as short-term storage depending upon experimental conditions.

The Glanzer and Cunitz data have been interpreted as evidence for long-term and short-term storage effects in free recall. Allowing greater rehearsal produces greater primacy but leaves recency unaffected; providing greater distraction reduces recency but leaves primacy unaffected. These results are consistent with the view that rehearsal transfers information to long-term storage while distraction inhibits its maintenance in short-term storage. Other studies have shown similar contrasting effects on the primacy and recency portions of the serial position function. Sumby (1963) compared the recall of lists of high-frequency words with that of low-frequency words. Words that were rated high in frequency (i.e., often used in speech and text) were recalled better than those rated lower in frequency for all list serial positions except those at the end. The recency effects were the same for both types of words. Essentially the same findings were obtained by Seamon and Murray (1976) in a free recall task that varied stimulus meaningfulness. Both studies demonstrate that variables such as word frequency and meaningfulness, which have traditionally been viewed as important determinants of learning (see Crowder, 1976), affect primacy but do not affect recency in free recall. The lack of an effect of these variables on the most recently presented items is consistent with the assumption that recency reflects the recall of information which has not yet been transferred from short-term to long-term storage. Similarly, the serial position function is strongly affected by the order in which items are free-recalled. A large recency effect is obtained only if the most recently presented items are recalled first; primacy is not affected by recall order (Tulving & Arbuckle, 1963). These data, together with those of Glanzer and Cunitz, suggest that the recency effect is based on information which is being maintained only temporarily in short-term storage.

Additional support for the view that primacy reflects long-term storage comes from Belmont and Butterfield (1971). They found that high-school students produced greater primacy than mildly retarded teenagers of comparable ages. Recency, however, was unaffected. Forcing the retarded students to engage in extra rehearsal significantly increased their amount of primacy, although not to the level of the normal students. These data support the hypothesis that extra rehearsal can enhance recall by producing greater transfer from short-term to long-term storage. The results further suggest that part of the difficulty faced by retarded individuals is their ineffective use of control processes such as rehearsal, which other individuals use spontaneously. Mental retardation is a topic of such complexity that it extends well beyond the scope of this book. We should note only that, in the present context, studies with retardates have supported the distinction between short-term and long-term storage by indicating an apparent difficulty in transferring information.

KORSAKOFF'S SYNDROME. Additional evidence for separate short-term and long-term storage comes from observations made on patients suffering from Korsakoff's syndrome. In 1889, Korsakoff found that chronic alcoholism could result in a set of mental disorders which included a particular form of amnesia. These patients had normal memory of events which occurred prior to the onset of their illness but no new long-term storage of events which occurred after their illness (Barbizet, 1970). Current thinking holds that excessive drinking and an inadequate diet may result in a prolonged vitamin deficiency which can produce permanent brain damage (Baddeley, 1976).

In a series of experiments, Baddeley and Warrington (1970) compared the memory performance of Korsakoff's patients with that of other hospitalized patients with no apparent memory disorders. In light of the Korsakoff's patients particular disorder, it was expected that these patients would show evidence of a deficit in long-term storage. On a free recall task, the non-Korsakoff patients produced a typical serial position function with both primacy and recency effects. The performance of the Korsakoff's patients was very different; they produced a strong recency effect but no primacy effect. Since the recency effect was the same for both groups of patients, Baddeley and Warrington concluded that Korsakoff's patients had a long-term storage impairment. This conclusion was supported by two additional observations. First, information was forgotten from short-term storage at the same rate for both Korsakoff's and non-Korsakoff's patients when a distractor task followed stimulus presentation. Second, the span of immediate memory for digit sequences was the same for both groups of subjects (Baddeley & Warrington, 1970). These data, which indicate a selective long-term storage impairment, imply a separation of short-term and long-term storage.

Recently, however, Cermak, Butters, and Goodglass (1971) found the rate of forgetting in immediate recall to be greater for Korsakoff's patients than for either normals or nonamnesic alcoholics. This finding is inconsistent with the results of Baddeley and Warrington (1970) and suggests that a short-term storage impairment may exist in Korsakoff's patients. While we may conclude that Korsakoff's patients have greater difficulty in either acquiring or remembering new experiences for longer than a very brief interval, we may not conclude that their short-term store is normal. Findings such as those by Cermak et al. weaken the value of the Korsakoff data since they imply that Korsakoff's patients may have a general memory disorder instead of a specific long-term storage problem. The finding of a general disorder would render the Korsakoff data less relevant to a theoretical distinction between short-term and long-term storage.

NEUROLOGICAL CASE STUDIES. Occasionally, case studies are reported of patients with brain changes due to accident or surgery. Although the number of case studies that are reported is quite small, the observations made on these patients are theoretically important since they support the separation of short-term and long-term storage.

Teuber, Milner, and Vaughan (1968) report the case of a patient, N. A., who was wounded by a fencing foil in a mock duel. During the duel, the tip of his opponent's foil passed through N. A.'s nostril and penetrated his brain. The resulting brain damage produced a state of amnesia similar to that found in Korsakoff's syndrome. Although N. A. appeared normal, he was unable to retain any new information over a period of seven years since the accident (Teuber et al., 1968).

Similar in gross respects to N. A. is the case of H. M., reported by Scoville (1968), Milner, Corkin, and Teuber (1968) and Wickelgren (1968). In an attempt to control severe epileptic seizures, Scoville removed a portion of H. M.'s brain known as the hippocampus. The operation was successful in reducing the frequency of H. M.'s seizures, but it left him with a complete loss of recent memory (Scoville, 1968). After recovering from the operation, H. M. had difficulty learning such commonplace things as his new home address and the location of objects around the house. He was able to do the same puzzles and reread the same magazines day after day without recognizing that he had done these things before (Barbizet, 1970). The impact of this profound memory disorder is probably best captured in H. M.'s own words. He said, "Every day is alone in itself, whatever enjoyment I've had, and whatever sorrow I've had" (Milner et al., 1968). Like a person who has just awakened from a dream, H. M. is not aware of what has happened before.

The studies of N.A. and H. M. suggest that the accidents and operations resulted in brain changes which produced an inability to transfer or retrieve information in long-term storage. Since these patients have little difficulty remembering events in their lives from before the brain trauma, it would appear that their problems lie more in the transfer than the retrieval of information. These data, based on unusual individuals, provide compelling evidence for the separation of short-term and long-term storage.

Rehearsal and Long-Term Storage

In this section, we will examine the widely held belief that rehearsal is an effective means of producing long-term memory. Different coding processes such as those involved in organizational and mnemonic schemes, will be treated in a later chapter (see Chapter Eight).

EFFECTS OF REHEARSAL. The Atkinson and Shiffrin (1968) model of memory specifies that rehearsal, while maintaining information in short-term storage, can also serve to transfer information to long-term storage. In a series of studies, Rundus attempted to specify the relationship between the amount of rehearsal a stimulus receives and the probability of its subsequent recall (Rundus, 1971; Rundus & Atkinson, 1970). Using a free recall task, Rundus required subjects to rehearse the stimuli orally while they were sequentially presented. The subjects were free to rehearse any stimuli whenever and as often as they wished providing they rehearsed out loud.

The results of the Rundus and Atkinson (1970) study are shown in Figure 6.5. Two functions are presented together to show the relationship between rehearsal and recall. The solid curve represents the probability of recall as a function of the serial position of each word in the twenty-item list. The typical serial position curve showing primacy and recency effects indicates that the task of oral rehearsal did not alter the basic recall phenomena. The dotted curve shows the amount of rehearsal each item received as the list was presented. This measure, which was obtained by tape-recording the subjects during list presentation, shows a large primacy effect and a gradual reduction in frequency across the re-

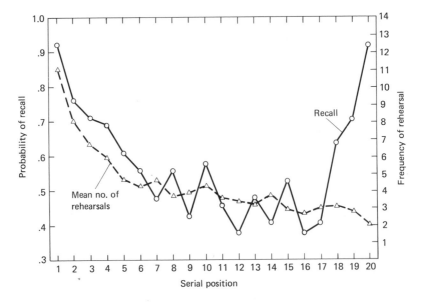

FIGURE 6.5. The serial position curve (solid line) for free recall of a twenty-word list and the rehearsal frequency of each item (dashed curve) during list presentation. (Adapted from Rundus & Atkinson, 1970)

maining serial positions. Overall, the initial items were rehearsed the most, and the terminal items were rehearsed the least. Excepting items from the end of the list, the data in Figure 6.5 show the probability of recall to vary directly with the frequency of rehearsal (Rundus & Atkinson, 1970).

In additional analyses, Rundus and Atkinson determined which items were being rehearsed at each point in time. Analyses of these rehearsal sets indicated that subjects typically rehearsed three to four words at any given time and that every word in the list was rehearsed at least once. Most importantly, the items in the last rehearsal set were usually from the end of the list and their probability of recall was very high (i.e., 96 percent). In terms of the Atkinson and Shiffrin (1968) model, if each rehearsal set is equated with the momentary contents of short-term storage, the primacy effect in Figure 6.5 can be attributed to recall from long-term storage by virtue of the additional rehearsals initial items received. Conversely, the recency effect can reflect recall from short-term storage since these items were being rehearsed at the time of recall.

Consistent with this interpretation, Rundus and Atkinson found that subjects recalled the items in the current rehearsal set first (i.e., recency) and then recalled the items in terms of the amount of rehearsal each item had received (i.e., primacy).

PROBLEMS WITH REHEARSAL. Before drawing any conclusions about the effects of rehearsal on long-term storage, we need to consider two points. First, the relationship observed by Rundus is correlational. Second, greater frequency of rehearsal has not always led to greater long-term storage. We will consider each of these points in turn.

A correlation merely states that two variables are related in either a positive or negative fashion. For example, body weight and grade level are positively correlated for grammar school children (i.e., the greater the weight, the higher the average grade level), but we would not infer that a particular body weight causes children to be placed in a particular grade level. As this example shows, causality cannot be inferred from correlational data. The same argument may be applied to Rundus's data, which show that recall probability is positively correlated with rehearsal frequency. While rehearsal may be sufficient to produce long-term storage, the data do not force this conclusion. It may be that rehearsal merely serves to maintain information in short-term storage so that coding processes have an opportunity to transfer the information to long-term storage. The longer the information is maintained in short-term storage by rehearsal, the greater the opportunity for transfer by coding processes. Rehearsal can thereby serve as either a direct or an indirect agent in information transfer, and the Rundus data cannot differentiate these possibilities.

The second problem with rehearsal is that different studies have reported different results. Ample evidence is available which indicates that greater rehearsal frequency facilitates short-term storage with no corresponding benefits in long-term storage (e.g., Craik & Watkins, 1973; Jacoby & Bartz, 1972; Modigliani & Seamon, 1974), while additional research demonstrates a strong effect of rehearsal frequency on long-term storage (e.g., Dark & Loftus, 1976; Darley & Glass, 1975). In order to highlight these discrepant results, we will examine two of these studies in greater detail.

In one study, Craik and Watkins (1973) presented subjects with a list of words and asked the subjects to remember the last word in the list that began with a critical letter. For a list such as "DAUGHTER, OIL, RIFLE, GARDEN, GRAIN, TABLE, FOOTBALL,

ANCHOR, GIRAFFE, CANDLE," if the critical letter was G, the subject, upon hearing the list, would first select GARDEN to remember, then drop it for GRAIN, only to drop GRAIN later for GIRAFFE, which was recalled. By this procedure, GARDEN was rehearsed in short-term storage for the shortest duration, while GRAIN was held in short-term storage for the longest duration. After many such lists with different critical letters, Craik and Watkins asked the subjects to free-recall as many words as possible. Their results show that rehearsal, when measured by the length of time a word was held in short-term storage, had no effect on the final recall test. These data suggest that rehearsal does not produce long-term storage.

Curiously, Darley and Glass (1975) used a procedure that was conceptually similar to that employed by Craik and Watkins, yet they obtained very different results. Using a visual search task (see Chapter Five), subjects were given word lists and asked to search for particular words, which could be located anywhere from the top to the bottom of each list. The subjects were told to read the target word at the top of a page and then search the list from top down, making sure that they found the target word since only one pass through the list was permitted. Over a series of lists, Darley and Glass varied the position of the target word. This procedure required the subjects to search each list for different periods of time and, consequently, to hold the corresponding target items for varying periods of time in short-term storage. In this manner, the rehearsal of the target items was systematically manipulated.

After completing a series of visual search trials, Darley and Glass gave the subjects a surprise free-recall test on all of the previously searched target words. The results showed recall to vary directly with the length of time that the subjects spent searching for each word during visual search. The probability of recall was higher for target words that were near the bottom of the search lists than for those near the top. These findings seem to contradict those of Craik and Watkins (1973) and suggest that rehearsal is capable of facilitating long-term storage. Similarly paradoxical are the findings from studies which have required subjects to rehearse orally so that rehearsal frequency could be precisely specified. Craik and Watkins (1973) found in a second study that rehearsal frequency did not affect long-term storage, while Dark and Loftus (1976) found that it did. Perhaps it is time to seek a better definition of rehearsal.

DIFFERENT TYPES OF REHEARSAL. Rehearsal which can be described as a rote, cyclic process of simply maintaining information in short-term storage has been called *maintenance rehearsal* (Craik & Watkins, 1973), *primary rehearsal* (Bjork & Jongeward, 1975; Woodward, Bjork, & Jongeward, 1973), and *echoing* (Darley & Glass, 1975). Rehearsal which attempts to relate items to be remembered and form associations to facilitate long-term storage has been termed *elaborative rehearsal* (Craik & Watkins, 1973), *secondary rehearsal* (Bjork & Jongeward, 1975; Woodward et al., 1973), and *attending* (Darley & Glass, 1975). Research by Bjork and his associates generally supports the above rehearsal distinctions.

Bjork and Jongeward (1975) presented subjects with sets of six words to be rehearsed in a rote, cyclic fashion (i.e., maintenance or primary rehearsal) or rehearsed by forming meaningful associations between the items (i.e., elaborative or secondary rehearsal). Following the presentation of the six words, there was a 20-second retention interval, during which the subjects engaged in one of the two types of rehearsal, and then a free-recall test of the six stimuli. After twenty trials of the same general type, the subjects were given either a surprise free-recall or recognition test for all of the words previously rehearsed. The recognition test consisted of all the words shown during the experiment and a larger number of words which were not shown previously. The subjects' task was to select the words that were earlier rehearsed.

Bjork and Jongeward found that both types of rehearsal produced high recall on the initial test of short-term storage, although primary rehearsal (their terminology) yielded higher recall than secondary rehearsal. On the final recall test based on long-term storage, the order was reversed; secondary rehearsal produced greater recall than primary rehearsal. These data imply that primary rehearsal is effective for maintaining information in short-term storage, while secondary rehearsal is effective for transferring information to long-term storage. Results from the subjects who were given a final recognition test, however, suggest that the situation is more complex. Although secondary rehearsal was still superior to primary rehearsal, subjects showed good long-term recognition performance for both primary and secondary rehearsal. Similar results by Woodward et al. (1973) indicate that these findings are reliable.

Apparently, the effects of rehearsal are complicated by the type of rehearsal and the type of memory test. Primary rehearsal is effective mainly for maintaining information in short-term storage, but it can produce transfer to long-term storage, as shown by the positive effect on long-term recognition. Secondary rehearsal, on the other hand, seems less effective than primary rehearsal at maintaining information in short-term storage but more effective at transferring information to long-term storage. If the terminology is altered slightly, we find that the distinction between primary and secondary rehearsal (or maintenance and elaborative or echoing and attending) was anticipated by Atkinson and Shiffrin (1968) in their discussion of rehearsal and coding processes over a decade ago. According to Atkinson and Shiffrin, rehearsal serves to maintain information in short-term storage so that coding processes have a chance to establish strong long-term traces. In the absence of elaborative coding, however, rote rehearsal was hypothesized to be able to establish weak long-term traces. This early view seems well supported by the research that has followed.

THE LEVELS OF PROCESSING APPROACH

Repetition and Memory Continuum

The view of memory as a collection of independent stores has not been universally accepted. A number of theorists view short-term and long-term storage as reflecting different points on a memory continuum rather than separate memory systems. Hebb (1961), for example, after arguing earlier (Hebb, 1949) for a distinction between activity and structural memory traces (i.e., short-term and long-term storage), rejected his former distinction on the basis of new data. Hebb presented subjects with sequences of nine digits for immediate recall. While the majority of the twenty-four trials employed a unique sequence each time, trials 3, 6, 9, 12, 15, 18, 21, and 24 repeated the same sequence. Hebb found that immediate recall was relatively poor and unchanging for those trials in which a unique digit sequence was employed each time. For the trials in which the sequence was repeated, however, there was a gradual and continuous improvement in recall from the sequence's first presentation (trial 3) to its last (trial 24). Hebb viewed these data as inconsistent with his earlier belief. In an immediate memory task, if each sequence presentation resulted in only short-term storage, no facilitation in performance should be found for stimulus repetitions that are spaced three trials apart. Hebb's finding of a repetition effect led him to conclude that each stimulus presentation resulted in long-term storage that was cumulative over repetitions.

Melton (1963) replicated and extended Hebb's (1961) findings by studying the effects of the number of repetitions and the spacing of repetitions in immediate recall. In a broad review of the experimental literature, Melton concluded that since specific variables, such as stimulus repetition and interference, produce common results in short-term and long-term memory tasks, it may be more appropriate to think of short-term and long-term storage as different points along a memory continuum. We will develop this approach more fully in the next section on memory formation and levels of processing.

Levels of Processing

INITIAL FORMULATION. Many researchers have realized that memory performance is intimately related to stimulus encoding procedures (e.g., Baddeley & Patterson, 1971; Cermak, 1972; Crowder & Morton, 1969; Tresselt & Mayzner, 1960). But it was Craik and Lockhart (1972) who outlined a framework for memory research which assumed that memory performance was best described by a processing continuum based on encoding operations.

The idea of processing levels in pattern recognition (see Chapter Five) has been available in psychology for a number of years (e.g., Selfridge & Neisser, 1960; Treisman, 1964). The perceptual analysis of a stimulus can be thought of as a series of stages or levels involving first the abstraction of physical features and later the abstraction of meaning. This progression of abstraction from physical features to an understanding of meaning is referred to as the depth or level of processing. Craik and Lockhart argued that the memory trace is an automatic by-product of a given perceptual analysis; it is not something that must be done in addition to perception. In this manner, perception and memory are intimately related (see also Jenkins, 1974). Craik and Lockhart further asserted that memory duration was a direct function of the level of stimulus processing: The deeper the processing, the stronger and more durable the memory trace. Figure 6.6 shows a particular visual stimulus, the different kinds of analyses that could be directed to that stimulus, and the hypothetical levels of processing. According to the levels-of-processing approach, memory for visual stimuli will be stronger if conceptual analyses are made of each item than if only visual or acoustic analyses are performed.

For Craik and Lockhart, memory duration is poorly described in terms of short-term and long-term storage. Instead, duration is assumed to fall along a processing continuum which ranges from

Stimulus	Perceptual classification	Type of analysis	Level of processing
	Is it red? Is it small?	Visual	Shallow
	Does it rhyme with chapel?	Acoustic	Moderate
	Is it edible? Is it good?	Conceptual	Deep

FIGURE 6.6. An example of the different kinds of perceptual analyses and their hypothetical levels of processing for a particular visual stimulus.

very brief memory durations resulting from physical analyses to much longer durations resulting from conceptual analyses. Similar to Atkinson and Shiffrin (1968), Craik and Lockhart do believe that stimuli can be maintained in a primary memory system (i.e., immediate memory) by 'recirculating information at one level of processing" (Craik & Lockhart, 1972, p. 676). By recirculating information, Craik and Lockhart mean the same thing that Atkinson and Shiffrin do when they discuss the main function of rehearsal. Craik and Lockhart refer to the recirculation of information at one level of processing in primary memory as *Type I* processing. This type of processing merely maintains information in primary memory without enhancing its duration once attention has been withdrawn. *Type II* processing involves directing attention to deeper levels of analysis, and it is this type of processing that enhances memory duration. Although Craik and Lockhart's Type I and Type II processing are analogous to Atkinson and Shiffrin's use of rehearsal and coding processes, the two formulations differ in a fundamental respect. Atkinson and Shiffrin's approach directs attention to memory storage systems, while Craik and Lockhart's approach directs attention to the relationship between encoding operations and retention. Whether more specific differences exist remains to be demonstrated (see also Glanzer & Koppenaal, 1977).

RESEARCH AND REFORMULATION. Many studies have been done on the relationship between encoding processes and memory performance. When viewed in terms of the levels-of-processing framework, much of this research is consistent, some of it suggests that the approach must be redefined, and some of it suggests areas in which the approach is in error. We will consider each body of research separately.

Research supporting the levels-of-processing approach is readily available in studies of incidental learning (e.g., Craik & Tulving, 1975; Hyde & Jenkins, 1969; Mechanic, 1962). In an incidental learning task, a subject is presented with a series of stimuli, asked to make some sort of perceptual classification of each stimulus, and then given a surprise free-recall or recognition test to assess what has been learned. Encoding operations are controlled by requiring different types of perceptual classifications, and the relationship between encoding and retention is measured by the memory performance on the surprise test. Hyde and Jenkins (1969) provide a representative example of many of these studies. In their study, Hyde and Jenkins presented subjects with a list of words. They required one group of subjects to count the number of letters in each word, another group to check for the presence of the letter E in each word, and a final group to rate the pleasantness of each stimulus. Since the subjects in the last group examined each stimulus in terms of its meaning, it was expected that this group would recall more of the stimuli on a surprise test than would either of the other groups of subjects, who were concerned with physical features. The results, like those of many similar experiments (e.g., Bobrow & Bower, 1969; Elias & Perfetti, 1973; Till & Jenkins, 1973), support the levels-of-processing assertion: The deeper the level of processing, the better the memory performance.

If memory performance is solely a function of encoding operations, then variables such as intention to learn and study time should have no effect. This seems to be the case. Hyde and Jenkins (1969) and Craik and Tulving (1975) found little difference in the performance of subjects who were forewarned of a free-recall test and those who were not. Retention varied only with the type of encoding task employed; knowledge of a subsequent memory test had no effect (see also Postman, 1964). Where intention to learn has shown positive effects, it may be that subjects spontaneously engaged in deeper levels of processing. Similarly, since deeper levels of processing typically take more time to complete than surface levels, more time is generally devoted to deep analyses than surface analyses. But study time, like intention, does not appear to be a key factor. Several studies have manipulated encoding processes so that surface analyses of physical features took more time than deep analyses of meaning (e.g., Craik & Tulving, 1975; Gardiner, 1974; Seamon & Murray, 1976). In each case, memory performance varied directly with the level of processing and not the total study time.

This approach, in spite of its successes, has not been without its critics. Nelson (1977) has presented the strongest critique to date in an attack based on the theoretical and empirical shortcomings of levels of processing. According to Nelson, different kinds of processing (e.g., visual analyses, acoustic analyses, and so forth) need not reflect different depths of processing. Differential depth of processing is an assumption based on different types of processing which produce different measures of memory performance. In the past, researchers have argued that their results supported the levels-of-processing approach without any means of verifying processing depth. A cynical view might hold that whatever produced good memory performance was deeply processed. To avoid a problem of circularity of definition, Nelson argued that it is necessary to order processing tasks in terms of their processing depths so as to independently determine their effect on memory performance. A recent study by Seamon and Virostek (1978) has provided a step in this direction. Using twelve different perceptual classification questions (e.g., Is the stimulus printed in upper-case letters? Is the stimulus a noun? Is the stimulus good?), one group of subjects rank-ordered the set of questions in terms of the amount of processing or degree of difficulty associated with answering each question. A second group of subjects was shown a list of words to be classified in terms of the different classification questions in an incidental learning task. Following the classification task, these subjects were asked to recall the stimuli on a surprise free-recall test. The results showed that recall was significantly correlated with the depth-of-processing order devised by the first group: The deeper the processing required by the classification question, the better the memory performance on the recall test.

Problems, however, still remain. Depth of processing is an ill-defined concept and likely to remain so until a better understanding of perceptual processing is obtained. It is noteworthy that recent studies (e.g., Craik & Jacoby, 1975; Craik & Tulving, 1975) have stressed the spread or elaboration of encoding in addition to the depth of processing. Craik and Tulving (1975) and Schulman (1974) report that within a given processing task, the more elaborate the encoding condition, the better the long-term recall. In one study subjects showed lower recall for words judged as appropriate for simple sentence frames (e.g., Does DRESS fit in the sentence, "The _____ is torn"?) than elaborate frames (e.g., Does DRESS fit in the sentence, "The small lady angrily picked up the red _____"?). Craik and Tulving still maintain, however, that a minimal semantic analysis is always more beneficial to retention than an elaborate physical analysis.

Although the relationship between memory performance and retrieval cues will be discussed in a later chapter, this issue must be mentioned briefly at this time. If retention varies with the spread of encoding, it may be that broader encodings provide more retrieval cues to facilitate remembering. If this is so, a number of researchers have speculated that perhaps the depth-of-processing findings can be explained simply in terms of differential availability of retrieval cues. Trying to remember a word in terms of whether it contained the letter E, for example, may be less effective as an aid to remembering than trying to remember a word that was encoded into a meaningful sentence. Several studies have tested this possibility and found that, while retrieval cues facilitated recall and recognition performance at all depths of processing, retention was still affected primarily by the initial encoding operations (e.g., Morris, Bransford, & Franks, 1977; Moscovitch & Craik, 1976). The availability of retrieval cues is a factor in memory performance, but it cannot account for the levels-of-processing data.

A REAPPRAISAL OF APPROACHES

In this closing section, we will reconsider the Atkinson and Shiffrin (1968) and Craik and Lockhart (1972) approaches with an eye toward integrating both positions. Before doing so, however, we must consider additional data which bear negatively on the Craik and Lockhart formulation.

First, as Baddeley (1976) notes, the levels-of-processing approach does not seem applicable to certain patients with neurological disorders. H. M., for example, is able to carry on a normal conversation which should entail deep levels of semantic processing, yet H. M. does not show evidence of new long-term storage. In this instance, retention is not related to depth of processing.

Second, Craik and Lockhart have distinguished between Type I and Type II processing and have asserted that Type I processing involves the repetitive processing of surface analyses and does not produce a more permanent memory trace. But recent studies by

Craik and Tulving (1975) and Nelson (1977) found that repetition of surface level encodings did improve long-term retention. Nelson forcefully argues that these data disconfirm the assumption about Type I processing (see Hintzman, 1976, for a review of repetition effects).

Finally, Nelson and Vining (1978) have shown Craik and Lockhart's basic assumption about the relationship between depth of processing and memory duration to be wrong. Deeper levels of processing result in longer-lasting memory traces only when the initial levels of learning have been free to vary. When learning has been equated over all levels of processing, memory duration is equivalent (Nelson & Vining, 1978). Moreover, physical analyses of stimuli need not always produce brief memory traces. Research indicates that physical aspects of stimulation can be retained for appreciable periods of time (e.g., Jacoby, 1975), in some instances for longer than one month (e.g., Kolers, 1975; Kolers & Ostry, 1974). What levels of processing affects, according to Nelson and Vining, is not the duration of the resulting memory trace but the speed with which a long-term trace is established. Seamon and Murray's (1976) data showing that levels of processing affects long-term, but not short-term, storage is compatible with this position.

The crucial implication of the above studies is that memory performance may not reflect a processing continuum, as Craik and Lockhart originally argued. Information may be conceptualized as existing in short-term or long-term storage, with the rate of transfer from short-term to long-term storage a function of the level of processing. When the degree of learning is permitted to vary across processing levels, memory performance may resemble a continuum; when the degree of learning is equated, memory performance across processing levels will be equivalent and no continuum will be seen. The Atkinson and Shiffrin (1968) and Craik and Lockhart (1972) approaches can be integrated in this manner to provide a unified account of memory performance with emphasis on both memory structures and control processes.

SUMMARY

1. Theorists since the time of William James have debated whether memory should be conceptualized in dichotomous terms or viewed as a continuum.

2. The Atkinson and Shiffrin (1968) approach separates memory into structures and control processes.

3. The memory structures are permanent features of memory and include the sensory registers, short-term store, and long-term store.

4. Control processes are used to interact with information in memory. Mental rehearsal is an example of a control process.

5. Learning, in the Atkinson and Shiffrin approach, involves the transfer of information from short-term to long-term storage.

6. Evidence for separate short-term and long-term storage comes from studies of free recall, Korsakoff's syndrome, and neurological disorders.

7. The serial position effect found in free recall showing primacy and recency effects has been interpreted as reflecting recall from long-term (primacy) and short-term (recency) storage.

8. Patients suffering from Korsakoff's syndrome show normal short-term storage and good long-term storage up to the time of their illness. After the onset of their illness, short-term storage may remain normal, but long-term storage becomes highly deficient.

9. Certain neurological patients, through accident or surgery, show normal short-term storage but deficient long-term storage. N. A. and H. M. are two examples.

10. Rehearsal may serve to maintain information in short-term storage and transfer a weak memory trace to long-term storage.

11. Experimental studies of the ability of rehearsal to transfer information to long-term storage have yielded conflicting results.

12. Recent research has attempted to distinguish between different types of rehearsal. Maintenance or primary rehearsal seems to hold information in short-term storage, while elaborative or secondary rehearsal serves to transfer information to long-term storage.

13. The levels-of-processing approach attempts to relate memory performance to stimulus encoding procedures. The basic assumption of the Craik and Lockhart (1972) position is that the deeper a stimulus is processed, the stronger and more durable will be the resulting trace.

14. Much evidence is available to show that retention varies with different types of processing even though the concept of depth of processing remains ill defined. Recent studies have emphasized the spread of encoding as a supplement to depth of processing.

15. Specific shortcomings of the levels-of-processing approach are: (a) it does not seem applicable to patients with neurological disorders, such as H. M.; (b) it does not predict the positive effects of repetition found with surface levels of analysis; (c) its claim that depth of processing enhances memory duration has not been supported.

16. An alternative position was presented in which information was conceptualized as existing in short-term or long-term storage, with the rate of transfer from short-term to long-term storage a function of the depth of processing. This unified approach emphasizes both memory structures and control processes.

CHAPTER SEVEN

Nonverbal Memory: Pictures, Images, & Faces

OBJECTIVES

1. To compare memory performance for pictures, images, and words.
2. To present evidence for both the subjective and psychological reality of mental imagery.
3. To discuss possible reasons for the observed superiority in retention of nonverbally coded information.
4. To provide a detailed review of facial recognition over time as an example of nonverbal memory.

INTRODUCTION

Up to now, we have focused primarily on verbal memory for digits, letters, and words. Except for the discussion of different sensory representations (e.g., iconic and echoic memories), the major emphasis has been on memory for stimulus names. But other types of memory representations are also available. Some things, such as our memory of people and places, can involve nonverbal representations that may last for considerable periods of time.

Almost everyone has had the experience of remembering some seemingly long forgotten event in the presence of an unexpected stimulus. Although these triggering stimuli can be verbal in nature, frequently they are not. On one occasion, a particular smell triggered the recall of an earlier experience that had not been on my mind for many years. While entering a nature trail on an early morning walk with my two sons, I stopped suddenly and realized that I had smelled this fragrance before. For a moment, I was completely taken back. No longer was I an adult idly walking with my young children; I was a boy of eight running along a trail with my friends at camp. Proust (1913) recalls a similar experience in his book *Remembrance of Things Past*. For Proust, it was the taste of a French pastry, a "petite madeleine," that led him to recall vividly a time in his youth. Each of these experiences, although anecdotal in nature, implies the presence of nonverbal long-term storage.

MEMORY FOR PICTURES AND WORDS

Early Verbal Superiority

Ebbinghaus's impact on the development of experimental psychology has already been noted in Chapter One. It was Ebbinghaus who invented the nonsense syllable in an attempt to plot the course of learning and retention. Such stimuli were felt to permit an assessment of pure learning and remembering since they were assumed to be uncontaminated by existing associations. Although it is now clear that even nonsense syllables differ in degree of meaningfulness (e.g., Underwood & Schulz, 1960), Ebbinghaus's research dictated an early preference for verbal stimuli in an attempt to ensure scientific rigor.

Subsequent studies have suggested that the choice of verbal stimuli was correct, for it seemed that subjects, when presented with pictorial stimuli, would code or represent the stimuli in terms of verbal descriptions and remember those descriptions. Carmichael, Hogan, and Walter (1932) presented subjects with a list of stimuli composed of picture and word pairs. Each picture was a line drawing which could be interpreted in one of two ways by an associated verbal label (e.g., O–O plus *eyeglasses;* O–O plus *dumb bell*). Two groups of subjects were shown the same set of pictorial stimuli but different associated labels. After a delay, the subjects were asked to reproduce the pictorial stimuli from memory. The results showed that the drawings were heavily influenced by the verbal labels; the subjects tended to draw the ambiguous pictorial stimuli in terms of the object names that were associated with them at the time of learning. Later work by Hebb and Foord (1945) found that verbal coding of pictorial stimuli occurred at the time of learning since varying the delay between presentation and test did not increase the degree of change.

Another demonstration of the importance of verbal coding of pictorial stimuli is found in Glanzer and Clark (1963). In this study, subjects were shown arrays of eight black or white figures. The subjects' task was to examine an array and then either provide a verbal description of the black-white sequence or reproduce the black-white sequence on a neutral array. The results indicated that the simpler the verbal description of an array, the more accurate the reproduction made from memory. Glanzer and Clark proposed that during perceptual processing, subjects engaged in covert verbalization and the length of this verbalization determined the ease of learning. Once again, the retention of pictorial stimuli seemed to be dependent upon verbal coding.

Later Pictorial Superiority

Later studies, while not denying that memory of pictorial stimuli could be directly influenced by their verbal contexts, showed that pictorial stimuli could be retained better than verbal stimuli when direct comparisons were made. Shepard (1967) gave subjects a deck of approximately 600 single words, English sentences, or pictures from magazines for self-paced viewing. After examining the stimuli, a forced-choice recognition test was presented in which subjects had to select which of two stimuli was seen previously. On each trial a previously shown stimulus was paired with a comparable stimulus not shown before. Although recognition scores were high in each instance, recognition of pictures (98.5 percent correct) significantly exceeded that of words (90.0 percent correct) and sentences (88.2 percent correct). Haber (1970) extended these findings by showing that individual subjects could recognize between 85 and 95 percent of 2,560 pictorial scenes after each had been shown for only 10 seconds. While these studies did not make a direct comparison of memory for pictures and their associated labels, these experiments and others (e.g., Bevan & Stegar, 1971; Nickerson, 1965; Standing, 1973) document the impressive ability of subjects to process and retain pictorial information.

Subsequent research has provided direct comparisons of pictures and their labels and found pictures to be remembered better (e.g., Paivio & Csapo, 1969; Paivio, Rogers, & Smythe, 1968). This is found over intervals as short as 10 minutes or as long as 3 months (Gehring, Toglia, & Kimble, 1976). Perhaps the clearest evidence of a long-term superiority for pictorial information comes from a study by Bahrick, Bahrick and Wittlinger (1975) in which memory for the faces and names of high-school classmates was examined over a span of 47 years. Using yearbooks from people who graduated as recently as 3 months or as long ago as 47 years, Bahrick et al. devised a series of tests to provide an accurate measure of memory for the faces and names of former classmates. On the face recognition test, the subjects were shown sets of five graduation pictures that were equated for age of picture, style, and so forth. The subjects' task was to select the one picture that was taken from their own yearbook. Chance performance on this task was 20 percent. The name recognition test was constructed in the same fashion, except that names were used instead of yearbook pictures.

Bahrick et al. found that within 14 years of graduation, subjects could recognize 90 percent of the faces and names of their classmates. Beyond this interval, a difference occurred between faces and names. Faces continued to be recognized at least 90 percent correct for up to 35 years after graduation. Only after 47 years did facial recognition drop to an accuracy level of 73 percent. Recognition memory for names, by contrast, dropped to the 78 percent correct level after 25 years and stayed at this approximate level through the 47th year. These data demonstrate two key points. First, information which is acquired over a long period of time (i.e., familiarization of at least 1 year for classmates) is retained, in large measure, for the life of the individual. Second, faces are retained at high levels longer than names. This study of memory for faces and names under natural learning conditions confirms the laboratory findings showing superior retention for pictorial information.

Collectively, the studies cited above indicate that subjects are better at remembering objects, pictures, and faces than names or verbal labels. Furthermore, these differences are magnified over repeated memory tests of the same stimuli since pictures show improved recall while words do not. This phenomenon, known as hypermnesia, has been reported by Erdelyi and Becker (1974) and Yarmey (1976). Before considering why a difference in memorability exists for pictures and words, we must examine research on mental imagery, since this will bear importantly on the theoretical explanation to be offered.

MENTAL IMAGERY

Evidence for Imagery

SUBJECTIVE EXPERIENCE. Count the number of windows in the home in which you live. When subjects are asked to perform this task, they frequently report that they count the windows by mentally walking through their homes, one room at a time (Shepard, 1966). Subjectively, this task provides a strong impression of visual imagery. Consider another example. Slowly read the eleven sentences in Table 7.1 and try to visualize the relationship provided in each instance. After reading the sentences, examine the four sentences in Table 7.2. In each case, determine whether the sentence was presented previously without looking back to Table 7.1. Complete this recognition test before continuing to read. Compared to subjects who were instructed to memorize the initial eleven sentences, subjects instructed to visualize the sentences were more

TABLE 7.1   A Demonstration of Visual Imagery

Read each sentence and visualize the relationship.

1. The lion is to the left of the bear.
2. The lion is to the left of the giraffe.
3. The bear is to the left of the moose.
4. The bear is to the right of the lion.
5. The moose is to the left of the giraffe.
6. The moose is to the right of the lion.
7. The giraffe is to the left of the cow.
8. The giraffe is to the right of the bear.
9. The giraffe is to the right of the moose.
10. The cow is to the right of the giraffe.
11. The cow is to the right of the bear.

(Adapted from Barclay, 1973)

TABLE 7.2   A Test of Visual Imagery

Which sentence did you read before?

1. The bear is to the left of the moose.
2. The moose is to the left of the bear.
3. The bear is to the right of the moose.
4. The bear is to the left of the giraffe.

(Adapted from Barclay, 1973)

accurate at recognizing sentence 1 and rejecting sentences 2 and 3 on a test of recognition memory. These same subjects, however, falsely recognized sentence 4 more often than those subjects using rote memory (Barclay, 1973). Although sentence 4 was never read, the information it contained was compatible with that in the images generated. Once more, a compelling impression of imagery is experienced.

Doubtless, many examples exist which provide imagerylike experiences. But these examples cannot be considered as evidence for the reality of visual imagery. The problem, as Bower (1970a) notes, is that subjective experiences provide no basis for agreement among observers. Introspective reports of imagery show so much variability in such things as intensity, vividness, and frequency that verbal reports of these inner experiences are of little value. What are needed are procedures whereby these heretofore hidden experiences can be revealed by observable responses made under precise and specific conditions. When this occurs, the study of imagery moves from the realm of speculation to that of experimental inquiry.

NORMAL IMAGERY. There are a number of established procedures in which the existence of mental imagery can be inferred. These procedures include free recall of high- and low-imagery words, modality-specific interference, and mental rotation. Each of these procedures will be reviewed in turn.

In the preceding section, we noted that pictorial stimuli are remembered better than verbal stimuli. It follows that the retention of verbal stimuli should be enhanced if subjects encode these stimuli in terms of visual imagery. Considerable research (see Paivio, 1971 for a review) indicates that this is true; high-imagery words (e.g., BUTTERFLY) are remembered better than low-imagery words (e.g., CITATION). When subjects are specifically instructed to study words in terms of either rote rehearsal or visual imagery, subjects who form images of the stimuli remember more items than those who do not (e.g., Schnorr & Atkinson, 1969). Data such as these indicate that imagery coding is an effective means of improving long-term retention. Related to this observation are the findings of Erdelyi, Finkelstein, Herrell, Miller, and Thomas (1976). They observed hypermnesia (i.e., improved recall over repeated attempts) for verbal stimuli encoded by visual imagery; previous research (Yarmey, 1976) has found this effect only with pictures. It would appear, then, that memory for pictorial stimuli and imagery-coded verbal stimuli are similar.

FIGURE 7.1. An example of a stimulus used by Brooks (1968) to study modality-specific interference. See text for details.

Studies of modality-specific interference have shown that subjects have more difficulty with a secondary task that requires the use of vision when they are simultaneously employing visual imagery in a learning task than when using some other coding strategy (e.g., Baddeley, Grant, Wight, & Thomson, 1974; Bower, 1972; Powell, Hamon, & Young, 1975). Brooks (1968), for example, presented subjects with a visual letter such as that shown in Figure 7.1. After study, the letter was removed and the subjects were asked to transverse the letter mentally by starting at the lower left and indicating whether each point was an extreme top or bottom point or an interior point. The correct sequence for the stimulus in Figure 7.1 is YES, YES, YES, NO, NO, NO, NO, NO, NO, YES. Brooks found that subjects were much faster at responding YES or NO verbally than at pointing to a column of Y-N pairs. Since pointing required visual guidance, it interfered with the subjects' ability to maintain an image of the letter stimulus and thereby slowed response times. Less interference in the verbal report condition resulted in faster response times since different modalities were used for stimulus storage and response. These data and others (e.g., Seamon & Gazzaniga, 1973) imply that some aspect of the visual system is activated when subjects use visual imagery during encoding or responding.

Finally, the studies of mental rotation by Shepard and others (see Shepard, 1978, for a review) provide strong evidence for visual imagery. Shepard and Metzler (1971) presented subjects with stimulus pairs such as those shown in Figure 7.2. The task was to determine if a stimulus pair contained different views of the same object or different objects. The subjects felt that they performed this task by mentally rotating one of the objects in each pair until it was found to be congruent or incongruent with the other. For stimulus pairs of the

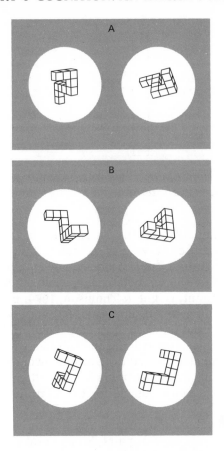

FIGURE 7.2. Selected examples of stimulus pairs used by Shepard and Metzler (1971) to study mental rotation. The stimuli can represent pairings of the same object (Pairs A and B) or different objects (Pair C).

same object, the response time data, which are shown in Figure 7.3, supported the introspective reports; response time was linearly related to the degree of angular rotation of the two objects. These data suggest that subjects rotated the stimuli at a fixed rate. The greater the degree of disparity of the objects, the greater the amount of rotation and the longer the response time. Other studies have extended these findings by showing that subjects can prepare for a rotated stimulus if they have sufficient time and knowledge as to the type of stimulus and degree of rotation required (e.g., Cooper &

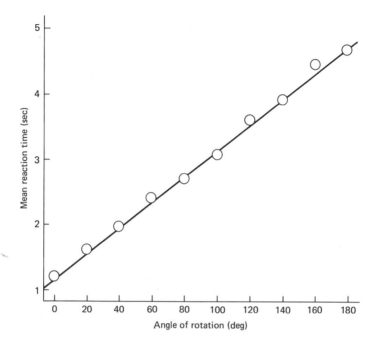

FIGURE 7.3. Mean response time for "same" pairs as a function of the degree of angular rotation for objects rotated on a picture plane. (Adapted from Shepard & Metzler, 1971)

Shepard, 1973). Without the benefit of visual imagery, it is difficult to see how this task and those from the other paradigms could have been performed. The data appear to require an inference of visual imagery for their interpretation. Subjective reports, although in accord, are not the primary data. The evidence for imagery rests on reliable findings such as those we have reviewed.

SUPERNORMAL IMAGERY. Virtually all subjects show evidence of using visual imagery when tested in any of the above paradigms. Individual differences, however, do exist. There are a number of people whose reported use of visual imagery far surpasses that of the norm. Unlike the professional mnemonists to be discussed in Chapter Eight, these individuals seem to possess special skills which render them different from other people. Luria (1968) reports the history of a man called S (Luria's abbreviation) who had the ability to reproduce arrays of fifty-two characters such as that

TABLE 7.3   A Stimulus Array that Could Be Held
in Eidetic Imagery by Luria's Subject, S

```
8 8 6 0
4 5 3 1
7 9 0 4
2 2 5 1
3 4 7 8
8 9 1 3
2 2 1 5
5 4 3 1
9 7 3 4
1 5 2 8
2 9 7 6
3 9 3 1
X 3 7 X
```

(Adapted from Luria, 1968)

shown in Table 7.3. After studying the array for 3 minutes, S took 25 seconds to recall the second vertical column, 30 seconds to recite the same column backward, and 50 seconds to recite all of the characters by rows. According to S, he was able to reproduce an image of himself studying the array so that recalling it from memory took little more time than that required to read the array initially. While it is impossible to veryify S's introspective reports, his performance is certainly unusual.

Another example in which visual images seem to persist for extended periods of time can be found in studies of *eidetic imagery* (e.g., Haber, 1969; Stromeyer, 1970; Stromeyer, & Psotka, 1970). This type of imagery can be described as a process of retaining visual information in the form of an accurate and highly detailed visual image. Stromeyer (1970), for example, discusses the case of a young woman who has the ability to form images and transpose them at will. In one demonstration Stromeyer presented this subject with two separate dot patterns. Each dot pattern contained 10,000 dots in a seemingly random arrangement. The patterns, if superimposed, would represent a number or letter. In this task, one of the dot patterns was presented for viewing by the subject's right eye only for 1 minute. It was then removed, and the second dot pattern was presented to the left eye alone. Stromeyer reports that the subject correctly saw the letter T. For most people, the letter would be visible only if the two dot patterns were superiposed. For Stromeyer's subject, eidetic imagery was apparently used to superimpose the squentially presented arrays. Although demonstrations such as these are intriguing, Gray and Gummerman (1975) report that interpretation problems exist with eidetic imagery. Not all people classified as eidetikers are able to perform like Stromeyer's subject when shown unpredictable dot patterns. Furthermore, not all eidetikers can produce accurate and detailed picture descriptions. Because studies of eidetic imagery have produced inconsistent results (see Gray and Gummerman, 1975, for a review), eidetic imagery remains a puzzle.

The Mental Picture Metaphor

In the preceding section, we reviewed different subjective experiences of imagery, various experimental procedures designed to make imagery processes observable, and special forms of imagery found in rare individuals. In each case, the temptation has been to view imagery metaphorically as a means of constructing mental pictures. But the experimental literature suggests that great caution must be used in discussing imagery in metaphorical terms ,(e.g., Anderson & Bower, 1973; Pylyshyn, 1973). Three specific studies indicate that the mental picture metaphor is incorrect.

HIDDEN AND EXPOSED OBJECTS. Neisser and Kerr (1973) compared the effects of instructions to form images of observable objects (e.g., "A harp is sitting on top of the torch held by the Statue of Liberty") with those to conceal objects within an image (e.g., "A harp is hidden inside the torch held by the Statue of Liberty"). Using an incidental learning paradigm, Neisser and Kerr reasoned that if the mental picture metaphor is appropriate, subjects should show poorer performance on measures of both imagery vividness and recall when objects are concealed within the images than when they are observable. According to the mental picture metaphor, the image should be examined in much the same way as a picture; objects hidden in images, like those hidden in pictures, should be poorly retained. In this study, the subjects read the sentences, tried to form images of each relationship, and then rated the images on a scale of vividness from 1 (most vivid) to 7 (least vivid). In some sentences the subjects constructed images of objects that were associated and either exposed or hidden (e.g., see above examples), while in other instances the subjects formed images of objects which were exposed but not associated (e.g., "Looking from one window, you see the Statue of Liberty; from a window on another

TABLE 7.4   Mean Recall and Vividness Ratings
             as a Function of Imagery
             Condition*

Condition	Recall†	Vividness
Hidden	4.12	3.19
Exposed	4.12	2.63
Separate	2.92	3.13

*Data are from Experiment 2.
†Maximum recall is 6.

(Neisser and Kerr, 1973)

wall you see a *harp*"). In the actual experiment, different sentences were used in each instance.

After rating the vividness of the images, a surprise cued recall test was presented. The subjects were given one object from each sentence (e.g., HARP) and asked to recall the other object from the same sentence (e.g., STATUE OF LIBERTY). The results, shown in Table 7.4, indicate that imagery vividness had no effect on cued recall. The subjects rated the Exposed Objects Sentences as significantly more vivid in imagery than either the Hidden Object or Separate Objects Sentences; yet, on the surprise recall test, recall from Hidden Objects Sentences was equal to that of Exposed Objects Sentences and superior to that of Separate Objects Sentences. These data are in disagreement with expectations based on the mental picture metaphor. Hiding an object within an image lowered its imagery vividness but did not affect its memorability. This suggests that an image is not like a mental picture.

CONGENITALLY BLIND SUBJECTS. The strongest evidence against the mental picture metaphor comes from studies of subjects who are congenitally blind. Jonides, Kahn, and Rozin (1975) compared paired associate learning in normally sighted students with that of students who were comparable except that they have been totally blind from birth. Both groups of subjects were presented with a list of paired associates composed of twenty noun pairs. The subjects' task was to listen to each noun pair and attempt to associate the nouns in some manner. After hearing all twenty pairs, the first member of each pair was presented as a stimulus and the subject was asked to recall the second member as a response. After one trial on all pairs, the recall of the normally sighted subjects was significantly better than that of the blind subjects. Prior to the start of a second trial on the same paired associates, all subjects were given relational imagery instructions in which they were told to form images of each noun and attempt to relate the images in each pair (e.g., ELEPHANT-BRIDGE might be imaged as an elephant walking on a narrow bridge). Not surprisingly, the performance of the normally sighted subjects improved since relational imagery has been demonstrated to be an effective learning strategy for paired associates (e.g., Bower, 1972). Furthermore, additional subjects who simply repeated the same task for two trials did not show an improvement, suggesting that the improved performance of the normally sighted subjects was due to the relational imagery strategy. What was surprising was the performance of the blind subjects. Although there could be nothing visual in the types of images generated by these subjects, their performance improved significantly with the aid of the relational imagery strategy.

These data and others which show that blind subjects can perform mental rotation tasks (e.g., Marmor & Zaback, 1976) forcefully imply that generating an image does not resemble looking at a picture. Imagery instructions may improve memory performance by coding information in terms of generated spatial relationships. This could resemble a picture in the sense that spatial relationships can exist in a picture, but these relationships need not be apprehended visually. Blind subjects, for example, can form spatial relationships to walk around their homes without the aid of vision.

Theories of Picture-Image Superiority

The evidence for the superiority of retention for pictorial or imagery-coded verbal information is strong. In this section, we will briefly review some of the more outstanding qualities of pictures and images that may serve to enhance the retention of their traces.

ATTENTIONAL FACTORS. Intuitively, memory for pictorial or imagery-coded information would seem to be enhanced when the stimuli are more distinctive than their verbal counterparts. Gehring, Toglia, and Kimble (1976), for example, note that frequency of stimulus usage is probably unequal. Words are used much more frequently prior to a laboratory experiment and may show substantial interference effects. Pictures, even of common objects, are more likely to be rendered in a unique format so as to limit the possibility of interference. Goldstein and Chance (1971) add that pictures can vary among themselves on many dimensions so that in tests of recognition memory only a fraction of these features need to be noted to differentiate old from new stimuli. Verbally coded information would not have these advantages. Finally, processing differences between pictorially coded and verbally coded information can also be present. Dhawan and Pellegrino (1977) found that pictures were encoded to a deep semantic level of processing faster than their verbal counterparts. For stimuli presented at short, fixed intervals, this indicates that pictorial information can be processed more deeply than verbal information and retained longer due to unequal learning.

DUAL-CODING THEORY. Levels of processing and attentional factors, however, will not fully explain the memory differences found for verbally and nonverbally coded information. The data showing modality-specific interference, in particular, call for some interpretation that is based on different representational codes. The most ambitious attempt to date along this line is Paivio's (1971) dual-coding theory. While not denying the importance of attentional factors, *dual-coding theory* holds that memory performance is based on the number of different traces produced for a given stimulus. Abstract (i.e., low-imagery) verbal stimuli have a high probability of generating only a verbal memory trace, while concrete (i.e., high-imagery) verbal stimuli may generate nonverbal traces as well as verbal traces. Concrete stimuli are remembered better than abstract stimuli because of the dual memory traces which produce better retention due to multiple storage and retrieval. With pictorial stimuli, dual-coding theory assumes that the probability of verbal and nonverbal memory representations is higher than for concrete words because generating a name of an object is faster than generating an image from an object's name.

A great deal of evidence has been amassed by Paivio (1971) and others (e.g., D'Agostino, O'Neill, & Paivio, 1977; Kosslyn, 1976) which supports the dual-coding assumption of separate verbal and nonverbal memory traces. Verbal traces may be conceptualized as abstract representations that bear no direct relationship to their corresponding object representations. Nonverbal-spatial representations are different. While we do not know what an image representation looks like, it is known that nonverbal traces resemble each other in ways that are analogous to their resemblances in the real world. Similar to direct perceptual comparisons, memory judgments are influenced by stimulus size (e.g., Moyer, 1973; Paivio, 1975) and shape (e.g., Shepard & Chipman, 1970). As an example, subjects are faster at deciding that a mouse is smaller than an elephant than they are at deciding that a mouse is smaller than a squirrel. Similarly, subjects are more apt to say that the shape of Oregon is more like that of Colorado than Florida even without an outline of each state present. These findings suggest that information can be coded nonverbally in memory on some basis which preserves the relationship found in perceptual comparisons. Verbal coding is simply not a likely candidate.

Dual-coding theory has not gone uncriticized (Friedman & Bourne, 1976; Nelson & Reed, 1976). Kintsch (1977) notes that dual-coding theory emphasizes only verbal and nonverbal-spatial codes. Other types of representations for other sensory modalities, such as audition and olfaction, must also be present. Perhaps because vision is the dominant sense (Posner & Nissen, 1976), theorists have concentrated on coding representations for dealing with visually presented information. This is a limitation, but not a failure, for dual-coding theory.

FACIAL RECOGNITION

Recognition Over Time and Change

Everyone is familiar with the old saw about forgetting a name but never a face. While this separation of verbal and nonverbal information is consistent with the kinds of data we have reviewed so far, faces are special in that they change over time yet still permit recognition. In this last section, we will review how faces change and how recognition might still be accomplished.

DYNAMIC CHANGES. According to Liggett (1974), the face is our most varied attribute. Fourteen bones provide the underlying structure to the face, and these bones differ in size and shape from one person to another. Also contributing to individual differences is a layer of fatty tissue which varies in thickness and smoothness across individuals. This tissue separates the skin from the interconnected and criss-crossing pattern of more than 100 muscles which permit variation in facial expressions (Liggett, 1974).

At birth, the forehead tends to be large and the cheeks shallow. With maturity, the underlying bone structure changes; the high forehead is lost, the distance between the level of the eyes and nose grows greater, and the nose, once small and concave, becomes broader and flatter. With increasing years, the eyes lose their luster and the skin loses its elasticity. Where once the skin recovered quickly from stretching due to a smile, the recovery becomes slower and may take as long as several seconds in elderly persons. Because of the loss of elasticity and the effects of gravity pulling down on the skin for many years, sags, wrinkles, and pouches begin to develop during one's twenties and become more noticeable after age forty (see Enlow, 1975; Guy, Converse, & Morello, 1977, for reviews). Although many factors, including bone structure, hair coverage, and so forth, are involved in facial aging, skin degeneration, which is especially noticeable around the eyes, appears to be a major sign of aging in the adult face. This fact has long been recognized by professional makeup artists to create an aged appearance (e.g., Buchman, 1973), and surgical procedures such as rhytidectomy (i.e., a face lift) provide only temporary restoration (Skoog, 1974).

DYNAMIC RECOGNITION. Almost everyone has had the experience of bumping into a former schoolmate or acquaintance who has not been seen in many years. Invariably, both viewers look at each other, note something familiar about each other's face, and then remember the person's name or at least the context in which each had formerly been acquainted. Faces change considerably over time, yet recognition appears to be surprisingly simple. These anecdotes, however, may fool us. Facial recognition over time may be the rule or only the exception to the rule that gets noted and remembered. Experimental verification under controlled conditions is necessary.

In a series of studies, Seamon (1980) has attempted to determine how well individuals can be recognized over periods of time which encompass facial change. In one study, subjects were presented with a list of faces of male college professors. The subjects looked at each face and indicated if they were familiar with the person. Familiarity was defined as having seen the professor on campus at any time prior to the experiment. The subjects were also informed that a recognition memory test on all of the faces would follow the stimulus presentation. The recognition test consisted of presenting the same professors in either the same pictures or pictures as they were approximately ten years earlier. Distractor pictures of professors not shown were also included. These pictures were similarly divided into current and older pictures of college professors. The subjects' task, which was explained at the onset, was to attept to recognize the person and not the particular picture.

The results showed that facial recognition over time was possible. Subjects achieved high recognition scores on those pictures that were repeated and for those professors who were judged as familiar. The subjects were also able to recognize pictures of the same professors as they were ten years earlier, whether they were familiar or not, significantly better than chance.

Additional research (Seamon, 1980) has attempted to measure this ability over a longer time span and greater developmental change. Facial recognition from infancy to young adulthood was examined by having college undergraduates obtain pictures of themselves from infancy (zero to two years old), childhood (seven to nine years old), early teens (thirteen to fifteen years old), and young adulthood (eighteen to twenty-one years old). In one study, subjects were presented with eight complete picture sets of individuals that had been randomly scrambled. The task was to sort all of the pictures so that each person had his or her young adult, teenage, childhood, and baby picture correctly associated. The percentage of correct young adult-teen pairings was 95 percent, young adult-childhood was 85 percent, and young adult-baby was 55 percent. The subjects associated faces of people over time better than chance (i.e., 20 percent) in each instance, although the ability to do so definitely decreased as the amount of time and facial change between the young adult standard pictures and the comparison pictures increased. Further research employing a forced-choice paradigm (e.g., Is this the same person in both pictures?) has produced comparable results. Facial recognition over time appears to be a demonstrable ability which is subject to the effect of time and change.

Toward a Theory

In Chapter Six we discussed the relationship between levels of processing and memory performance. Faces, as visual stimuli, should show the same effects of encoding operations on recognition memory as other types of stimuli. Research shows this to be true. A number of studies of facial recognition have employed an incidental learning paradigm and asked subjects to make superficial (e.g., Is the person male or female?) or deep (e.g., Is the person honest?) analyses. The general result is that recognition is superior when subjects attend to a face in terms of a personality variable than when they attend to a particular physical dimension (e.g., Bower & Karlin, 1974; Patterson & Baddeley, 1977; Winograd,

1976). Presumably, personality factors require more thorough processing than physical factors.

If attention is an important determinant of performance, it is important to know what people attend to while looking at a face. Data from several different sources suggest that the eyes and mouth command the most attention. This can be seen, for example, in the eye movement recordings of individuals looking at a picture of a face. While the eyes scan the entire facial area, they focus again and again on the eyes and mouth (Walker-Smith, Gale, & Findlay, 1977; Yarbus, 1967). Similarly, recognition paradigms have shown that changes involving the eyes and mouth are more likely to be noticed than a change in the nose (Davies, Ellis, & Shepherd, 1977; Fisher & Cox, 1975), and the eyes and mouth are better recognized than the nose in an incidental recognition test of isolated features following exposure to an entire face (Seamon, Stolz, Bass, & Chatinover, 1978). The eyes and mouth are what people attend to when given free viewing, and these are the features that are best retained.

Why do people attend to the eyes and mouth, and how might these features mediate the recognition of individuals over time and dynamic change? We will examine each of these questions separately and, in the process, put forth a sketchy and quite tentative hypothesis on facial recognition.

The reason the eyes and mouth command attention does not appear to be mysterious. Through movement (e.g., smiles, frowns, and so forth), the eyes and mouth convey information to the viewer. This information may either supplement what is being said or act as the sole input if verbal information is not available. The eyes and mouth are the expressive parts of a face; viewers look at these in order to understand the moods, thoughts, and feelings of other people. This attention to expressive features must be an acquired skill that develops in early childhood and may be refined through adulthood. If this view is correct, facial recognition is accomplished not because of any conscious attempt to remember a face but rather incidentally in the process of picking up information for the purpose of communication and understanding. As yet, this hypothesis has said nothing about how recognition occurs over dynamic changes; it merely states that the eyes and mouth of a face will be remembered because attention was directed to them. This hypothesis would further assume that attending to features for the purpose of understanding the meaning of the thought being expressed would constitute a deep level of encoding and thereby facilitate learning and retention.

The fact that twenty-one to twenty-five week-old infants show good facial recognition (e.g., Fagan, 1973) is not damning to this hypothesis. While it is unlikely that infants are preset to look at the eyes and mouth for nonverbal communication cues, human beings of all ages are attracted by movement (see Lewis & Brooks, 1975). Attention to movement may be an innate process which can provide a basis for infant facial recognition; memory is related to attention, attention is attracted by movement, and the eyes and mouth are those facial features most capable of movement. The experience of looking at live models with smiling eyes and cooing mouths might generalize to static facial representations so as to mediate recognition performance at a very young age.

This hypothesis holds that facial recognition is a function of attention primarily to the eyes and mouth. Children and adults attend to these features because they convey nonverbal information which facilitates understanding. Infants, who also show facial recognition, may attend to these features because they are associated with movement. Up to this point, the hypothesis is capable of accounting for the recognition of nonchanging faces in terms of encoding processes.

Faces, however, do change. There are characeristic head changes in size and shape that all people undergo over time (e.g., Enlow, 1975; Pittenger & Shaw, 1975). These changes and others already noted enable a viewer to determine the age of another person, but they do not provide clues for individual recognition over time. A more realistic possibility is that the ability to recognize a person after dynamic changes have occurred is actually a fringe benefit that is picked up by virtue of having attended to the features of a face that have remained relatively stable. Preliminary studies (Seamon, 1978) suggest that the eyes and mouth change less than the nose over time. These data, while offered tentatively, are based on the ratings of various dimensions of each feature from picture sets of individuals from infancy to young adulthood. The results show that ratings of eye and mouth dimensions change less over time than those for the nose. If these data are supported by additional research, they may provide a basis for understanding a complex cognitive ability. Dynamic facial recognition may be achieved because viewers attend to the structural aspects of a face which change least over time. Infants are attracted by movement, and the eyes and mouth move more than other features. During childhood and adulthood, the eyes and mouth continue to attract attention, but not so much because of movement as for the purpose of providing information through nonverbal communication. Dynamic facial recognition is thus posited to be a valuable cognitive ability that is picked up incidentally as a fringe benefit of attention.

Additional Considerations

As attractive as the above hypothesis might appear to be, it is limited in several important respects. First, much additional research is needed to check the reliability of the preliminary findings. Second, and equally important, given the assumptions made by the above hypothesis, facial recognition is undoubtedly more complex than this view assumes. In the closing paragraphs, we will examine some of the factors which render facial recognition complex and show why any simple hypothesis should be viewed as incomplete.

Aside from the eyes and mouth, facial recognition is facilitated by the presence of unique features (e.g., Fisher & Cox, 1975). This fact, long known by caricaturists (see Gombrich, 1972), implies that any facial feature, providing it is sufficiently different or unusual, can mediate recognition by drawing attention to itself.

Another approach would emphasize the interaction of facial features. It may be that the relationship among the various features is more important than the contribution of each individual feature (see Carey & Diamond, 1977). Galton (1879) recognized this possibility in his study of composite photography. By superimposing photographs of members of the same family, it was possible to create a prototypical person who represented the sum of each member. Recent research by Psotka, Norris, and Currie (1978) suggests that subjects may generate composites in a recognition memory test for faces. Perhaps the most compelling argument for the importance of the whole face (i.e., feature relationships) is found in the work of Harmon (1973). Figure 7.4 shows a portrait of a man in which all of the detailed features have been removed. All that remains is a grid composed of various shades of gray. Although any individual feature is completely unrecognizable (e.g., look at only an eye or the nose), the person in the picture, Abraham Lincoln, is recognizable. Harmon has created an artificial situation in which recognition is possible because the feature relationships have been preserved.

At present, we know that both individual features and interrelationships can be recognized. Part of the complexity of facial recognition may be the realization that recognition can be accom-

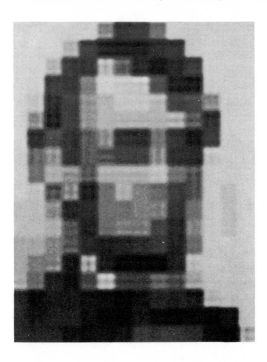

FIGURE 7.4. A block portrait of Abraham Lincoln (from Harmon, 1973). See text for details.

plished on a number of different levels and that no one factor may be paramount.

SUMMARY

1. Early research by Ebbinghaus and others stressed the importance of verbally coded memory representations.

2. Subsequent research has consistently shown that pictures are remembered better than their corresponding verbal labels. One study showed that faces of high-school classmates were retained over a period of years better than the associated names.

3. Numerous examples exist which provide a subjective experience of mental imagery. These experiences, however, cannot be considered as evidence for the existence of imagery because introspective reports vary both quantitatively and qualitatively.

4. Studies of free recall, modality-specific interference, and mental rotation provide experimental evidence that supports the reality of imagery.

5. In studies of free recall, high-imagery words are remembered better than low-imagery words.

6. Studies of modality-specific interference have shown that subjects have difficulty on a secondary task which requires vision when they are simulteneously attempting to use visual imagery.

7. Studies of mental rotation suggest that subjects make mental comparisons of objects by generating and rotating memory images.

8. A number of unusual individuals, called eidetikers, appear to have a supernormal form of imagery which allows for highly accurate and detailed recall. Because of inconclusive results, eidetic imagery remains a puzzle.

9. One approach to imaging is to view it metaphorically as a means of constructing mental pictures.

10. Research comparing images of hidden and exposed objects and normally sighted and congenitally blind subjects suggests that the mental picture metaphor is inaccurate. Imagery may improve memory by providing a spatial framework.

11. Although attentional factors may contribute to the differences in memory performance for verbally and nonverbally coded information, the dual-coding theory attributes the major effect to the number of memory codes.

12. According to dual-coding theory, the probability of verbal and nonverbal coding is lowest for abstract verbal information, higher for concrete verbal information, and highest for pictorial information.

13. Faces are a type of nonverbal stimuli that change over time, yet allow for recognition.

14. One possibility is that people attend to those features in a face that remain relatively stable over time, so that recognition is possible. The eyes and mouth may command attention by providing nonverbal communication. These same features, if they change less over time than other features, could mediate recognition.

15. Other cues, such as unique features and the relationship among the features, may serve to mediate recognition. The complexity of the problem of facial recognition is underscored by the number of different stimuli potentially capable of permitting recognition.

CHAPTER EIGHT

Organizing & Memorizing

OBJECTIVES

1. To demonstrate that patterns of organization can be observed in perceptual tasks involving vision and speech.
2. To show how organizational processes assist memory performance in different mnemonic schemes.
3. To show that organizational processes can enhance memory performance by providing a plan for remembering.
4. To speculate on the source of organizational effects in terms of memory storage and memory retrieval.

INTRODUCTION

When people are asked to list all of their acquaintances, the list of names that is generated is not a haphazard recollection but a structured output that is organized in terms of relationships. People who are close in terms of their relationships are named together during recall. Relatives, neighbors, and business acquaintances are grouped separately rather than interspersed among the others. Similar structured outputs are obtained with other taxonomic categories, such as animals or automobiles (Bousfield & Sedgewick, 1944). This grouping of recall suggests that people organize information on the basis of conceptual relationships.

Organizational processes have important implications for an understanding of remembering. Norman (1976), for example, likens remembering to the retrieval of a book from a library. Without an efficient filing system, retrieving a book would be a difficult, if not impossible, task. Long-term storage may similarly employ various conceptual schemes to permit fast and efficient information retrieval. In this chapter, we will review how these schemes may be used as plans for remembering. Before doing so, however, we should note that patterns of organization can be observed in tasks involving not only memory but also perception as stimulus elements are grouped or organized into meaningful wholes.

ORGANIZATIONAL PATTERNS

Visual Organization

Much of the credit for the study of organization in visual perception belongs to the Gestalt psychologists—Wertheimer, Kohler, and Koffka—who derived organizational principles during the 1920's and 1930's to account for the perception of form (Allport, 1955). Perhaps the easiest way to appreciate some of these principles is to view a set of stimuli and note how the features are structured. Figure 8.1 presents a number of different examples of visual organization.

For most people, the dot matrices viewed in Figures 8.1a and 8.1b are perceived differently. There is a strong tendency to see the dots in Figure 8.1a as four rows of four dots, while those in Figure 8.1b are seen as four columns of four dots. According to the Gestalt psychologists, similarity acts as an organizing principle since similar features tend to be grouped together. In Figures 8.1a and 8.1b, shading seems to produce similarity by either rows or columns and thereby determines the structure of each matrix.

Another organizing principle discussed by the Gestalt psychologists is that of good form. Figures 8.1c and 8.1d show two examples of similar stimuli that are organized quite differently on the basis of good form. The brackets in Figure 8.1c tend to be seen as enclosing three squares. Even though the innermost brackets are closer to each other, each member is seen as belonging to a separate form. Just the opposite is true of the brackets shown in Figure 8.1d. No longer are the brackets perceived as enclosing squares; now the adjacent brackets are seen as separate columnlike figures standing in front of a blank surround. In each instance, the brackets are

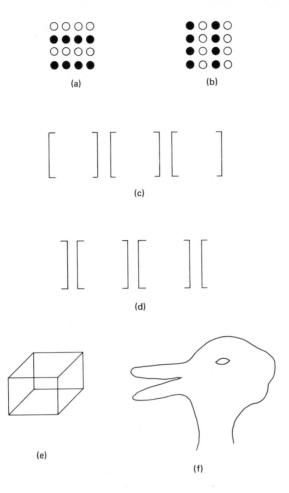

FIGURE 8.1. Demonstrations of visual organization. See text for details.

organized on the basis of a simple symmetrical scheme which is the essence of good form (Allport, 1955).

Good form can be easily destroyed in Figures 8.1c and 8.1d by simply adding another bracket to the sequence (e.g., add] to the right of Figure 8.1d). The additional bracket creates conflict because it enables competing organizations to exist for the same stimuli. We can see the brackets as enclosing squares or forming columns, but we cannot see both simultaneously. Figures 8.1e and 8.1f show additional examples of competing organizations. In Figure

8.1e, the Necker cube is reversible so that the front and back of the figure can be made to alternate at will. We cannot, however, see the cube both ways simultaneously. Similarly, it is easy to see either the duck (looking left) or the rabbit (looking right) in Figure 8.1f, but both cannot be seen at the same time. These examples indicate that a structure is imposed on visual stimuli to organize the information into a meaningful whole. While multiple organizations of the same stimuli may be possible, only one organization can be apprehended at any particular time.

Grammatical Organization

The organizational patterns that are seen with visual stimuli were once felt to be observable in speech perception. Early research by Ladefoged and Broadbent (1960) and Fodor and Bever (1965) suggested that speech perception was organized on the basis of the grammatical segments or phrase structure of a sentence. To use an example from Fodor and Bever, Sentence A has two major phrases with a break between *happy* and *was*. The phrase structure serves to organize the words into smaller, more manageable subunits. Violating the phrase structure, as in Sentence B, serves to render the sentence less comprehensible.

> Sentence A (That he was happy) (was evident from the way he smiled.)

> Sentence B (That he was) (happy was) (evident from the way he smiled.)

Support for the psychological reality of phrase segmentation in speech perception was obtained by dichotically presenting subjects with a sentence in one ear and a click in the other ear. The subjects' task was to recall the sentence and indicate where in the sentence the click had been presented. If subjects perceived the sentences in terms of their phrase structure, they might be reluctant to break those units for a click occurring during a phrase. If so, errors in the form of a tendency to hear the click as occurring between phrases might be expected. The strongest support for this hypothesis was obtained by Garrett, Bever, and Fodor (1966). Using acoustically similar sentences which had different phrase structures (e.g., Sentences C and D below), subjects tended to report the click that occurred simultaneously with the word *Anna* in each instance as occurring before the word *Anna* in Sentence C and after the word

Anna in Sentence D. These data suggested that subjects perceived the sentences in terms of their phrase structure.

Sentence C (In her hope of marrying) (Anna was surely impractical.)

Sentence D (Your hope of marrying Anna) (was surely impractical.)

Subsequent research by Seitz and Weber (1974), however, has revealed a limitation. Click displacement toward a phrase boundary is found only if the subjects must first recall the sentence before noting the location of the click. When the subjects are given the sentence for click notation, there is no click displacement. This finding indicates that phrase structure is important for remembering sentences but may not be necessary for perceiving them. Additional support for this position is found in research which has shown that subjects, while trying to recall sentences, make more errors (e.g., Johnson, 1968) and take more time (e.g., Wilkes & Kennedy, 1969) going between phrase boundaries than going between words within phrase boundaries. According to Jarvella (1971), when subjects are trying to remember sentences, they organize the sentences in immediate memory on the basis of the phrase structure. As Aaronson and Scarborough (1976) have shown, this method of organizing sentences is adopted only when subjects are trying to remember them. No evidence for the importance of phrase structure is found when subjects are simply asked to listen to the sentences for the purpose of comprehension (Aaronson & Scarborough, 1976). This notion that remembering can be facilitated by organizing information into smaller, more manageable subunits is one which we shall discuss more fully in the next section. For the present, we should note that organizational processes seem to reduce the complexity of a task by grouping stimuli into more meaningful or more manageable units.

ORGANIZATIONAL FACTORS IN MEMORY

Mnemonics

BACKGROUND. The word *mnemonic* comes from the Greek word *mnene*, which means memory or the effect of past experience. Over time, mnemonics have come to be defined as schemes for assisting memory. Their use is quite old and dates back at least to the times of the ancient Greek and Roman civilizations, when effective mem-

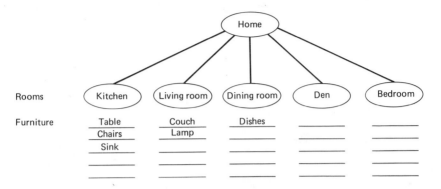

FIGURE 8.2. The home as a hierarchical structure.

orization was a highly valued skill. People such as actors or orators, who needed to remember large bodies of information, used these techniques to ensure effective retention. Although there are many different types of mnemonic techniques, we will focus primarily on the method of loci as a representative example.

The method of loci was a favored device for retaining a sequence of information such as a story or speech. To use the method with a speech, for example, a person was told to examine the speech and divide it into a number of major sections or topics. Within each section, the speech was then divided further into a sequence of key ideas. After the speech was so divided, the person was instructed to perform a mental walk through a series of familiar places (i.e., loci), as would be found in a town or home. In the case of a home, the person was told to associate the speech with the home by mentally walking through the home and attaching key ideas to objects or pieces of furniture along the way. Relational imagery was used to associate ideas and objects by visualizing the ideas in concrete form and relating them in some fashion to the objects in a home. The method of loci works because it organizes a large body of information in terms of a familiar, well-defined structure. As shown in Figure 8.2, the home can be represented by a three-level hierarchical structure which is divided into rooms and objects within rooms. The mental walk through the home is used to associate sections of the speech with rooms of the house and ideas in each section with objects in each room. Since a mental walk must have a beginning, middle, and end, the method of loci ensures that the sequencing of the speech will be in the correct order.

By the above method, a large body of information can be organized by breaking it into smaller, more manageable subunits and relating it to an existing structure that is already well learned. Two principles of effective memorizing are thereby employed. First, it is usually easier to deal with small amounts of information than large amounts; second, it is usually easier to remember new things if they are related to things already known.

PLANS FOR REMEMBERING. As seen in the above example, the method of loci provides a scheme for remembering. Like any good plan, it satisfies a number of minimal requirements; it tells where to begin, how to proceed, and when the task is completed (Bower, 1970a). Miller, Galanter, and Pribram (1960) demonstrate how a rhyme scheme can be used in place of the geographical locations in the method of loci with the same positive results. This variation, called the *pegword mnemonic*, requires the memorizer to learn the rhyme scheme shown in Table 8.1. Since demonstrations can facilitate understanding, try to learn the rhymes by reciting them several times and testing yourself by saying each number and recalling the word before proceeding. Table 8.2 presents a list of ten words which can be memorized with the pegword mnemonic. Using relational imagery, go down the list, one word at a time, and visualize the object that each word represents and associate it in some fashion with the appropriately numbered word in the rhyme scheme of Table 8.1 (e.g., Associate TELEPHONE to BUN by imagining a bun talking into a telephone or a telephone sitting on a large bun, and so forth). Take a moment to form your images and make sure that the visualized objects from the word list and the appropriately numbered objects from the rhyme scheme interact in some manner. After you have finished, you should be able to recite the list for-

TABLE 8.1   The Pegword Mnemomic Rhyme Scheme

ONE IS A BUN
TWO IS A SHOE
THREE IS A TREE
FOUR IS A DOOR
FIVE IS A HIVE
SIX ARE STICKS
SEVEN IS HEAVEN
EIGHT IS A GATE
NINE IS A LINE
TEN IS A HEN

(After Miller, Galanter, & Pribram, 1960)

TABLE 8.2   A Word List for Memorization

1   TELEPHONE
2   PENCIL
3   CAR
4   MOUSE
5   HAMMER
6   COAT
7   DISH
8   BOOK
9   HAT
10   SCISSORS

ward or backward or in any order you wish. Not only will you know each item, but you will also know each item's position in the list (e.g., What was the position of the word DISH?).

The pegword mnemonic is a fast and seemingly effortless way to learn a sequence of information. It does, however, have its limitations. In a detailed study of this mnemonic, Bower (1970a) has listed a number of factors which influence its effectiveness. The factors are listed below.

1. *The list of memory pegs or loci serve as retrieval cues. They must be known and available at the time of learning and remembering.*
2. *The memory loci need not be images of geographical locations. Any visualized object or context can serve as a memory peg.*
3. *The memory loci and the information to be remembered must be associated during information input. The loci can function as retrieval cues only if the items are associated.*
4. *Multiple items can be associated with the same memory loci with no decrement in performance if the items are elaborated into an interactive scene. Unless they are united by relational imagery, interference may result.*
5. *Association of memory loci and items to be remembered by relational imagery is critical.*
6. *Unusual or bizarre images are not necessary for the mnemonic to be effective. Bizarreness may serve to maintain attention and thereby provide motivational assistance, but common images can function just as well.*
7. *If study is repeated over trials, the information should be associated with the same loci used previously. Associating the same information with different loci produces interference.*

For lists longer than ten items, the pegword mnemonic cannot be used, but the method of loci, of which the pegword mnemonic is a variant, is ideally suited. Ross and Lawrence (1968) found that college students recalled thirty-eight words from a list of forty by the method of loci when they used their college campus for memory loci. In some circumstances, it is possible to forego the use of loci altogether. Professional mnemonists such as Lorayne and Lucas (1974) use a mnemonic called the *link*. By this method, items are retained by chaining them together with relational imagery. The words in Table 8.2, for example, would be memorized by relating TELEPHONE with PENCIL, PENCIL with CAR, and so forth. This is an effective system that permits forward or backward recitation, although it does not provide information about numerical location in the sequence. If this information is necessary, other schemes are incorporated by Lorayne and Lucas.

The effectiveness of these mnemonics rests on the use of relational imagery to form strong associations and use of a segmental structure to organize the information. Relational imagery produces a deep level of stimulus processing, and the memory loci provide a plan for remembering. The result is efficient learning and retrieval.

RHYMES AND RULES. Different memory aids are available, and not all mnemonics work in the same manner. Virtually every child has learned the alphabet by the song shown in Table 8.3. This song makes use of rhymes to break the long string of letters into smaller groups that are easier to retain. The rhymes serve as accents or boundary markers to impose an organization on the long letter series. Rhyming facilitates learning by limiting the number of response alternatives that are possible in any row (Bower & Bolton, 1969). In many instances, a rhyme permits subjects to generate a list of possibilities and check the list for the correct alternatives. This can change a recall task into an implicit recognition task.

Of course, rhymes may be used in a different way. Rhymes can be used to learn a rule (e.g., I before E, except after C; Thirty days hath September, April, June, and November). When a person is asked how many days are present in December, the person can recite the rhyme and by the rule obtain the correct response of 31. Under these circumstances, remembering is more of a problem-solving task since the mnemonic provides the rule for solution. Space does not permit a discussion of other mnemonic systems (see Yates, 1966), but the general principles we have noted seem applicable to many. The notable exceptions are the mnemonic rules just

TABLE 8.3   The Alphabet as String and Song

ABCDEFGHIJKLMNOPQRSTUVWXYZ

ABCD	EFG
HIJK	LMNOP
QRS	TUV
WX	Y & Z

Now I know my ABC's,

Next time won't you sing with me?

(Source unknown)

discussed, which result in a rule rather than specific information being retained in long-term storage.

Evidence for Organization

Although the importance of organizational processes has been known for many years (e.g., Müller & Schumann, 1893), research proceeded slowly on this topic following the publication of Katona's book *Organizing and Memorizing* in 1940 and papers by Bousfield (e.g., Bousfield, 1953) until the 1960's and 1970's. With the publication of Miller, Galanter, and Pribram's book *Plans and the Structure of Behavior* in 1960, psychologists took an increasingly cognitive orientation in their study of memory. Heavy emphasis was placed upon the interaction of the person and the material to be learned. Instead of viewing people as passive recipients of information, the cognitive approach viewed them as active organizers of information. A good deal of research has since been accumulated which supports this view. For our purposes, we will review several studies of free recall and serial learning which provide experimental data on organizational processes.

FREE RECALL. There are a number of ways of demonstrating organizational effects in free recall. Experimenters can impose an organization on a list of stimuli by inserting pauses or accents between subsets of sequential items (e.g., Bower & Springston, 1970; Müller & Schumann, 1893) or by using stimuli which are associatively or categorically related (e.g., Cofer, Bruce, & Reicher, 1966; Deese, 1959; Jenkins & Russell, 1952). Alternatively, it is possible to observe subjective organizational patterns in the recall of unrelated items for each subject. In this section, we will consider examples of experimenter-imposed and subjective organization in turn.

Jenkins and Russell (1952) provided early evidence of experimenter-imposed organization in free recall. Subjects were presented with a list composed of twenty-four associatively related word pairs (e.g., TABLE-CHAIR; MAN-WOMAN). Although the words were presented individually in a random order, Jenkins and Russell found that subjects tended to recall the list items in pairs by their associative relationships. Bousfield (1953) found similar evidence for organization in the free recall of categorized word lists. Bousfield presented subjects with a sixty-item list composed of four categories (e.g., ANIMALS) of fifteen items each (e.g., HORSE, SHEEP, and so forth). Like Jenkins and Russell, Bousfield found that, although the words were presented randomly, their recall was clustered in terms of the categorical relationships. This clustering of recall on an associative or categorical basis constituted early evidence for organizational processes in free recall. In this context, organization may be defined as the reordering or restructuring of information on the basis of previously learned relationships (e.g., associative or categorical relationships).

One reason why subjects might organize information is that the structure may serve as a plan to guide subsequent retrieval. Bower, Clark, Lesgold, and Winzenz (1969) studied organizational processes by presenting subjects with a large number of words shown in either their true hierarchical arrangements or in random arrangements. Further 8.3 shows one of the stimulus sets for the hierarchy of minerals. The subjects saw four different hierarchies, each containing twenty-eight words, for 56 seconds each. Half of the subjects saw the words in a true hierarchical arrangement such as that shown in Figure 8.3, and half saw the same words in each set with the order scrambled. Confirming earlier results, Bower et al. found that subjects who studied the words in their correct conceptual arrangements recalled 73 of the 112 words (4 sets of 28 words) after one trial, while those who viewed the random arrangements recalled only about 20 words (see also Cofer et al., 1966). After three attempts at study and recall, subjects with the correct orders recalled all 112 words, while the other subjects managed to recall only 53 words. This is a large effect of stimulus organization on recall.

How did organization affect performance in the above study? Bower et al. suggest that the subjects who had words presented in their correct hierarchical relationships used the hierarchical structure as a retrieval plan to guide their recall. This is supported by the finding that subjects in both groups differed in terms of how

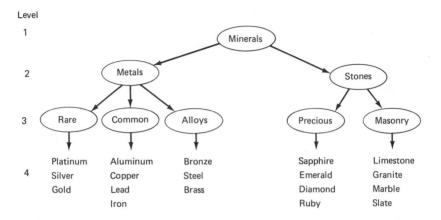

FIGURE 8.3. A conceptual hierarchy for the category of MINER-ALS. (Adapted from Bower et al., 1969)

they recalled the list items. Subjects who saw the hierarchical word arrangements recalled the words in terms of their conceptual order. They typically started at the top of a hierarchy, such as that shown in Figure 8.3, and worked down the inverted tree either branch by branch (e.g., MINERALS, METALS, RARE, COMMON, and so forth) or level by level (e.g., MINERALS, METALS, STONES, RARE, COMMON, and so forth). By and large, recall of the lower items in the hierarchy was heavily dependent upon prior recall of the upper items (e.g., GRANITE would be recalled only if MASONRY was recalled first). Subjects who studied the word lists in the randomly arranged sets did not show these effects. Their recall showed no structural pattern since the recall of each word appeared to be independent of all others. Much as in our discussion of mnemonics, the hierarchical organization of the words seemed to function as a plan for remembering in that it told the subjects when to begin, how to proceed, and when they were finished.

Hierarchically arranged stimuli are not, however, a necessary condition for observing organization. Tulving (1962) demonstrated that subjects will organize unrelated lists of words on the basis of relationships that are unique for each subject. Once again organization is revealed by the pattern of recall, but now it is shown by the consistency of recall on successive trials. Even though a word list is presented in a different order on each trial and there are no apparent relationships among the words used, Tulving found that the words tended to be recalled in the same order over trials. Tulving's subjective organization is a measure of the repetition of word pairs from one trial to another. The actual order of recall might vary greatly from subject to subject, but all subjects are similar in that they recall the items in a consistent manner over trials (e.g., Pellegrino & Battig, 1974). Recently, Buschke (1977a) has developed a new technique whereby subjective organization can be revealed after a single trial by having subjects write all the words that were recalled together in the same location. With this technique, as with Tulving's repetition measure noted above, subjective organization is based on stimulus proximity since items are recalled in either the same order or at the same time. As the measure of subjective organization increases, so too does the recall performance level (see Shuell, 1969, and Sternberg & Tulving, 1977, for reviews). This relationship is strengthened by the finding that, providing the material to be remembered is organized, recall does not improve by telling subjects that they will be tested for recall (e.g., Mandler, 1967; Ornstein, Trabasso, & Johnson-Laird, 1974). Organization appears to be a sufficient condition for learning.

SERIAL LEARNING. In studies of serial learning, subjects are presented with a sequence of items to be recalled in the same order as shown during presentation. In the serial anticipation method, the subjects are first shown the items one at a time for study. Following the study trial, the subjects are asked to anticipate each list item by recalling it before it is shown again in the same sequence. Each item thereby serves as a cue for the succeeding item. In the study-test method, the subjects simply attempt to recall all of the items in their correct order; no cues are provided. Early research tended to use the serial anticipation method developed by Ebbinghaus in the late nineteenth century. Since that time, serial learning has been viewed as a chain of associations from one item to another in a sequential list.

Later research, however, has come to favor the use of the study-test procedure since it has revealed organizational phenomena similar to those found in free recall. The view of serial learning as a stimulus-response chain was effectively destroyed by Lashley (1951), who recognized that such chains were not sufficient to account for the complexity of serial order behavior. Tasks involving language or motor skills, such as playing a piano or hitting a baseball, were performed too quickly to be guided by a stimulus-response chain. According to Lashley, skilled behavior necessitated the hierarchical organization of the basic elements into higher-level units—with these units, in turn, organized into a larger unit to represent the entire sequence. In dealing with information which must be temporally ordered, subjects first acquire some of the basic elements, cluster these adjacent elements into relatively independent units, and then cluster the units into an overall structure. Subjects learn the order of items within each unit and then learn the order of units in the entire sequence (see Estes, 1972, and Johnson, 1972).

Recent research by Bower and Martin, among others, has provided evidence for organizational processes in serial learning which mimic those found in free recall. Bower found evidence for experimenter-induced organization in serial learning by showing that the learning of digit sequences was based on the consistency of the stimulus grouping pattern. In one study, Bower and Winzenz (1969) presented subjects with twelve trials of serial learning by the study-test method. On each trial a nine-digit sequence was presented for study and recall. The same digit sequence was used for trials, 3, 6, 9, and 12, while unique sequences were used on all other trials. In addition to studying the effects of stimulus repetition, as Hebb (1961) did earlier, Bower and Winzenz organized the digit sequences by reading the numbers in groups (e.g., 176839452 could be read as "Seventeen, Six hundred eighty-three, Nine hundred forty-five, Two"). In some instances the repeated sequence was grouped in the same fashion for four trials, while in other instances the grouping pattern was changed four times. The results, shown in Figure 8.4, indicate that the number of errors subjects made on repeated strings with different grouping patterns on trials 3, 6, 9, and 12 was comparable to that of new strings used on the remaining trials. There was a decrease in errors with stimulus repetitions only if the same grouping pattern was employed each time. These results are analogous to the effects of same versus different grouping patterns found in free recall by Bower, Lesgold, and Tieman (1969). No improvement in recall is found if the stimuli are organized differently each time.

Additional research by Bower and others (e.g., Johnson, 1968; Lesgold & Bower, 1970; Restle & Brown, 1970) has shown evidence for organization in terms of the types of errors made by subjects during serial recall. Subjects make more errors in reciting serial lists as they move between organizational groupings within a list than they do when reciting items within each subset. With well-learned, organized sequential information, subjects no longer make errors, but they do take more time between grouped subsets than

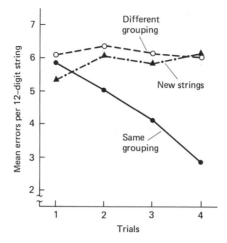

FIGURE 8.4. *The average number of errors made over trials for stimuli organized in (a) the same manner each time, (b) a different manner each time, or (c) for new stimuli each time. (Adapted from Bower & Winzenz, 1969)*

within grouped subsets (e.g., McLean & Gregg, 1967; Seamon & Chumbley, 1977; Wilkes & Kennedy, 1970). These data, showing organizational processes in serial learning, were based on experimenter-imposed stimulus grouping procedures.

If organizational processes are important for serial learning, it should be possible to demonstrate not only effects of experimenter-imposed organization but effects of subjective organization as well. Only recently have such effects been observed in serial learning. Martin and Noreen (1974) presented subjects with serial lists of thirty-two unrelated words to learn by the serial anticipation method. They found that during list learning, the subjects tended to anticipate correctly the same clusters of adjacent items on each trial. On a subsequent free-recall test, Martin and Noreen found that list recall was grouped in terms of the same clusters seen during serial learning. This suggests that the same principles of subjective organization found in free recall also apply to serial learning. These data and others emphasize the importance of organizational factors in memory. As Bower has noted, ". . . a preferred strategy of the adult human in learning a large body of material is to 'divide and conquer'; that is subdivide the material into smaller groups by some means, and then learn these parts as integrated packets of information . . ." (Bower, 1970b, p. 41).

Locus of Organization

Given that information is organized, we may ask whether organization affects memory performance by enhancing the storage or the retrieval of information (Postman, 1972). From the studies of clustering in free recall, it is clear that organization affects retrieval since organization is inferred from the patterns of recall. But it is not clear whether the recall patterns are based on information which has been stored and retrieved in terms of an organized format or stored in some unknown manner and simply recalled in terms of a convenient and organized retrieval scheme. At the time of encoding, subjects might organize information and store it in terms of that structure. During recall, the output is structured because the input has been structured. Alternatively, at the time of encoding, subjects might store the information as it is shown while simultaneously devising a retrieval plan based on the relationships noted between the stimuli. During recall, the output is structured because the input has been subjected to the structure of that plan. Although the end result is the same in each instance, the means to the ends are fundamentally different.

The conceptualization of organization as having its locus in either storage or retrieval processes, while easy to draw, is difficult to test. The problem, as noted by Wood (1972), is that there is no way to assess storage independently of retrieval; storage cannot be assessed directly. This being so, questions about the locus of organization cannot be answered precisely. Organization affects retrieval, but it is unclear whether organization affects storage as well. Be that as it may, the effectiveness of organizational processes for enhancing memory performance remains unquestioned.

SUMMARY

1. *When subjects recall lists of items, their recall is not a haphazard recollection but an organized output based on conceptual relationships.*

2. *Organizational effects can be found in perceptual tasks in which subjects group features of a stimulus to form a meaningful whole.*

3. *The Gestalt psychologists of the 1920's and 1930's derived organizational principles, such as similarity and good form, to account for the perception of form.*

4. Speech perception reveals organizational patterns based on the phrase structure of sentences. Organization by phrase structure helps subjects to remember sentences by breaking the sequential string of words into smaller, more manageable parts.

5. Mnemonics are schemes that have been devised for the purpose of assisting memory. Use of various mnemonics dates back to antiquity.

6. The method of loci is a mnemonic which involves associating new information with a preexisting structure such as the plan of a town or home. This mnemonic provides a plan for remembering in that it tells the person where to begin, how to proceed, and when remembering is completed.

7. The pegword mnemonic requires that the memory pegs be available at the time of learning and remembering to serve as retrieval cues. Association between the information to be remembered and the memory pegs must be made at the time of learning. Consistency of encoding for repeated presentations is also important since associating the same information with different memory pegs produces interference.

8. The link is a mnemonic device which associates a series of items by chaining adjacent items in a series by relational imagery.

9. Rhymes and rules can also function as mnemonics to facilitate memory performance. Rhymes serve to structure information by providing a rhythmic sequence. They are easy to learn because they restrict the number of response alternatives. Rules function differently in that they specify conditions under which certain events are possible. If a rule is remembered, it is not necessary to remember isolated instances; they can be generated from the rule.

10. Organization in memory can be defined as the reordering or restructuring of information from that which was originally presented. Studies of free recall indicate that subjects cluster words that are associatively or categorically related even if such words were not presented together at list input. Lists of unrelated items show evidence of subjective organization since the same items are recalled in either temporal or spatial proximity.

11. Studies of serial learning show comparable effects of experimenter-imposed and subjective organization in the patterns of recall.

12. Organizational processes can facilitate memory perfor-
    mance by enhancing memory storage or retrieval. Since
    there is no way to assess storage independently of retrie-
    val, questions about the locus of organization cannot be
    answered precisely. Organizational processes affect retrie-
    val, but it is not known whether they affect storage as well.

CHAPTER NINE

Remembering Events

OBJECTIVES

1. To examine basic processes in item recognition and recall, such as memory scanning and encoding specificity.
2. To review the ways in which recognition and recall differ.
3. To examine memory for complex stimuli to determine which factors contribute to the retention of gist and which favor the retention of detail.
4. To present evidence for reconstructive processes and to show that remembering is frequently a combination of what was and what must have been.

INTRODUCTION

For many of us, November 22, 1963, is a date that continues to evoke strong memories of a now-distant event. Livingston (1967) states that many people vividly remember where they were and what they were doing at the time of hearing of the assassination of President John F. Kennedy. A common factor in everyone's recall seems to be a perceptlike clarity of the events surrounding the news report that appears undiminished by time. On that occasion, I can recall hearing the first reports of the assassination over a car radio as I was driving down a hill a short distance from my home.

The scene through the windshield still seems vivid today, although other details, such as the type of car I was driving, are no longer available. In a study of these types of experiences, Brown and Kulik (1977) have likened the recall of traumatic events to a photograph obtained from a flashbulb exposure which momentarily and indiscriminately preserves objects in its field. These "flashbulb memories" are not a form of photographic memory since people might remember who told them of a traumatic event but not what the informant was wearing. The flashbulb metaphor is intended only to highlight the brevity and the surprise with which such news is received. The important factors for producing flashbulb memories seem to be a high level of surprise and a high degree of consequentiality or emotional arousal (Brown & Kulik, 1977). By these criteria, December 7, 1941, is a date capable of evoking its own flashbulb memories for an earlier generation of Americans.

In this chapter, we will find that remembering, whether it deals with trivial or traumatic events, can entail a host of complex cognitive processes. This multiprocess view may be easily appreciated by considering the different kinds of remembering involved in such things as recalling your name, how to kick a football, or the location of your car keys. The underlying processes, as Reitman (1970) notes, are not likely to be the same. Although there is yet no general theory of remembering, much basic data on retrieval processes are available. These processes, and the factors which affect them, are the subject matter of this chapter.

BASIC PROCESSES IN RECOGNITION AND RECALL

Item Recognition in Short-Term Storage

REACTION TIME DATA AND RETRIEVAL MODELS. In studies of item recognition in short-term storage, a subject must indicate if a particular stimulus occurred in the immediate past. This seemingly simple task offers no hint as to its underlying mental operations by introspective analysis. Consider, for example, the sequence of target items on the left side of Table 9.1 and the corresponding probe items on the right. For a given row, read the target items and then the probe item. Without looking back at the targets, determine if the probe item was a member of the preceding targets as quickly and accurately as possible. Table 9.1 contains three examples with different target set sizes (i.e., 1, 3, and 7 targets). While most people find this task to be trivial, it offers no insight into the fundamental

TABLE 9.1 An Item Recognition Task Involving Short-Term Storage

Examples	Target Items for Short-Term Storage	Probe Item for Classification	Correct Response
A	1	9	"No"
B	7-3-5	6	"No"
C	9-2-8-7-5-3-6	8	"Yes"

Instructions: For each example, read the target items and then the corresponding probe item to the right. Without looking back at the target, classify the probe in terms of target membership as quickly and accurately as possible (see text for details).

operations which permit fast and accurate responding. Introspection is of no help because the task is performed too quickly. In this instance, consciousness lags behind processing.

The stimulus classification task is a means of demonstrating item recognition in short-term storage. If the probe occurred in the immediate past, the subject makes a positive response; if the probe did not occur recently, the subject makes a negative response. A logical analysis of the demands of this task suggests that several subprocesses are necessary. First, the target stimuli must be encoded and held in immediate memory. If there is a time delay between the presentation of the target items and the probe, the target items must be rehearsed to prevent forgetting. Second, the probe item must be encoded and recognized by the pattern recognition operations in the same manner as the target stimuli. Third, the probe item must be compared to each of the target stimuli to determine if it was a member of that set. Finally, a positive or negative response must be made on the basis of the target and probe stimuli comparisons. These processing stages imply that if a subject is timed from the moment a probe is presented until a response has been made, the reaction time will be a measure of probe encoding time, memory comparison time, and response execution time. Since performance on this task is virtually error free, reaction time is the principal performance measure.

Assuming independent stages of probe encoding, memory comparisons, and response execution, different models of processing may be formulated by varying the assumptions about the nature of the comparison process. Although more complex models are possible (see Townsend, 1971; 1972), the three simple models shown in Figure 9.1 are sufficient for the present purposes. Figure 9.1a shows a parallel classification model in which the representation of the encoded probe stimulus is simultaneously compared to

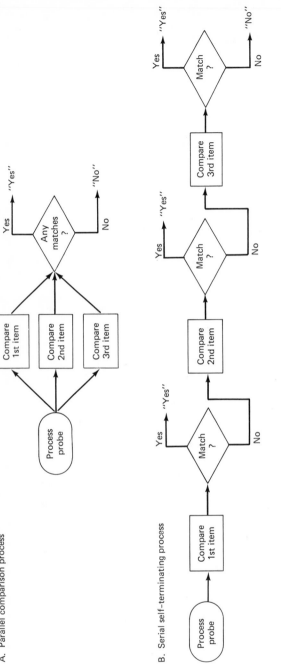

A. Parallel comparison process

B. Serial self-terminating process

C. Serial exhaustive process

FIGURE 9.1. Three models of item recognition in short-term storage. The models differ in terms of the assumptions made about the stimulus comparison process. In each instance, the target set consists of three stimuli and the probe is always a single stimulus.

each of the target item representations. Figure 9.1b and 9.1c show serial classification models in which the representation of the probe is compared to the representations of the target items in a sequential, one-at-a-time fashion. In Figure 9.1b, the serial process is labeled *self-terminating* because the comparisons stop as soon as a match is found in positive instances or after all representations have been examined in negative instances. In Figure 9.1c, the process is called *serial exhaustive* because the probe is compared to each and every item in the target set; a response is made only after all comparisons have been completed.

Each of the models shown in Figure 9.1 makes a different prediction about the effect of the number of target stimuli on reaction time. As the number of target stimuli increases from 1 to 7, the number of comparisons between the target items and the probe increases accordingly. Hypothetical data functions suggested by each of the retrieval models are shown in Figure 9.2. According to the parallel comparison model, an increase in the number of target stimuli should have no effect upon reaction time since all of the comparisons are made simultaneously. Figure 9.2a shows the predicted results. Serial models, since they assume sequential comparisons, should show measurable effects of the number of targets. If each comparison in the serial self-terminating model takes the same amount of time, the reaction time functions should be linear for both positive and negative responses. Moreover, positive responses should be faster than negative responses since, on the average, only half of the targets will have to be searched for a positive response, while all the targets must be compared for a negative response. Data supporting the serial self-terminating assumptions are shown in Figure 9.2b. Finally, the serial exhaustive model predicts reaction time to increase linearly over the number of targets at the same time for positive and negative responses since all target items are compared before each response. Results supporting this model are shown in Figure 9.1c. Each model, by making different assumptions about the underlying comparison process, yields different predictions about the effects of the number of target stimuli and type of response on reaction time.

From the studies of visual search cited previously (see Chapter Five), it might be expected that the serial self-terminating model would provide the best performance description. Studies by Sternberg (1966), however, and many others subsequently (see reviews by Nickerson, 1972; Sternberg, 1975), have consistently found evidence in support of the serial exhaustive model. According to

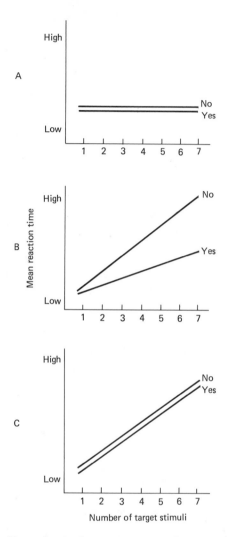

FIGURE 9.2. Hypothetical reaction time data predicted by the three item recognition models shown in Figure 9.1. In each instance, reaction time is plotted as a function of the number of target stimuli in short-term storage.

Sternberg (1966), the linear increase in reaction item for positive and negative responses implies that subjects scan the target items in immediate memory to make a recognition response. The 38 millisecond increase in reaction time for each additional target item suggests that subjects scan at a rate of approximately 26 digits per second (i.e., 1000 msec/38 msec = 26.32 items per sec). The fact that the rate of comparison is so fast has led Sternberg to conclude that items in immediate memory are recognized on the basis of a high-speed, serial exhaustive scan. With short sequences of up to seven items, the speed with which the entire set can be scanned apparently offsets any loss in time due to exhaustiveness. By way of contrast, in visual search tasks where the rate of visual scanning is much slower, performance is maximized by searching the display in a serial self-terminating manner.

MEMORY REPRESENTATIONS. In earlier chapters, we saw that pattern recognition processes can entail different levels of stimulus analysis (see Chapter Five), and that information in short-term storage can be represented in a variety of ways (see Chapter Six). It is not surprising that data from stimulus classification experiments suggest the same variability in memory codes. Subjects may make memory comparisons on the basis of stimulus appearance (e.g., Posner & Taylor, 1969; Seamon, 1978) or a more abstract quality such as stimulus name (e.g., Bracey, 1969; Sternberg, 1967). The conclusion that subjects may encode and compare stimuli in a variety of ways seems inescapable. Task demands determine the level of abstraction necessary for stimulus recognition.

FACTORS AFFECTING SCANNING. Three factors which have produced reliable effects on response time in the item recognition task are practice, stimulus organization, and expectancy. In the earlier review of visual search, it was noted that practice produced significant improvements in search rates. The same observation is found in memory scanning (e.g., Burrows & Murdock, 1969; Kristofferson, 1977). Figure 9.3 shows the results of the study of Burrows and Murdock (1969). Subjects were presented with three to six target digits followed by a probe digit for recognition. The data in Figure 9.3 were obtained by plotting the average reaction times for positive and negative responses combined at each target set size for three stages of practice: early (Sessions 1–5), middle (Sessions 6–10), and late (Sessions 11–14). Each practice session consisted of approximately one hour per day. Not only was there an overall

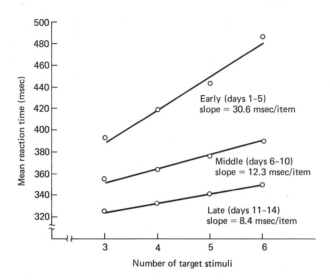

FIGURE 9.3. *Mean reaction time as a function of the number of target stimuli and the degree of practice on the item recognition task. (Adapted from Burrows & Murdock, 1969)*

reduction in reaction times across all stages of practice, but the slope of each function also decreased. By dividing the slope value into 1 second, an estimate of the number of stimuli that could be classified per unit of time was obtained. The results indicated that in the early stage of practice, subjects scanned at a rate of about 33 digits per second. With additional practice, the rate of scanning increased to approximately 81 digits per second in the middle sessions and 119 digits per second in the late sessions. As in visual search, memory scanning performance can be described as a serial process that is affected by the subject's degree of practice.

Studies of target stimulus organization suggest that under some conditions a scan of the target items is not necessary for probe classification. Rosenbaum (1974) used rule-defined digit sets as targets (e.g., 4,8; 3,6,9; 2,4,6,8) and found that reaction time did not increase over the number of target stimuli, as it did with unrelated digit sets (e.g., 1,7; 4,7,9; 1,5,6,8). DeRosa and Tkacz (1976) found similar results with target stimuli of pictures that were ordered to show a meaningful sequence. Reaction time did not increase with the number of target pictures if the sequence was coherent. In each of these instances, target stimulus organization served to reduce response time by permitting subjects to make a probe classification on some basis other than scanning. Rosenbaum (1974) suggests that subjects may use the organization to generate a rule and then test the probe in terms of the rule. If the rule is satisfied, a positive response ensues; if it is not, a negative response is made.

Studies of the effects of expectancy on reaction time have a long history in experimental psychology (Boring, 1950). By the 1860's and 1870's it was evident that expectancy and preparation were important determinants of performance (e.g., James, 1890; Kulpe, 1895; Titchner, 1908), and continued interest in this topic is evident by the fact of ongoing research (see Egeth & Bevan, 1973; Pachella, 1975). Studies of stimulus classification have shown that expectancy can influence encoding and response processes (e.g., Hacker & Hinrichs, 1974; Shiffrin & Schneider, 1974). Expecting the probe serves to reduce probe encoding time and, to a lesser extent, response execution time (e.g., Seamon, 1976; 1978; Seamon & Wright, 1976). It does not serve to enhance the rate of scanning or eliminate the need for scanning, as the effects of practice and target stimulus organization seem to demonstrate.

Item Recognition in Long-Term Storage

The serial exhaustive scanning model has been extended to item recognition in long-term storage. Atkinson and Juola (1973; 1974) have presented a retrieval model which holds that items in long-term storage can be recognized by one of two processes. First, items can be recognized on the basis of the amount of familiarity associated with their memory traces in long-term storage. Items with high familiarity will be recognized as repeated stimuli, while those with low familiarity will not. Second, items which have neither high nor low familiarity may be recognized by scanning the set of relevant item representations in memory to determine if the test item is present. This view extends the item recognition research by arguing that information can be recognized on the basis of its current state of familiarity or by a scan of the set of relevant memory representations.

Data consistent with the Atkinson and Juola model include the results of Fischler and Juola (1971), who found that repetitions of target stimuli held in long-term storage produced faster response times and fewer errors. Fischler and Juola suggest that responses to repeated stimuli were faster and more accurate because repetitions increased the familiarity of the stimuli and thereby eliminated the need for a decision based on scanning.

Further support for the model is found in the study of Juola, Fischler, Wood and Atkinson (1971). Subjects were presented with sets of ten, eighteen, or twenty-six words to learn in serial order. Following list mastery, the subjects were tested by presenting individual words and measuring the time needed to classify each stimulus in terms of target set membership. Half of the test trials presented stimulus words from the original set of ten, eighteen, or twenty-six words (i.e., positive response words) and half presented distractor words not included in any of the original sets (i.e., negative response words). Juola et al. found during initial trials that positive responses were longer than negative responses, and response time for both response types increased as a function of the size of the memory set (i.e., ten, eighteen, or twenty-six words). With additional testing, positive responses became faster than negative responses and less affected by target set size.

In terms of the Atkinson and Juola model, during the initial trials of the Juola et al. experiment, negative responses should be faster than positive responses because items that were not presented previously should have low familiarity and may be rejected directly on this basis. Stimuli to which positive responses are made should have higher familiarity than those for negative responses because these stimuli were seen previously. But the amount of familiarity may not be sufficient to permit recognition on this basis alone. Under these conditions, subjects must scan the target set before making a positve response. With continued testing, the situation changes since all stimuli used in the experiment gain in familiarity. Because of the increase in familiarity by repeated testing, distractor items can no longer be rejected on the basis of low familiarity and now necessitate a memory scan. Positive items, which formerly required a scan, now have sufficient familiarity to permit recognition on this basis alone. Since a scan is no longer needed for positive instances, an effect of memory set size is no longer found. These data and others are well described by the Atkinson and Juola model of item recognition. Although research is still in progress (e.g., Atkinson, Herrmann, & Wescourt, 1974; Mohs, Wescourt, & Atkinson, 1975), the model remains the most comprehensive statement about item recognition processes in short-term and long-term storage made to date.

Item Recall in Long-Term Storage

AVAILABLE BUT INACCESSIBLE TRACES. The study of item recall has followed a different course from that of item recognition. While some research has been directed at determining the processes involved in recall (e.g., Anderson & Bower, 1972), more attention has been focused on the conditions which affect recall probability. This concern is understandable since we are sometimes aware of knowing more than we can remember. Everyone has had the experience of failing to recall something that is said to be on the tip of the tongue. In the case of words, people experiencing these states generally know the word's meaning and something about its sound and appearance even though they cannot recall the specific word (Brown & McNeill, 1966). Since it is often possible to recognize stimuli which cannot be recalled (e.g., Blake, 1973; Hart, 1967), these data indicate that not all information in long-term storage is equally accessible. At times, information may be available but inaccessible.

A procedural change from recall to recognition is not a necessary condition for retrieving previously inaccessible information. Tulving and Pearlstone (1966) demonstrated that recall can be enhanced by the use of cues. Using lists composed of subsets of categorically related words, subjects were asked to recall the stimuli under conditions of either free or cued recall. In the free recall condition, the subjects simply listed as many words as they could remember on a blank sheet for recall. In the cued recall condition, the recall sheet contained the category names for each of the stimulus subsets in the list (e.g., the word WEAPONS served as a cue for the words BOMB and CANNON). Not surprisingly, Tulving and Pearlstone found that cued recall performance was greater than free recall performance, indicating that cues can facilitate performance. Following the first recall, all subjects recalled the list again under the cued condition. In the second recall, it was found that subjects who had previously free-recalled the stimuli showed a substantial improvement with cued recall. This finding indicates that more information was available than was accessible on the first recall attempt. Performance was determined by the accessibility of the information in long-term storage, and accessibility was influenced by the cues available to the subjects at the time of recall. What determines the effectiveness of a particular retrieval cue is the subject matter for the next section.

THE PRINCIPLE OF ENCODING SPECIFICITY. On the basis of many studies of cuing in free recall (e.g., Tulving & Osler, 1968; Tulving & Thomson, 1973), Tulving has put forth a principle which attempts to specify the conditions under which a particular cue will be effective in recall. The principle, called *encoding specificity,* states that "a retrieval cue can provide access to information available about an event in the memory store if and only if it has been stored as part of the specific memory trace of the event" (Tulving & Thomson, 1973, p. 16). Encoding specificity represents an extension of the available-but-inaccessible approach to remembering. It states not only that cues may facilitate recall by making accessible that information which was previously inaccessible, but that such cues will be effective only if they were encoded with the stimuli to be remembered at the time of learning.

Empirical tests of the encoding specificity principle have been largely supportive. Thomson and Tulving (1970) tested subjects in a recall task and manipulated the availability of cues during study and testing. Nine groups of subjects were employed to test all combinations of three different cuing conditions (i.e., no cues, weak cues, or strong cues) at list input or output. Table 9.2 shows how cuing conditions were manipulated at list input and output for the nine groups and provides examples of the kinds of cues used for the list items. The subjects were presented with a list of twenty-four words which could have no cues, weak cues, or strong cues paired with the stimuli at the time of list input and no cues, weak cues, or strong cues provided at the time of recall. Recall performance, also shown in Table 9.2, supports the principle of encoding specificity. In most instances, performance is best when the retrieval conditions match the encoding conditions. If cues were provided at input, those same

TABLE 9.2   Experimental Conditions, Results, and Sample Stimuli and Cues

Stimulus Presentation Condition	STIMULUS RECALL CONDITION		
	No Cues	Weak Cues	Strong Cues
No Cues	(1) 14.0	(2) 11.1	(3) 19.0
Weak Cues	(4) 10.7	(5) 15.7	(6) 13.9
Strong Cues	(7) 12.2	(8) 9.2	(9) 20.2

Possible List Stimuli	Possible Stimulus Cues		
	No Cues	Weak Cues	Strong Cues
BLACK	—	train	white
STEAK	—	knife	meat
LIGHT	—	head	dark

(From Tulving and Thomson, 1970)

cues produced the best output. As can be seen in Table 9.2, shifting from weak cues at input to strong cues at output diminished rather than enhanced recall. These results are in agreement with predictions based on encoding specificity.

Seemingly discordant with the encoding specificity hypothesis are the data from those subjects shown in Table 9.2 who had no cues at input but strong cues at output. Their high recall, however, might be expected if these subjects spontaneously encoded the stimuli in terms of strong associates (e.g., STEAK is a cut of meat) at the time of list presentation. To test this possibility, Thomson and Tulving (1970) performed an additional study which induced the subjects to encode a list of words exclusively in terms of either weak or strong associates. This was done by presenting subjects with a series of recall tasks in which they were consistently given either weak or strong associates at both list input and output. On a subsequent list, the cuing conditions were shifted between list input and output for all subjects (i.e., weak cues at input and strong cues at output, or strong cues at input and weak cues at output). The results showed that strong cues at recall did not facilitate performance relative to a control group of subjects who had not been given any cues. These data support the encoding specificity principle by demonstrating that a retrieval cue must be encoded with a stimulus at the time of learning in order to be effective. Merely presenting a cue at the time of recall, regardless of its preexperimental association with the stimulus item, did not enhance recall.

Encoding specificity has not gone unchallenged. Some researchers have questioned its generality (e.g., Horowitz & Manelis, 1973; Postman, 1975; Reder, Anderson, & Bjork, 1974), while others have questioned its basis in fact (e.g., Santa & Lamwers, 1974). This is an area of research that is still being actively investigated (e.g., Tulving & Watkins, 1977), and a final statement has yet to be made. At present it seems clear that recall is facilitated by the presence of cues that were available at the time of stimulus encoding. The conditions under which other cues can facilitate performance are still hotly debated. In this context, the results of Anderson and Pichert (1978) may be viewed as a challenge to the generality of encoding specificity. Subjects read a story involving a house from the perspective of either a burgler or a real estate prospect. Following the initial recall of the story, the subjects were asked to recall it once more. This time the perspectives were shifted. The results showed that on the second recall, subjects recalled more information relevant to the new perspective and less information relevant to the old perspective than they had recalled on the first attempt. Anderson and Pichert hold that these data indicate that recall can be independent of the subject's perspective at the time of encoding. Such a finding suggests flexibility in the retrieval processes used in accessing information in long-term storage.

Differences Between Recall and Recognition

To complete our review of basic processes, it is necessary to examine whether recall and recognition tasks involve basically the same or substantially different operations (see Brown, 1976). One possibility is that performance differences for recall and recognition are based on differences in memory trace strength. If less memory strength is needed for recognition than for recall, then recognition performance will be superior. Another possibility is that recall is harder than recognition because some of the underlying processes differ; recall may require a memory search, while recognition may not. Although recall and recognition processes are not yet fully understood, several types of data have been considered as relevant to the issue. These data include studies of stimulus and instructional variables, effects of stimulus organization, and the recall of unrecognized stimuli. Each will be reviewed briefly in turn.

STIMULUS AND INSTRUCTIONAL VARIABLES. It is widely held that recall and recognition memory are differentially affected by variations in stimulus materials and instructional sets. Studies have shown that words rated high in frequency or meaningfulness are better recalled than words of low frequency or meaningfulness (e.g., Deese, 1961; Hall, 1954; McNulty, 1965) but that the reverse is true for word recognition (e.g., McCormack & Swenson, 1972; McNulty, 1965; Shepard, 1967). Other studies have shown that recall is usually better following intentional learning instructions than incidental learning sets (e.g., Estes & DaPolito, 1967), while recognition is either unaffected or may show an advantage for incidental learning (e.g., Eagle & Leiter, 1964; Estes & DaPolito, 1967). Recent research on levels of processing, however, has clouded these distinctions. When processing levels have been equated in incidental learning, high-meaningful stimuli have yielded higher recall and recognition than low-meaningful stimuli (Seamon & Murray, 1976). Moreover, for comparable levels of processing, studies which have varied intentional and incidental learning sets have not found qualitative differences in recall or recognition performance (e.g., Bower & Karlin, 1974; Craik & Tulving, 1975). At present, the status of stimulus and instructional variables with regard to the differentiation of recall and recognition processes is problematic.

STIMULUS ORGANIZATION AND MEMORY SEARCH. One view of the differences between recall and recognition memory is that recall necessitates a search of long-term storage to locate the desired trace. Recognition, on the other hand, has no need for a memory search since the trace for an item may be directly accessed to check for some indication of recency or familiarity. Since stimulus organization is felt to have beneficial effects on recall because it provides a plan for memory search, it follows that stimulus organization should not affect recognition performance if a memory search is not a component of this process. Although some researchers have failed to find positive effects of list organization in studies of recognition memory (e.g., Kintsch, 1968; McCormick, 1972), the bulk of the evidence seems heavily in favor of a small but significant effect of list organization on recognition performance (e.g., Bower et al, 1969; D'Agostino, 1969; Mandler, 1972; Mandler & Boeck, 1974). According to Mandler (1972), the effect of list organization on memory performance is smaller in recognition tasks than in recall tasks because memory search may not be needed in each instance. As in the Atkinson and Juola (1973; 1974) retrieval model for item recognition, Mandler holds that stimuli can be recognized either on the basis of sufficient familiarity or by engaging in a memory search to determine if the information can be located in long-term storage. To the extent that memory search is necessary, stimulus organization will benefit recognition performance, and recall and recognition will be comparable.

THE RECALL OF UNRECOGNIZED STIMULI. The search for differences between recall and recognition memory is predicated on the fact that recognition is generally easier than recall. As witnessed by the tip-of-the-tongue phenomenon, we can often recognize things that we cannot recall. But the recent findings of Tulving and his associates (e.g., Flexser & Tulving, 1978; Tulving & Watkins, 1977) demonstrate that it is possible to create conditions whereby items that cannot be recognized may, with appropriate cues, be recalled. At face value these data raise problems, with explanations of recall and recognition differences assumed to be due to differences in memory strength (i.e., less trace strength needed for recognition than for recall) or component processes (i.e., a memory search is needed for recall but may not always be necessary for recognition).

As noted earlier, our understanding of recall and recognition memory is still incomplete. It may be, as Craik (1979) has suggested, that recall and recognition involve similar processes but different types of information (see also Brown, 1976; Flexser & Tulving, 1978; Rabinowitz, Mandler, & Patterson, 1977). Recall involves the retrieval of a stimulus trace given a specific context, while recognition entails the retrieval of an earlier context given a specific stimulus. This thorny issue awaits additional research.

MEMORY FOR GIST AND MEMORY FOR DETAIL

Information Abstraction

In order to study memory under natural learning conditions, much current research has focused on the retention of sentences and stories instead of the more traditional lists of related or unrelated stimuli. This is not so much a new approach (see Bartlett, 1932) as it is a belated recognition of the variety and richness of cognitive functioning when dealing with complex, meaningful stimuli. Where earlier we saw that subjects interacted with the learning material by imposing an organization on a list of seemingly unrelated items (see Chapter Eight), we will now examine different forms of subject-material interactions in order to describe more adequately the processes of remembering.

That subjects interact with the learning material is easily demonstrated by the fact that not all stimuli are equally well retained. Johnson (1970) had one group of subjects read a story and rate each sentence in terms of the importance of its ideas to the whole story. Another group of subjects read the same story and recalled it after 15 minutes, 7 days, or 63 days. The results showed that although recall decreased as the retention interval increased, important ideas were retained better than unimportant ideas at each interval. While this result may not be surprising, it demonstrates that the subjects' evaluations of the stimulus material have important consequences for remembering; important things are retained, unimportant things are not.

The manner in which ideas are retained has also been the subject of several recent studies. Sachs (1967) read subjects a story and then provided a recognition memory test of selected sentences from either the middle or the end of the story. The task was to determine if each sentence had been heard before. Sachs repeated some of the sentences in their original form (e.g., "He sent a letter about it to Galileo") while changing others in terms of formal wording (e.g., "He sent Galileo a letter about it"), active-to-passive voice (e.g., "A letter about it was sent to Galileo"), or meaning (e.g., "Galileo sent him a letter about it"). She found that subjects were very accurate in recognizing any type of sentence change if the sentences were obtained from the end of the story. Presumably, this information was still available in some form for comparison since it had been presented recently. Performance on sentences from the middle of the story, however, fared differently. Only changes in the meaning of the sentences were detected much above chance; for the most part, all other types of change went unnoticed. These data suggest that initially subjects have fairly accurate information about the sentences from a story as they are heard. With the passage of time and additional information, however, surface details such as formal word order are lost and only the gist of each sentence remains. Since, in most cases, comprehension and not memorization is the goal, these data imply that we abstract and retain the gist of what we hear in connected discourse.

Most compelling is the demonstration by Bransford and Franks (1971) that people not only abstract ideas from sentences but also abstract partial ideas into a complete representation that was never presented in its entirety. Bransford and Franks read sentences which expressed one, two, or three ideas (e.g., "The sweet jelly was on the table. The ants in the kitchen ate the jelly") and subsequently asked subjects to distinguish repeated sentences from new sentences formed by combining previously expressed ideas. The results showed that the subjects erroneously recognized a sentence which expressed all of the partial ideas in a complete form (e.g., "The ants in the kitchen ate the sweet jelly which was on the table"). Sentences of this type, which were recognized with highest confidence, were never presented in the initial set. These data and others (e.g., Anderson & Paulson, 1977; Brewer, 1975; Pezdek, 1977) demonstrate that memory for meaning lasts longer than memory for the syntactic vehicles used to convey meaning. People retain the gist of meaningful information in long-term storage and may later be fooled by stimuli which are comparable in meaning but different in surface features.

While verbatim memory was not found in any of the above studies, evidence for verbatim memory does exist. Several studies have demonstrated that memory for sentence surface features such as formal wording can be demonstrated over periods of days, weeks, and, in one case, years (e.g., Rubin, 1977). Aside from the obvious case of rote memorization, verbatim memory has been found when sentences are presented in unusual formats, such as reading upside-down sentences (e.g., Kolers, 1975), or when they express wit, sarcasm, or criticism (e.g., Keenan, MacWhinney, & Mayhew, 1977; Kintsch & Bates, 1977). Not surprisingly, since humor depends in part on the wording of an event, jokes would appear to fall in this category as well. While no single explanation may account for these instances of verbatim memory, their presence demonstrates the versatility of the memory system in its ability to retain only gist or specific detail as well.

The Importance of Context

In Chapter Five we discussed how stimulus context can supplement data driven processing with powerful conceptually driven processing. If we view the processes of perception as fundamental to an understanding of memory, it follows that context should have important consequences for remembering as well as for perception. Data from Bransford and Johnson (1973) support this view. Subjects who read an ambiguous story in which they were first provided with a context or theme recalled significantly more ideas than those subjects who were given the context after the story (Bransford & Johnson, 1973). In this example, a context may have enabled the subjects to abstract meaningful and related ideas in the formation of gist. When context is lacking, this may no longer be possible and subjects may remember different types of information. Anderson and Bower (1973), for example, read one group of subjects a story in which the context was preserved by presenting the sentences in their correct sequential order. For another group of subjects, the story context was destroyed by presenting the sentences in a scrambled sequence. A subsequent recognition memory test for the formal wording of the sentences showed that subjects did better if they heard the sentences out of context than within a story frame. The presence of a context permitted the subject to abstract meaning and skim over surface details. Without context, it was more difficult to abstract meaning, and only surface details were noted and retained.

As with stories, visual scenes which form a meaningful sequence are also capable of demonstrating context effects. Jenkins,

Wald, and Pittenger (1978) showed subjects a series of slides of a woman making a cup of tea. Enough slides were shown in sequence so that the subjects were aware that they were experiencing a single event at different points in time. Following the viewing of the slides, the subjects were given a recognition test consisting of some of the slides seen previously, some slides not seen but clearly belonging to the event (e.g., slides of the woman making a cup of tea from the original sequence which were not shown before), and some control slides which violated an aspect of the original sequence (e.g., the woman pouring water with her left hand instead of her right). Jenkins et al. found that subjects correctly recognized 80 percent of the original stimuli and falsely recognized 50 percent of the previously unseen belonging slides. Control slides were erroneously recognized less than 1 percent of the time. These data contrast sharply with the results of a second experiment, which used slides showing scenes from a party with no unifying sequential framework. In this study, subjects recognized 83 percent of the original stimuli and made errors on less than 10 percent of the belonging and control slides.

According to Jenkins et al., the recognition of an event (e.g., the woman making a cup of tea) has important implications for what is remembered. Each slide that is shown may give rise to a specific memory trace, but these individual traces can be overridden by an event context or schema (Bartlett, 1932). Whether subjects retain the gist of what they perceive or only isolated details depends upon the availability of a stimulus context. When a meaningful context is present, subjects abstract the gist of the stimuli and have difficulty distinguishing those stimuli which were seen before from those which are merely consistent with the present context. For stimuli presented without contextual support, only isolated elements can be retained. In these instances, there is no gist to abstract.

Reconstructive Processes

Our review of memory for complex events is not yet complete. Studies by Kintsch (1976) indicate that when there is a delay between perception and recall, reconstructive processes may lead to gross inaccuracies in recall. In one experiment, Kintsch read subjects a biblical story of Joseph and his brothers. When tested for recall immediately after the story, the only errors subjects made were errors of omission; less material was recalled than was presented. But when a 24-hour delay was imposed between hearing the story and recalling it, the results showed a lack of differentiation between the story as heard and the subjects' prior knowledge of the story. Many of the subjects simply recalled everything they knew about Joseph and his brothers. This lack of differentiation implies that the subjects had gaps in their memories which they filled with relevant information from long-term storage. The story was reconstructed on the basis of what was abstracted from the story as heard and what was already known.

Studies of eyewitness testimony provide additional examples of reconstructive processes in memory. Many people are aware of how faulty eyewitness reports can be, yet, paradoxically, these reports may still sway courtroom proceedings. Loftus (1974), for example, found that the proportion of subjects who voted guilty in a simulated trial increased from 18 to 72 percent with eyewitness testimony. Muensterburg (1908) and later Buckhout (1974), however, showed that eyewitness reports are exceedingly inaccurate. In a staged assault on a professor before a class of students, Buckhout found 7 weeks after the incident that many students could not describe the assault accurately and only about 40 percent of the students could pick out the assailant from a set of six pictures. Approximately 60 percent of the students selected the picture of an innocent person. In criminal cases, Buckhout reports that eyewitness testimony may initially be incomplete and fragmented, but with repeated recalls from the first police report to the final courtroom testimony, the remembrance becomes a coherent, well-integrated story. Eyewitness reports are inaccurate because eyewitnesses generate a context within which they fit the initial sketchy details that were perceived and from which they unknowingly make inferences about details that were missed. The result is a reconstructed recall based partly on what was and partly on what must have been.

Since, in any complex event, some details will be perceived while others will be missed, it is not surprising that people will integrate information from other sources in an attempt to present a reasonable and coherent testimony. As one example, the wording of questions can change the quality of recall. Loftus and Palmer (1974) showed subjects a film of an automobile collision and found that speed estimates were greater for the question "How fast were the cars going when they smashed into each other?" (estimated speed = 41 mph) than for "How fast were the cars going when they hit each other?" (estimated speed = 34 mph). After viewing the film of the accident and being asked either the *smashed* or *hit* question, the subjects were questioned again one week later. When asked on the subsequent test if they had seen any broken glass, Loftus and Palmer found that subjects were more apt to say that they had seen broken glass if they were previously given the *smashed* question. In reality, no broken glass was shown in the film. These inaccurate remembrances indicate that subjects integrated information from the initial event with that provided by the examiner after the event. The result, as Bartlett noted many years ago, is that remembering is often "an imaginative reconstruction, or construction, built out of the relation of our attitude towards a whole active mass of organized past reactions or experience..." (Bartlett, 1932, p. 213).

Inference and Semantic Memory

If recall is a reconstruction based on memory and inference, some means of representing inferential knowledge is necessary. Tulving (1972), for example, has distinguished between episodic and semantic memory. For him, episodic memory represents our memory of events, while semantic memory represents our knowledge of the world. Facts such as "two plus two equals four" and "most fire engines are red" are examples of information from semantic memory. Although little is known about how semantic memory specifically affects event memory, a brief review of different semantic models is necessary because inferences are based on our knowledge of the world. We will consider a network model by Collins and Quillian (1969), a propositional model by Anderson and Bower (1973), and a feature comparison model by Smith, Shoben, and Rips (1974) as representative of different approaches to semantic memory (see Smith, 1978, for a review of semantic memory theory).

A NETWORK MODEL. Collins and Quillian (1969) proposed that *semantic memory* could be represented as a nonredundant, hierarchical structure composed of nouns and their defining features. A portion of this proposed hierarchical memory structure can be seen in Figure 9.4. Besides hypothesizing that information is categorically organized, the most salient aspect of the model is the assumption that information is stored in a nonredundant manner. The features which serve specifically to define canaries are stored with the representation for "canary"; other features which serve to define birds in general are stored with the representation for "bird."

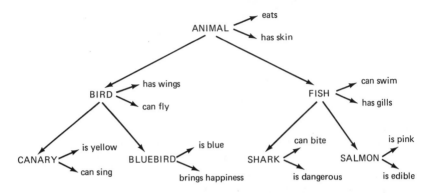

FIGURE 9.4. A portion of the hierarchically organized memory structure assumed by the network model of Collins and Quillian. (Adapted from Collins & Quillian, 1969)

In this manner, Collins and Quillian posit that much of what we know is based on inferential processing (e.g., a canary has wings because a canary is a bird and a bird has wings).

The assumption of inferential processing leads to the obvious prediction that response times to verify statements such as "A canary is yellow," "A canary has wings," or "A canary has skin" should vary directly with the number of inferential steps needed for sentence verification. Although early data were supportive (e.g., Collins & Quillian, 1969), subsequent studies have found instances in which the predictions were not upheld. Rips, Shoben, and Smith (1973), for example, found that while a cantaloupe is a melon, and a melon is a fruit, subjects were faster at verifying the sentence "A canaloupe is a fruit" than "A cantaloupe is a melon." As attractive as the nonredundant, hierarchical semantic structure may be, it is conceivable that people are not so logically organized and that information is redundantly stored.

A PROPOSITIONAL MODEL. A different kind of network model has been proposed by Anderson and Bower (1973). This model, called HAM (an acronym derived from human associative memory), holds that the basic unit in memory is a proposition. According to Anderson and Bower, a proposition is a cluster of associations among elementary concepts. Figure 9.5 shows how the proposition "In the park the hippie touched the debutante" might be represented by four basic associations. The context-fact association indicates where the event occurred and what happened. Information about context is

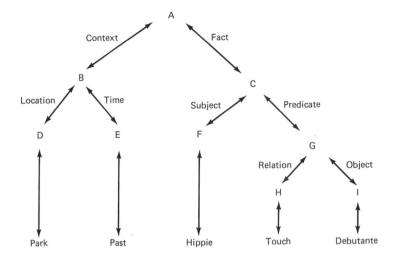

FIGURE 9.5. A propositional representation of the sentence "In the park the hippie touched the debutante." (Adapted from Anderson & Bower, 1973)

based on a *location-time* association which more adequately defines where and when the event occurred. A fact is defined by a *subject-predicate* association which indicates who or what the fact is about and what happened to the subject. Finally, a *relation-object* association further specifies what action the subject took with respect to the object.

The words at the bottom of Figure 9.5 are memory representations of concepts and the various associations show how these concepts have been related by experience. Each of these representations is assumed to have ties to other propositions such that a tracing of all of the associations involving "hippie," for example, would reveal everything a person has learned about this concept. In this manner the Anderson and Bower model, while it is a network model, is unconcerned about information redundancy.

Although we may sometimes make use of inferential reasoning in answering questions (e.g., "Did Martha Washington have a mouth?" Anderson & Bower, p. 383), many propositions may be stored directly rather than inferred from a nonredundant structure. To account for the reaction time difference for verifying sentences such as "A canary is a bird" and "A canary is an animal," Anderson and Bower hold that the latency difference is based on the speed of the retrieval process and need not be construed as evidence for a hierarchical memory structure. Sentence verification is based on tracing the associative pathways for *canary* and *bird* or *canary* and *animal*. HAM, for example, would generate a list of previously stored propositions involving birds. This list, which would be ordered on the basis of the most recently or frequently encountered experiences, would provide a measure of the preestablished associative strength of the various concepts. For most people, *canary* would be higher on the list of *bird* experiences than it would be on a list of *animal* experiences. Assuming that people retrieve information on the basis of recency and frequency of occurrence, an association between *canary* and *bird* will be retrieved faster than an association between *canary* and *animal*.

This review, while dealing with only a limited aspect of the complex Anderson and Bower model, indicates that an assumption of nonredundant, hierarchical information storage need not be necessary to account for the sentence verification data. As Anderson and Bower note, there is no compelling reason to believe that human memory does not contain redundant information. Such a concern may be important for computers where storage space can be limited, but the human brain may not be an analogous structure.

A FEATURE COMPARISON MODEL. Another model which assumes redundant information storage is the feature comparison model of Smith, Shoben, and Rips (1974). This model assumes that each concept or noun representation has stored with it in semantic memory a list of both defining and characteristic features. Among the defining features for the word *robin*, for example, would be the facts that a robin has feathers, wings, and a red breast. The characteristic features for this concept would include that it flies, perches in trees, is small, and so forth. Statements such as "A robin is a bird" are verified by a process which matches the defining and characteristic features of each concept (i.e., robin and bird). As shown in Figure 9.6, the result is a two-stage process which compares defining and characteristic features in Stage 1. If the similarity between the feature sets for each concept is either high or low, the process is stopped and a response of True or False is made. For intermediate levels of feature agreement, a second stage follows in which only the defining features of each concept are matched. If all of the defining features match in Stage 2, a positive response, is made; if they do not, a negative response follows.

The two-stage comparison process based on matching redundant features can account for the Collins and Quillian (1969) data

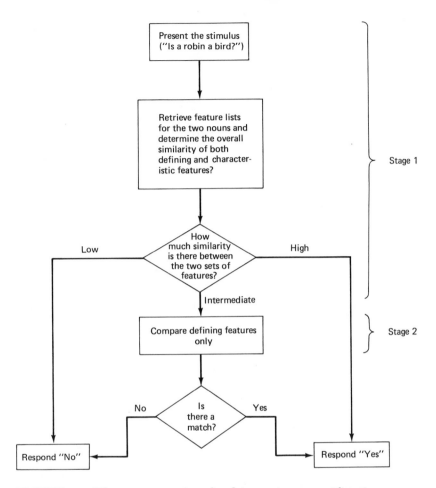

FIGURE 9.6. The processes involved in sentence verification according to the feature comparison model of Smith, Shoben, and Rips. (Adapted from Smith, Shoben, & Rips, 1974)

by assuming that response time for sentence verification varies directly with the number of shared features in each concept or the number of stages for verification. In addition, this model has the important property of predicting that the type of response a subject makes to a statement such as "A bat is a bird" will depend on the level of analysis required. If subjects are asked to verify the above statement in a casual manner, most people respond quickly and affirmatively. But when subjects are presented with the same statement and asked to verify it strictly, most subjects respond more slowly and negatively. According to the feature comparison model, the type and speed of response will depend on the level of analysis. A fast preliminary analysis based only on Stage 1 will suggest that a bat is a bird, while a slower analysis involving Stage 2 will reveal that a bat is not really a bird. To its credit, this model has more versatility than the strict hierarchically organized structure proposed by Collins and Quillian (1969). But what the ultimate outcome will be for this model, as well as other models of semantic memory (e.g., Anderson, 1976), is still too early to determine. At present, the various approaches say precious little about how our knowledge of the world influences our memory of events.

SUMMARY

1. Studies of item recognition in short-term storage suggest that recognition is based on a high-speed, serial exhaustive scan.

2. Stimulus representations may involve physical or nonphysical aspects such as stimulus name. Task demands determine the level of abstraction necessary for recognition.

3. Among the factors which have been shown to affect memory scanning are the amount of practice on the task, the presence of an organizing format for the stimuli, and the expectancies generated by the subject.

4. For item recognition in long-term storage, subjects may recognize information by either a fast decision process based on the degree of stimulus familiarity or a slower serial scanning process.

5. Studies of item recall have demonstrated that information may be available but inaccessible in long-term storage. This is evidenced by the tip-of-the-tongue phenomenon and the fact that cued recall is generally superior to free recall.

6. The principle of encoding specificity states that a cue will facilitate recall only if it has been encoded with the stimulus to be remembered at the time of learning and is available to the subject at the time of remembering. Empirical support for this principle is available.

7. Various findings suggest that recall and recognition memory tasks involve different underlying processes. These

data include differential effects of stimulus and instructional variables and unequal effects of stimulus organization.

8. The finding that recall may sometimes be superior to recognition raises problems for approaches which assume that differences between recall and recognition are due to differences in memory strength (i.e., less strength needed for recognition) or component processes (i.e., only recall necessitates a memory search).

9. With complex information, it is possible to see evidence for the abstraction of gist as subjects relate ideas from stories and remember the meaning of what they experienced.

10. Verbatim memory can be demonstrated when information is presented in an unusual format, such as a sentence printed upside-down.

11. Context serves to structure complex information; it provides a schema that guides the processing and subsequent retention of the information.

12. When stimuli are presented within a meaningful context, people abstract the gist of the event and have trouble distinguishing stimuli that were experienced before from those that are merely consistent with the context. When no context is available, the abstraction of gist is not possible, and only specific elements are perceived and retained.

13. Recall is frequently a reconstruction based partly on what was and partly on what must have been. Eyewitness reports, for example, may start out fragmentary and incomplete, but over time, because of reconstructive processes, the reports become coherent, full-blown stories.

14. Events occur within a context, yet events which occur frequently may eventually lose their contextual ties. This information may then become a permanent part of the person's knowledge of the world.

15. Semantic memory contains our knowledge of the world; it is important because it can influence the manner in which we perceive and remember new experiences.

16. Our knowledge of semantic memory is still incomplete, and various approaches are possible. Three approaches examined briefly were a network model based on inferential processing, a propositional model based on associative relationships, and a feature comparison model based on redundant feature matching.

CHAPTER TEN

Developmental & Pathological Aspects of Memory

OBJECTIVES

1. *To review how the memory system develops in infancy and childhood.*
2. *To consider the types of memory problems that can occur due to psychological or neurological impairment.*
3. *To examine the possibility that all experiences produce permanent memory traces.*

INTRODUCTION

Some years ago, a Canadian neurosurgeon named Penfield made a surprising discovery. During an operation he found that memories of previous events were recalled when the brain of an awake patient was stimulated by a mild electrical current. The patient reported seeing or hearing things that had been experienced many years before. Probing in one spot produced the report of an orchestra playing a song that had been popular years earlier; probing another spot produced a different recall from a previous time. These remembrances were not confused with reality even though they contained sharp, vivid details. For Penfield, the recall of what appeared to be common, everyday events suggested that all of our experiences, the great and the small, are recorded somewhere in the brain (Penfield, 1952; 1975).

In this final chapter, we conclude our review of how the memory system works by considering normal and pathological aspects of memory functioning. Previous chapters have dealt with the sensory memories, attentional and pattern recognition processes, methods of memory formation, and organizational and retrieval processes. What has been neglected so far is a review of how the memory system develops, the types of problems that can occur due to psychological or neurological difficulty, and whether, as Penfield suggests, the brain permanently records the stream of consciousness over the lifetime of the individual. It is to these topics that we now turn.

DEVELOPMENTAL BASES OF MEMORY

Infant Memory

CASUAL OBSERVATIONS. Our review of the developmental bases of memory will begin with an examination of the memory capabilities of infants. Casual observations indicate that infants exhibit a variety of behaviors from which it may be inferred that they possess the means for establishing short-term and long-term storage. Among the memory-related behaviors that children under the age of one year are capable of demonstrating are imitation, object permanence, and attachment (Cohen & Gelber, 1975). When an infant imitates the action of another person, this behavior implies that the infant has stored, at least temporarily, information about the other person's behavior. The fact that an infant can imitate a mother's intonation pattern during vocalization implies a short-term storage system capable of representing and articulating sound patterns. In object permanence, a toy or other desired object is taken from the infant and placed under a blanket. Infants between the ages of four and eight months will search for the object providing part of it is exposed; infants between eight and twelve months will search even if the entire object is concealed (Ault, 1977). Object permanence, according to Piaget (1929), demonstrates knowledge that an object exists even though it is no longer visible. In this instance, short-term storage is again implied, although the representational basis for such storage is not obvious. Finally, attachment or fear of strangers demonstrates that infants are capable of distinguishing among people on the basis of familiarity. Fear of strangers, which normally develops between six and eight months of age, involves recognition memory and provides evidence of long-term nonverbal storage. Whether person recognition is based solely on visual appearance or a cluster of personal factors involving sight, smell, and sound is not clear.

SYSTEMATIC OBSERVATIONS. As compelling as the various casual observation methods are for demonstrating memory in infants, a number of problems are inherent which limit their usefulness in experimental psychology. Cohen and Gelber (1975) note that memory indicants, such as imitation or attachment, involve complex social interactions. In an early stage of research, it is often desirable to study processes under less complex, more tightly controlled settings. For this reason, two paradigms which share in experimental rigor have been widely adopted for the study of memory in infants. These methods, which have been reviewed earlier in our discussion of selective attention (see Chapter Four), are the habituation paradigm and the paired-comparison technique.

In the habituation paradigm, the infant is presented with the same stimulus over a series of trials and a response measure, such as time spent viewing the stimulus, is obtained. Performance over trials typically shows a response increment for the early trials followed by a decrement in later trials. The decrement is termed habituation and is assumed to reflect memory rather than fatigue since a change in the stimulus will result in increased performance once more. Studies have shown that stimulus habituation is easier to obtain in older than younger infants (Fantz, 1964), although in some instances habituation has been reliably demonstrated in infants less than three days old (e.g., Friedman & Carpenter, 1971).

In the paired-comparison technique, the infant is presented with a pair of identical visual stimuli, one on the left and one on the right. After a period of time, the identical stimuli are replaced by a pair consisting of a familiar stimulus from the preceding set and a novel stimulus not seen before. The response measure is the percentage of time spent looking at each stimulus over a given temporal interval. Memory is demonstrated by the infant selecting one stimulus, usually the novel stimulus, for viewing longer than the other. If no memory is present, no viewing preferences should be obtained and each stimulus should show equivalent viewing times.

Studies by Fagan (1973) have employed the paired-comparison technique with infants to measure the duration of memory for abstract and concrete stimuli by varying the length of time between

TABLE 10.1 Mean Percent Fixation to Familiar and Novel Abstract Visual Patterns in Infants

| Study-Test | Stimuli | |
Interval	Familiar	Novel
Immediate	34	66
24 hours	39	61
48 hours	41	59

(Adapted from Fagan, 1973, Exp. 1)

the study and test trials. In an experiment which measured the duration of memory for abstract stimuli, Fagan presented four- to six-month-old infants with a pair of identical visual patterns consisting of random lines, concentric circles, or checkerboards for 2 minutes of free viewing. Immediately after the stimulus familiarization period, the infants were presented with a repeated pattern and a novel pattern. The location of the familiar stimulus was counterbalanced over all subjects (i.e., some of the subjects saw the familiar pattern on the left, and others saw it on the right). Either 24 or 48 hours after the immediate test, the same testing procedure was repeated on all infants. Viewing preferences, expressed in terms of the percentage of time spent viewing the familiar and novel stimuli over a period of 40 seconds, are shown in Table 10.1. A clear preference for the novel stimulus is readily seen when the test immediately follows the familiarization period. With delays of 24 and 48 hours between the first test and the retest, a reduction in preference for the novel stimulus can be seen as the viewing time for each stimulus begins to approximate an even split. These data imply that infants can retain information about an abstract stimulus for up to 2 days following a 2-minute initial exposure.

In a second study, Fagan employed the same procedure to test infant memory for pictures of faces. Immediately after a 2-minute familiarization period, infants were presented with a picture of a familiar face or a novel face and the time spent viewing each stimulus was again recorded. As before, a retest of viewing preferences was provided 24 hours, 48 hours, 1 week, or 2 weeks after the initial test. Consistent with the results from the abstract stimuli, the data in Table 10.2 show a strong preference for the novel stimulus. These findings indicate that infants are capable of storing information about faces in memory over a period of time as long as 2 weeks. While we would not want to conclude that these studies demonstrate that concrete stimuli are remembered better than ab-

TABLE 10.2 Mean Percent Fixation to Familiar and Novel Pictures of Faces in Infants

Study-Test Interval	Stimuli	
	Familiar	Novel
Immediate	36	64
24 hours	38	62
48 hours	35	65
1 week	39	61
2 weeks	43	57

(Adapted from Fagan, 1973, Exp. 2)

stract stimuli (e.g., even at this early age, infants would have had more experience with facial stimuli than abstract patterns), it does seem clear that infants are capable of demonstrating effects of long-term storage even though they cannot express themselves verbally. In such instances, the ingenuity of the experimenter offsets the limitations of the subjects.

Differences Between Children and Adults

In order to determine how the memory system develops, it is important to examine the ways in which children differ from adults. Toward this end, we will examine differences in attentional processes, strategy selection, and memory duration prior to speculating on the developmental bases of memory.

ATTENTIONAL PROCESSES. Successful memory performance is dependent upon the selection of appropriate information from the environment. While the ability to attend selectively may be largely innate (see Chapter Four), a considerable body of evidence indicates that information selectivity is subject to age-related differences. Vurpillot (1968), for example, recorded the eye movements of children between the ages of six and nine in a task which required them to decide if two pictures were the same or different. Her results showed that younger children looked at only parts of the pictures and consequently made more errors than older children, who systematically scanned each picture before a decision was made (see also Mackworth & Bruner, 1970).

But the lack of systematic attentional processes is not the only shortcoming of young children. Research by Hagen (1972) and others indicates that young children have difficulty separating relevant from irrelevant information in learning situations. In one study by Hale, Miller, and Stevenson (1968), school-age children were shown a film and then asked to recall relevant information about the film's plot and irrelevant information about characters in the film (e.g., "What color dress was the woman wearing?"). Hale et al. found that recall of relevant information improved with age, while recall of irrelevant features increased up to age thirteen and then decreased. With increasing age, children selectively attended to the more meaningful features of the film.

Research by Bach and Underwood (1970) is consistent with the view that meaningful aspects of stimulation tend to assume dominance as a child increases in age. In a study of recognition memory for words, Bach and Underwood found that false recognition of words acoustically related to list items tended to decrease between ages seven and eleven, while false recognition of words associatively related to list items significantly increased. For the older children, word meaning was clearly the most important factor. More recent research by Kail and Siegel (1977) has examined word meaning in terms of its denotative and connotative aspects. Denotative characteristics, which supply specific meaning, are available to young children, while connotative aspects, which supply associative significance, are available only to older children, and in some instances only to adolescents and adults. In sum, these findings indicate that as children get older, they examine information more systematically and choose the more meaningful aspects of that information for attention.

USE OF STRATEGIES. Various types of evidence indicate that as children get older, their spontaneous use of effective retention strategies shows a dramatic increase. Flavell, Beach, and Chinsky (1966) measured the immediate memory span of children in kindergarten, second grade, and fifth grade. The children were presented with a series of two to five object pictures (e.g., a flag, an apple, and so forth) to which the experimenter pointed in a particular order. The task was to recall the series by pointing to the pictures in the same order. The results showed that memory span, when defined as the largest set of pictures a child could sequentially order correctly, increased directly with the age of the child. An analysis of the spontaneous use of rehearsal to retain the ordered sequence showed developmental changes as well. By employing a lip reader, Flavell et al. were able to determine the number of observable rehearsals each item received prior to the recall test. The results showed that most of the kindergarteners never spontaneously rehearsed the items, while the majority of the fifth graders rehearsed each item three or more times prior to recall. Second graders were intermediate; some of them never rehearsed, and others rehearsed as often as fifth graders. Subsequent research by Keeney, Cannizzo, and Flavell (1967) and Kingsley and Hagen (1969) indicates that although young children do not spontaneously use rehearsal, with training they can adopt this strategy and improve their performance to the level of those children using rehearsal spontaneously.

In the Flavell et al. study, the change in memory performance with increasing age appears closely related to the adoption of an effective strategy for maintaining information in short-term storage. Consistent with this interpretation are the results of Sabo and Hagen (1971), who report that when a rehearsal prevention task was employed between a series of stimuli to be remembered and a recall test, the presence of a distractor had little effect on young children but a significant negative effect on older children. A distractor could inhibit performance only if it interfered with an ongoing process, such as mental rehearsal.

As with rehearsal, organizational strategies show an increase in spontaneous use as the child grows older (e.g., Moely, Olsen, Hawles, & Flavell, 1969; Neimark, Slotnick, & Ulrich, 1971). Kindergarten and first-grade children demonstrate little awareness that clustering items in a free-recall task can improve performance, while older children become increasingly concerned with using effective strategies to improve recall. Between the ages of ten and twelve, spontaneous category clustering can be found in free recall, followed by subjective organizational schemes a few years later (Moely, 1977). As might be expected from our review of attentional variation in children, the basis for list organization in free recall is likewise variable. Rhyming and syntactical relations may be observed in the recall of young children, while semantic clustering becomes more important as children get older (e.g., Cole, Frankel, & Sharp, 1971; Rossi & Wittrock, 1971).

Finally, studies employing mental imagery as a relational strategy also show age-related effects. While it was once believed that kindergarteners could not benefit from instructions to remember paired associates by means of relational imagery, subsequent research has shown that even young children can improve their performance if appropriately instructed (e.g., Varley, Levin, Severson, & Wolff, 1974; Yuille & Catchpole, 1973). But, as Reese (1977) carefully points out, with complex strategies, more extensive prompting is required for young children and, even with such prompting,

TABLE 10.3 Percent Recognition as a Function of Age of Subject and Delay Between Stimulus Exposure and Test

Subjects and Experiment	Unit of Time Between Study and Test			
	Day	Week	Month	Year
College Students (Nickerson, 1968)	92	90	78	63
Preschool Children (Brown & Scott, 1971)	84	74	58	—

Note: Chance performance in each experiment is 50%.

young children do not always continue to use the strategy when the prompts are eliminated. With age, it seems that the use of complex strategies spontaneously increases, and the ability to take advantage of strategy instruction becomes greater (Reese, 1977).

LONG-TERM RECOGNITION MEMORY. Given the differences found in attentional processes and strategy selection, it is not surprising that comparisons of long-term recognition memory between children and adults show large differences in performance over time. In one study, Nickerson (1968) presented college students with a deck of 100 pictures of black and white objects obtained from magazines. After viewing the picture stimuli, the subjects were given a delayed recognition test 1 day, 1 week, 1 month, or 1 year later. The test consisted of the 100 pictures previously viewed and 100 new pictures of comparable quality. The task was to indicate which of the 200 test stimuli had been seen before. The results, shown in Table 10.3, indicate that, while recognition performance is initially quite high, with the passage of time, performance deteriorates so that after one year it is only slightly better than chance.

A similar qualitative change in recognition memory over time was obtained by Brown and Scott (1971). In their study, preschool children between the ages of three and five were presented with 50 pictures of colored objects obtained from children's books. Immediately after viewing the stimuli, the children were given a recognition test consisting of the initial 50 stimuli and 50 stimuli not seen before. On this test, the children recognized 98 percent of the stimuli correctly. Following the test, the subjects were tested again 1 day, 1 week, or 1 month later. Percent recognition, based on the same test, is shown in Table 10.3. Once more, performance deteriorates over time, but, in contrast to Nickerson's (1968) data for adult subjects, recognition performance for children is near chance level after only 1 month. While it is difficult to make direct comparisons between different experiments, the results indicate that retention in preschool children is not comparable to that of adults (see also Buschke, 1977b).

CONCLUSIONS. The review of attentional processes, strategy selection, and long-term recognition memory has revealed important aspects of the development of memory. To recapitulate, studies of attention have shown that with increasing age, children examine information more systematically and attend to more meaningful features. Studies of strategy use have demonstrated that the spontaneous use of complex strategies increases with age, as does the ability to profit from instructions in their use. Finally, studies of long-term recognition memory suggest that retention is poorer in preschool children than in college-age adults.

Coupled with the above developmental changes is the emergence of a type of memory processing called *metamemory*. According to Flavell (1971), metamemory refers to a person's awareness about memory and performance. An awareness of the memory demands of a task or the fact that some stimuli will be harder to remember than others are examples of metamemory. Young children, for example, show limited metamemory as they overestimate their memory capabilities, while older children are more realistic in their estimates (e.g., Flavell, Friedrichs, & Hoyt, 1970). As children get older, not only do they process different information, they also become more aware of what each situation demands and how best to use available resources for successful performance (e.g., Brown, 1975; Kreutzer, Leonard, & Flavell, 1975). Developmentally, memory performance changes because children become more planful and adaptive in changing environmental situations (Flavell & Wellman, 1977).

MEMORY PATHOLOGY

Not all changes in memory functioning reflect positive growth and development. Some changes, because of psychological or neurological problems, result in memory impairment. In this section, we will consider selected memory pathologies because they are interesting in their own right and because they can serve as an additional source of information about normal functioning.

Psychopathology

Dissociative neuroses constitute a group of problems which involve alterations in states of awareness (Sarason, 1976). Two such dissociative reactions are amnesia and fugue states. In *amnesia,* psychological stress or trauma, under conditions associated with great fear, rage, or humiliation, can produce a memory loss in order to satisfy a specific emotional need for a particular period of time (Linn, 1967). Psychologically, the loss of memory serves the person by removing the unwanted experience from conscious awareness. Such amnesias, which begin and end abruptly (Kirschner, 1973), reduce the anxiety associated with a specific event by preventing the event from becoming conscious. According to Sarason (1976), this type of response to psychological pressure does not seem to involve brain damage or other organic factors. It is a form of failure to face reality and is found in persons who are characterized as emotionally immature.

When the avoidance of a problem involves literally running away from the traumatic situation as well as repressing its associated memories, the disorder is called a *fugue state.* According to Linn (1967), a fugue state may follow a severe emotional trauma in which the person escapes the situation in a state of panic followed by a complete memory loss of all personally identifying information. Upon recovery, the person will remember nothing of what transpired during the state, but, with therapy, such memories are usually recovered. The recovery of previously repressed information indicates that amnesia which is caused by a psychological problem is the result of a blockage of retrieval; encoding or storage processes do not seem to be affected. In line with the view of available but inaccessible traces (see Chapter Nine), we saw that inaccessible information could be made accessible by the provision of appropriate retrieval cues (e.g., Tulving & Pearlstone, 1966). Studies of amnesia and fugue states indicate that the reverse is also possible; previously accessible information can be made inaccessible by the involvement of personal motivational factors (see Freud, 1951).

Neuropathology

Memory problems may also be found in instances where psychological problems are not present. Amnesia may result from physical trauma as well as psychological trauma. Old age and senility produce disturbances in memory functioning, as do surgical operations involving the cerebral cortex. Since these topics are discussed in great detail elsewhere (e.g., Birnbaum & Parker, 1977; Pribram & Broadbent, 1970; Talland & Waugh, 1969), the present coverage will be limited to examining the major findings and noting their relevance to normal functioning.

ANTEROGRADE AND RETROGRADE AMNESIA. Although anterograde and retrograde amnesia are similar in that both involve a loss of memory, *anterograde amnesia* involves memory loss for events subsequent to traumatic events, while *retrograde amnesia* entails memory loss for events prior to a physical trauma. Since examples of anterograde amnesia have already been discussed in terms of patients suffering from Korsakoff's syndrome or various brain injuries such as N.A. (see Chapter Six), this topic will not be considered further.

Retrograde amnesia is almost always found in some degree following an accident in which there is a cerebral concussion. According to Russell and Nathan (1946), the more severe the concussion, the further the memory loss extends backward in time. Gradually, as the patient recovers from an injury, the amnesia becomes progressively smaller, with older memories returning before more recent memories. Except under special circumstances, there is a short period of time just prior to an accident which usually does not return. Whether the events preceding an accident are recalled does not seem to depend on the severity of the concussion, but, rather, on what the person was doing at that time. If the person had been particularly attentive or if the circumstances of the accident had been exceptional, the events prior to the accident may be recalled. If, however, the person was not paying close attention, the events prior to the accident tend not to be recalled (Barbizet, 1970). The relationship between the recovery of prior events and the degree of attention is similar to that found between memory performance and depth of processing (see Chapter Six). In the present context, events that received conscious analysis may be recovered, while those that failed to reach consciousness may not have been sufficiently processed to ensure storage and subsequent retrieval.

A concussion following an accident is not the only source of traumatic amnesia. Electroconvulsive shock also produces retrograde amnesia which is comparable to that produced by a head injury (Williams, 1969). This procedure, which is used in the treatment of severe depression, involves the presentation of a brief elec-

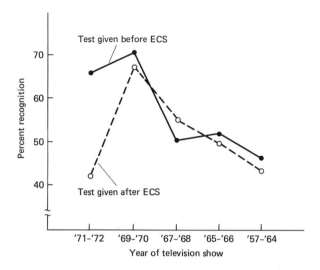

FIGURE 10.1. Percent recognition of television shows as a function of presentation of electroconvulsive shock (ECS) and year of show. (Adapted from Squire, Slater, and Chace, 1975)

trical current to the head of a patient in sufficient magnitude to produce a seizure and temporary loss of consciousness. In one study of the effects of electroconvulsive shock on memory, Squire, Slater, and Chace (1975) tested patients about prime-time television programs which were shown briefly in prior seasons. The task required the patients to recognize which program from a set of four names was actually shown in a given year. In each instance, only one name was real; the other three names were fictitious. Different versions of the television test were presented to hospitalized patients prior to their first shock treatment and again 1 hour after their fifth treatment. The results, shown in Figure 10.1, indicate that memory for television programs declines with the passage of time (i.e., performance becomes poorer as the programs become more distant) and, most importantly, electroconvulsive shock has a disruptive effect on only the most recent year tested; memory for programs of earlier years is unaffected. This disruption, however, is only temporary. According to Squire et al., within 2 weeks of the last shock treatment, memory for the most recent programs returned to its pretreatment level.

In terms of encoding, storage, and retrieval processes, the Squire et al. data, as well as the data on amnesia from psychological trauma, indicate that retrograde loss is the result of retrieval difficulty for a period of time following a physical or psychological shock. Encoding and storage processes, however, are also implicated by the findings reported by Barbizet (1970) relating attention and memory recovery. Although we cannot be more specific about the locus of amnesia, it is clear that retrograde loss does not result from simply a loss of consciousness. Anesthetists indicate that, providing premedication has not been too strong, patients remember the last instructions they are given before losing consciousness (Barbizet, 1970). A traumatic disruption of ongoing processes seems necessary to produce memory loss.

OLD AGE AND SENILITY. Just as memory functioning changes with the development of the child, so, too, does functioning change as a person advances in age. Beyond age sixty, characteristic changes occur which seem to undo some of the positive skills acquired as a child. These changes are common and not to be confused with the pathological changes wrought by senility or arteriosclerotic brain disease, to be discussed subsequently.

It is common knowledge that memory functioning is hampered in old age. The old are aware of their deficient memories, but apparently they lack the ability to use more effective retention strategies (Reese, 1976). Studies by Craik (1968), Raymond (1971), and Arenberg (1973) have demonstrated that the old are impaired in long-term storage. Craik, for example, found no difference in subspan memory lists between subjects aged twenty-two and sixty-five, but significant differences were found for lists longer than the memory span. Data from free-recall studies showed that both groups produced equivalent recency effects, but the young group produced a greater primacy effect than the old group (Craik, 1968).

Why do the old show deficiencies in long-term memory tasks? A study reported by Craik (1977) suggests that older subjects are capable of encoding stimuli on a deep semantic basis, but such encoding strategies are often not spontaneously employed. When groups of young and old subjects were induced to encode words on the same semantic level, performance between groups was equivalent when memory was tested by recognition but not when memory was tested by recall. With recall, the young subjects did better than the old subjects. Since encoding processes were equated for young and old, the difference in recall may reflect retrieval deficiencies in the aged (see also Buschke, 1977b, and Hultsch, 1975). Based on similarities between young children and adults over age sixty,

Reese (1977) has argued that memory deficiencies in the aged reflect deficiencies in the use of effective strategies. Why the aged should no longer employ those strategies which served them so well in earlier years is unclear. It may be that, with increasing years and decreasing learning opportunities, such strategies are simply forgotten (Reese, 1977).

Two types of memory problems found in people between the ages of sixty and ninety serve to differentiate those problems which are normal from those which suggest neuropathology. According to Kral (1969), one problem, common to all people to some extent, is that old people are increasingly subject to forgetting names, places, and dates of distant experiences. This problem affects males and females equally and is unrelated to the death rate.

In contrast to the familiar forgetting of distant details, Kral found that some old people failed to recall recent events. People with this problem tended to be disoriented and engaged in confabulation (i.e., filling memory gaps with reasonable but inaccurate events). It is noteworthy that this problem is observed more frequently in women than men and is associated with a higher than average death rate. Studies of senile brain disease indicate that half of the cases studied show evidence of cerebral arteriosclerosis, which involves thickening of the arteries and a resultant reduction in the supply of oxygen to the brain (Busse, 1967). Autopsies of people who suffered from senile brain disease reveal general brain atrophy, which is usually most obvious in the frontal lobe of the cerebral cortex. This brain disease is relevant to this section because it rarely occurs before the age of sixty-five. It is more frequently found in women than men, and it results in memory loss for recent events which is concealed by confabulation. Unlike other old people who merely forget isolated details from the distant past, these people suffer a neuropathological memory impairment which signals a breakdown in the cognitive system and eventually a cessation of life.

CEREBRAL SURGERY. Although a discussion of brain structures and anatomy is beyond the scope of this text, an examination of gross cerebral organization is appropriate since it bears on normal memory functioning. For this reason, observations dealing with cerebral lobectomies and other surgical procedures will be considered briefly.

The human brain is dominated by two large hemispheres which constitute the entirety of the cerebral cortex. The two hemispheres, which are responsible for the higher forms of behavior in man, seem different in terms of the type of information each is most suited to process. Studies by Milner (1970) and others have shown that when a portion of either the left or right hemisphere (i.e., the left or right temporal lobe) is removed in patients suffering from severe epilepsy, characteristic memory disorders are produced. Following a left temporal lobectomy (i.e., removal of a portion of the left temporal lobe), patients show selective impairment on verbal memory tasks. Recall of short passages, verbal paired associates, and duration of immediate memory show diminished performance, compared to those patients with comparable portions of their right hemisphere removed or control patients who received no surgical intervention (e.g., Corsi, 1969; Milner, 1967). Patients with right temporal lobectomies show a different type of memory impairment. These patients, when compared to the appropriate controls, show deficits in dealing with complex visual or auditory patterns. Nonverbal tasks, such as maze learning or recognition of nonsense figures, are especially difficult for these patients (e.g., Kimura, 1963; Milner, 1968). The finding of different deficits associated with left and right temporal lobectomies implies differences between the two hemispheres. The left hemisphere seems best equipped for dealing with verbal memory tasks, while the right hemisphere seems more suited for handling nonverbal-spatial memory tasks.

There is much converging evidence to support the view of dichotomous processing on a hemispheric level in man. Studies of stroke patients have shown a loss of verbal ability (e.g., aphasia) in many patients who suffer a stroke in the left hemisphere, while nonverbal deficits, such as a difficulty in facial recognition (e.g., prosopagnosia), can be found when strokes occur in the right hemisphere (e.g., Hécaen & Angelergues, 1962). Perhaps the most compelling evidence for cerebral laterality differences is found in the split-brain studies of Sperry and Gazzaniga (e.g., Gazzaniga, 1967, 1970; Sperry, 1968). In severe circumstances, a number of epileptic patients have had their hemispheres split by an operation which completely severs the corpus callosum. The corpus callosum is a thick bundle of nerve fibers which serves to connect the left and right hemispheres and acts as a communication link between both cerebral structures. While this operation has been shown to reduce the severity of subsequent epileptic seizures, it has also revealed general differences in the information-processing capabilities of each hemisphere. As in the studies involving cerebral lobectomies, patients who have undergone the split-brain procedure show the left hemisphere to be language dominant and most capable for verbal tasks, while the right hemisphere is best for nonverbal-spatial tasks (see Nebes, 1974, for a review). Although individual variation exists (see Hardyck, 1977), this dichotomy represents the cerebral organization found in the majority of people who are right-handed and have a family history of right-handedness (see also the behavioral data of Geffen, Bradshaw, & Wallace, 1971, and Seamon & Gazzaniga, 1973).

The data on cerebral organization are important because they indicate that when a person suffers a cerebral disorder, damage to a particular hemisphere is likely to produce a particular type of memory impairment. Damage to the left hemisphere may result in language or speech deficits and verbal memory loss, while assault to the right hemisphere may produce a decrement in nonverbal-spatial abilities. Because of the known relationships between site of disorder and type of memory deficit, neurologists may use this information as a diagnostic device for detecting brain damage.

THE QUESTION OF PERMANENCE

The issue of trace permanence is a fitting topic to close both this chapter and this book. Providing an individual has developed normally and remains free of psychological and neurological impairment, are there data to support the contention of Penfield that all prior experiences leave permanent traces in memory? Relevant to this issue are observations involving electrical stimulation of the brain, hypnotic age regression, and the relearning of a childhood experience. Each will be considered in turn before closing thoughts are presented.

Electrical Stimulation of the Brain

Penfield's (1952; 1975) belief that all experiences leave permanent traces in memory was based on his studies of electrical stimulation of the brain (see Introduction). Numerous difficulties, however, suggest that this conclusion may not be warranted. As noted by Barbizet (1970), recall during electrical stimulation has been found only with epileptic patients who were stimulated in an area of the brain showing abnormal (i.e., epileptic) functioning; on no occasion has the effect been observed with a healthy brain. These experiences, when they occurred, were rare (e.g., less than 8 percent of the epileptic patients showed the effect) and were never verified to determine if they actually occurred. Finally, since patients could not add to these recalls in any way to make them more precise in terms of time or place, Barbizet suggests that such reports represent a pathological memory process. Because of these shortcomings, Penfield's observations are insufficient to conclude that all experiences leave permanent traces in memory.

Hypnotic Age Regression

If all memory traces are permanent, they should be recoverable by reinstating prior contexts. Childhood experiences, for example, should be recalled if people could be mentally regressed to an appropriate age. While demonstrations purporting to show hypnotic age regression have been available since the end of the nineteenth century (see Hilgard, 1977), experimental analyses are more recent. In an early study of hypnotic age regression, True (1949) asked age-regressed subjects to recall the day of the week of their birthday at different ages. He found that college students were 92 percent correct when age regressed to age ten, 84 percent correct at age seven, and 62 percent correct at age four. Similarly high were scores obtained when age-regressed subjects were asked to state the day of the week of Christmas. While seemingly supporting the idea of permanent memory traces, two problems negate the value of these findings: first, performance was better than it should have been (i.e., generally, four-year-olds are not sensitive to the days of the week); second, subsequent studies have attempted to replicate these results and found performance to be no better than chance (see Barber, 1962).

Reiff and Scheerer (1959) performed a more recent study of memory and hypnotic age regression. They compared the recall of age-regressed subjects with that of nonhypnotized control subjects and found that age-regressed subjects were more accurate in remembering the names of their grammar school teachers. Methodological flaws, however, limit the usefulness of this study. Instead of comparing the recall of hypnotically age-regressed subjects with that of nonhypnotized subjects, both groups of subjects should have been hypnotized and only one group age-regressed. At present, the difference in recall may be due to an effect of hypnosis (e.g., recall is greater under hypnosis than in a normal, awake state) or an effect of age regression. This experiment cannot differentiate these possibilities.

Although occasional reports suggesting remarkable instances of hypnotically induced memory recovery occur from time to time (e.g., Walker, Garrett, & Wallace, 1976), the history of research on this topic indicates that a healthy skepticism is appropriate. Until such claims have been substantiated by other researchers and shown to be unexplainable by simpler formulations, it seems more reasonable to agree with Neisser (1967), who wrote that, with regard to hypnotic age regression, the age of miracles is over. As with the observations from brain stimulation, the findings from studies of hypnotic age regression are not sufficient to conclude that all experiences produce permanent memory traces.

Relearning Ancient Greek

A sensitive measure of memory not yet discussed is the performance measure of relearning called the *savings score*. A savings score is the difference between the number of trials to learn material initially and the number of trials needed to relearn the material subsequently. This measure, originally adopted by Ebbinghaus, was used by Burtt (1941) in a test of permanent childhood memory. Using his infant son as his only subject, Burtt read passages of Sophocles in the original Greek to the child from the age of fifteen months to three years. Over this period of time, twenty-one passages, each twenty-two lines long, were read ninety times. Later, when his son was eight, fourteen, and eighteen years old, Burtt measured the number of trials the child needed to learn each of ten passages of Sophocles. At each age, seven of the passages were from the original twenty-one read to the child in infancy, while the remaining three were new. In comparing the average performance for the novel passages with those previously heard, Burtt found a savings of 27 percent for the previously heard passages at age eight, and 8 percent savings at age fourteen, and only 1 percent savings at age eighteen. These data, although based on only one subject, show no evidence of a permanent trace of an early childhood experience. In view of the fact that attentional processes and strategy use change as a child matures, perhaps these results are understandable.

Closing Thoughts

Our review of the studies of electrical stimulation of the brain, hypnotic age regression, and the relearning of a childhood experience provide no support for the view that all experiences leave permanent traces in memory. This is not to say that such traces do not exist; rather, the present studies fail to provide supporting evidence. But in light of the evidence marshaled here and throughout this text, it seems clear that a view which assumes that all experiences produce permanent memory traces is probably wrong. As noted in Chapter Two, some memories may last a lifetime, some may last only a few days or hours, some perhaps thirty seconds, and some are so brief that they last but a quarter of a second.

While all memories may not be permanent, certainly some memories may last a lifetime. Neisser (1967) discusses anecdotal evidence of familiar faces being recognized forever and skilled performances such as bicycle riding or swimming or well-learned lines from a play or poem lasting for the life of the individual. Bahrick et al.'s (1975) study of name and face recognition of former high-school classmates over a span of forty-seven years clearly supports this view. What makes memories such as these permanent is difficult to say. It may be that the memories which last are those that are recalled and, in a sense, reexperienced and refreshed from time to time. Alternatively, perhaps these memories were so well learned and highly practiced initially that even the passage of time cannot completely erase their deep and lasting imprint. It seems fair to say that while we know how to improve the duration of memory and we know what makes some experiences more memorable than others, we still do not know why some experiences last forever and others for far shorter periods of time. This will probably remain a mystery until we have a more satisfactory theory of cognition which includes such factors as motivation and personality. As Neisser (1967) stated over a decade ago, cognition is only one aspect of psychology, and it cannot exist alone.

SUMMARY

1. Casual observations indicate that infants exhibit a variety of behaviors, from which it may be inferred that they possess memory.

2. Among the memory-related acts that children under the age of one year are capable of demonstrating are imitation, object permanence, and attachment.

3. The habituation paradigm and the paired-comparison technique are two approaches used in the systematic study of memory in infants.

4. Studies employing the paired-comparison technique have demonstrated that infants may show evidence of stimulus memory for up to 2 weeks.

5. Memory differences between children and adults were examined in terms of attentional processes, strategy selection, and long-term recognition memory.

6. Studies indicate that as children get older, they examine information more systematically and select the more meaningful aspects of that information for attention. These differences in attentional processes are coupled with an increasing spontaneous use of effective retention strategies which result in greater long-term memory performance.

7. Developmentally, memory performance changes because children become more planful and adaptive in changing environmental situations.

8. Psychological and neurological impairments can result in various types of memory disorders. Stress resulting from psychological problems may produce a dissociative neurosis, such as amnesia or a fugue state, in which memory loss serves a person by removing an undesirable event from conscious awareness.

9. Memory loss may also result from physical trauma. A concussion from an accident or a severe electroconvulsive shock can produce retrograde amnesia that may extend backward in time over a period of years. With time, the amnesia usually recovers, with older memories returning first.

10. Beyond age sixty, memory changes occur which appear to undo the positive skills acquired as a child. The forgetting of details from distant events is a common occurrence in old age.

11. Pathological changes produced by senility or arteriosclerotic brain disease produce memory disruption of recent events in which entire episodes rather than fine details are lost. These changes signal a breakdown in the cognitive system and an eventual cessation of life.

12. Studies of patients who have undergone cerebral surgery indicate that, for many people, the left hemisphere of the brain is language dominant and excels at verbal tasks, while the right hemisphere is more suited for nonverbal, spatial tasks. Damage to a particular hemisphere is likely to result in a particular (i.e., verbal or spatial) memory impairment.

13. Observations involving electrical stimulation of the brain have been interpreted to mean that all experiences produce permanent memory traces.

14. A fine examination of the conditions under which electrical stimulation produces recall suggests that the conclusion that all traces are permanent is unwarranted. Studies of hypnotic age regression as well as a study involving the relearning of a childhood experience likewise produce no support for the permanent trace position. A view of memory which assumes that all traces are permanent is probably wrong.

15. While all memories may not be permanent, some memories may last a lifetime. What makes some memories permanent is a mystery and is likely to remain so until we have a more satisfactory theory of human cognition.

References

Aaronson, D., & Scarborough, H. S. Performance theories for sentence coding: Some quantitative evidence. *Journal of Experimental Psychology: Human Perception and Performance*, 1976, *2*, 56–70.

Aderman, D., & Smith, E. E. Expectancy as a determinant of functional units in perceptual recognition. *Cognitive Psychology*, 1971, *2*, 117–129.

Allport, F. H. *Theories of perception and the concept of structure.* New York: Wiley, 1955.

Alpern, M. Muscular mechanisms. In H. Davson (Ed.), *The eye.* Vol. 3. New York: Academic Press, 1962.

Anderson, J. R. *Language, memory, and thought.* Hillsdale, N.J.: Erlbaum, 1976.

Anderson, J. R., & Bower, G. H. Recognition and retrieval processes in free recall. *Psychological Review*, 1972, *79*, 97–123.

Anderson, J. R., & Bower, G. H. *Human associative memory.* Washington, D.C.: Winston, 1973.

Anderson, J. R., & Paulson, R. Representation and retention of verbatim information. *Journal of Verbal Learning and Verbal Behavior*, 1977, *16*, 439–451.

Anderson, R. C., & Pichert, J. W. Recall of previously unrecallable information following a shift in perspective. *Journal of Verbal Learning and Verbal Behavior*, 1978, *17*, 1–12.

Arenberg, D. Cognition and aging: Verbal learning, memory, and problem solving. In C. Eisdorfer and M. P. Lawton (Eds.), *The psychology of adult development and aging.* Washington, D.C.: American Psychological Association, 1973.

Arnheim, R. *Art and visual perception. The new version.* Berkeley, Calif.: University of California Press, 1974.

Atkinson, R. C., Herrmann, D. J., & Wescourt, K. T. Search processes in recognition memory. In R. L. Solso (Ed.), *Theories in cognitive psychology.* Potomac, Md.: Erlbaum, 1974.

Atkinson, R. C., Holmgren, J. E., & Juola, J. F. Processing time as influenced by the number of elements in a visual display. *Perception & Psychophysics*, 1969, *6*, 321–326.

Atkinson, R. C., & Juola, J. F. Factors influencing speed and accuracy of word recognition. In S. Kornblum (Ed.), *Attention and performance IV.* New York: Academic Press, 1973.

Atkinson, R. C., & Juola, J. F. Search and decision processes in recognition memory. In D. H. Krantz, R. C. Atkinson, R. D. Luce, and P. Suppes (Eds.), *Contemporary developments in mathematical psychology.* San Francisco: Freeman, 1974.

Atkinson, R. C., & Shiffrin, R. M. Human memory: A proposed system and its control processes. In K. W. Spence and J. T. Spence (Eds.), *The psychology of learning and motivation: Advances in research and theory.* Vol. 2. New York: Academic Press, 1968.

Ault, R. L. *Children's cognitive development.* New York: Oxford University Press, 1977.

Averbach, E., & Coriell, A. S. Short-term memory in vision. *Bell System Technical Journal*, 1961, *40*, 309–328.

Averbach, E., & Sperling, G. Short-term storage of information in vision. In C. Cherry (Ed.), *Information theory: Proceedings of the Fourth London Symposium.* London: Butterworth, 1961.

Bach, M. J., & Underwood, B. J. Developmental changes in memory attributes. *Journal of Educational Psychology*, 1970, *61*, 292–296.

Bachrach, A. J. Diving behavior. In *Human performance and SCUBA diving.* Proceedings of the symposium on underwater physiology. Chicago: The Athletic Institute, 1970.

Baddeley, A. D. *The psychology of memory.* New York: Basic Books, 1976.

Baddeley, A. D., Grant, S., Wight, E., & Thomson, N. Imagery and visual working memory. In P. M. A. Rabbitt and S. Dornic (Eds.), *Attention and performance V.* New York: Academic Press, 1974.

Baddeley, A. D., & Patterson, K. The relationship between long-term and short-term memory. *British Medical Bulletin*, 1971, *27*, 237–242.

Baddeley, A. D., Thomson, N., & Buchanan, M. Word length and the structure of short-term memory. *Journal of Verbal Learning and Verbal Behavior*, 1975, *14*, 575–589.

Baddeley, A. D., & Warrington, E. K. Amnesia and the distinction between long- and short-term memory. *Journal of Verbal Learning and Verbal Behavior*, 1970, *9*, 176–189.

Bahrick, H. P., Bahrick, P. O., & Wittlinger, R. P. Fifty years of memory for names and faces: A cross-sectional approach. *Journal of Experimental Psychology: General*, 1975, *104*, 54–75.

Barber, T. X. Hypnotic age regression: A critical review. *Psychosomatic Medicine*, 1962, *24*, 286–299.

Barbizet, J. *Human memory and its pathology*. San Francisco: Freeman, 1970.

Barclay, J. R. The role of comprehension in remembering sentences. *Cognitive Psychology*, 1973, *4*, 229–254.

Barlow, H. B. Eye movements during fixation. *Journal of Physiology*, 1952, *116*, 290–306.

Bartlett, F. C. *Remembering: A study in experimental and social psychology*. London: Cambridge University Press, 1932.

Baxt, N. Über die Zeit, welche nötig ist, damit ein Gesichtseindruck zum Bewusstsein kommt. . . .*Pflügers Arch. ges. Psysiol.*, 1871, *4*, 325–336. (Cited in Murray, D. J. Research on human memory in the nineteenth century. *Canadian Journal of Psychology*, 1976, *30*, 201–220.)

Belmont, J. M., & Butterfield, E. C. Learning strategies as determinants of memory deficiencies. *Cognitive Psychology*, 1971, *2*, 411–420.

Bernbach, H. A. Rate of presentation in free recall: A problem for two-stage memory theories. *Journal of Experimental Psychology: Human Learning and Memory*, 1975, *104*, 18–22.

Bevan, W., & Stegar, J. A. Free recall and abstractness of stimuli. *Science*, 1971, *172*, 597–599.

Biederman, I. Perceiving real-world scenes. *Science*, 1972, *177*, 77–80.

Biederman, I., Glass, A. L., & Stacy, E. W., Jr. Searching for objects in real-world scenes. *Journal of Experimental Psychology*, 1973, *97*, 22–27.

Biederman, I., Rabinowitz, J., Glass, A. L., & Stacy, E. W., Jr. On the information extracted from a glance at a scene. *Journal of Experimental Psychology*, 1974, *101*, 597–600.

Birnbaum, I. M., & Parker, E. S. (Eds.). *Alcohol and human memory*. New York: Wiley, 1977.

Bjork, R. A., & Jongeward, R. H., Jr. Rehearsal and mere rehearsal. Cited in Bjork, R. A. Short-term storage: The ordered output of a central processor. In F. Restle, R. M. Shiffrin, N. J. Castellan, H. R. Lindman, and D. B. Pisoni (Eds.), *Cognitive theory*. Vol. 1. New York: Wiley, 1975.

Bjork, R. A., & Whitten, W. B. Recency-sensitive retrieval processes in long-term free recall. *Cognitive Psychology*, 1974, *6*, 173–189.

Blake, M. Prediction of recognition when recall fails: Exploring the feeling-of-knowing phenomenon. *Journal of Verbal Learning and Verbal Behavior*, 1973, *12*, 311–319.

Blake, R. R., Fox, R., & Lappin, J. S. Invariance in reaction time classification of same and different letter pairs. *Journal of Experimental Psychology*, 1970, *85*, 133–137.

Bobrow, S. A., & Bower, G. H. Comprehension and recall of sentences. *Journal of Experimental Psychology*, 1969, *80*, 455–461.

Boring, E. G. *A history of experimental psychology* (2nd ed.). New York: Appleton-Century-Crofts, 1950.

Bousfield, W. A. The occurrence of clustering in the recall of randomly arranged associates. *Journal of General Psychology*, 1953, *49*, 229–240.

Bousfield, W. A., & Sedgewick, C. H. An analysis of sequences of restricted associative responses. *Journal of General Psychology*, 1944, *30*, 149–165.

Bower, G. H. Analysis of a mnemonic device. *American Scientist*, 1970, *58*, 496–510. (a)

Bower, G. H. Organizational factors in memory. *Cognitive Psychology*, 1970, *1*, 18–46. (b)

Bower, G. H. Mental imagery and associative learning. In L. W. Gregg (Ed.), *Cognition in learning and memory*. New York: Wiley, 1972.

Bower, G. H., & Bolton, L. S. Why are rhymes easy to learn? *Journal of Experimental Psychology*, 1969, *82*, 453–461.

Bower, G. H., Clark, M. C., Lesgold, A. M., & Winzenz, D. Hierarchical retrieval schemes in recall of categorized word lists. *Journal of Verbal Learning and Verbal Behavior*, 1969, *8*, 323–343.

Bower, G. H., & Karlin, M. B. Depth of processing pictures of faces and recognition memory. *Journal of Experimental Psychology*, 1974, *103*, 751–757.

Bower, G. H. Lesgold, A. M., & Tieman, D. Grouping operations in free recall. *Journal of Verbal Learning and Verbal Behavior*, 1969, *8*, 481–493.

Bower, G. H., & Springston, F. Pauses as recoding points in letter series. *Journal of Experimental Psychology*, 1970, *83*, 421–436.

Bower, G. H., & Winzenz, D. Group structure, coding, and memory for digit series. *Journal of Experimental Psychology Monograph Supplement*, 1969, *80*, No. 2, Part 2.

Bracey, G. W. Two operations in character recognition: A partial replication. *Perception & Psychophysics*, 1969, *6*, 357–360.

Bransford, J. D., & Franks, J. J. The abstraction of linguistic ideas. *Cognitive Psychology*, 1971, *2*, 331–350.

Bransford, J. D., & Johnson, M. K. Considerations of some problems of comprehension. In W. Chase (Ed.), *Visual information processing*. New York: Academic Press, 1973.

Brewer, W. F. Memory for ideas: Synonym substitution. *Memory & Cognition*, 1975, *3*, 458–464.

Broadbent, D. E. *Perception and communication*. London: Pergamon Press, 1958.

Brooks, L. R. Spatial and verbal components of the act of recall. *Canadian Journal of Psychology*, 1968, *22*, 349–368.

Brown, A. L. The development of memory: Knowing, knowing about knowing, and knowing how to know. In H. W. Reese (Ed.), *Advances in child development and behavior*. Vol. 10. New York: Academic Press, 1975.

Brown, A. L., & Scott, M. S. Recognition memory for pictures in preschool children. *Journal of Experimental Child Psychology*, 1971, *11*, 401–412.

Brown, J. An analysis of recognition and recall and of problems in their comparison. In J. Brown (Ed.), Recall and recognition. New York: Wiley, 1976.

Brown, J. A. Some tests of the decay theory of immediate memory. Quarterly Journal of Experimental Psychology, 1958, 10, 12–21.

Brown, R., & Kulik, J. Flashbulb memories. Cognition, 1977, 5, 73–99.

Brown, R. W., & McNeill, D. The tip-of-the-tongue phenomenon. Journal of Verbal Learning and Verbal Behavior, 1966, 5, 325–337.

Bruce, D. R., & Crowley, J. J. Acoustic similarity effects on retrieval from secondary memory. Journal of Verbal Learning and Verbal Behavior, 1970, 9, 190–196.

Buchman, H. Film and television make-up. New York: Watson-Guptill, 1973.

Buckhout, R. Eyewitness testimony. Scientific American, 1974, 231, 23–31.

Burrows, D., & Murdock, B. B., Jr. Effects of extended practice on high-speed scanning. Journal of Experimental Psychology, 1969, 82, 231–237.

Burtt, H. E. An experimental study of early childhood memory: Final report. Journal of Genetic Psychology, 1941, 58, 435–439.

Buschke, H. Two-dimensional recall: Immediate identification of clusters in episodic and semantic memory. Journal of Verbal Learning and Verbal Behavior, 1977, 16, 201–215. (a)

Buschke, H. Retrieval in the development of learning. In N. J. Castellan, Jr., D. B. Pisoni, and G. R. Potts, Cognitive theory. Vol. 2. Hillsdale, N.J.: Erlbaum, 1977. (b)

Busse, E. W. Brain syndromes associated with disturbances in metabolism, growth, and nutrition. In A. M. Freedman and H. I. Kaplan (Eds.), Comprehensive textbook of psychiatry. Baltimore: Williams & Wilkins, 1967.

Calfee, R. C. Human experimental psychology. New York: Holt, Rinehart and Winston, 1975.

Carey, S., & Diamond, R. From piecemeal to configurational representation of faces. Science, 1977, 195, 312–314.

Carmichael, L., Hogan, H. P., & Walter, A. A. An experimental study of the effect of language on the reproduction of visually perceived form. Journal of Experimental Psychology, 1932, 15, 73–86.

Cermak, L. S. Human memory: Research and theory. New York: Ronald Press, 1972.

Cermak, L. S., Butters, N., & Goodglass, H. The extent of memory loss in Korsakoff patients. Neuropsychologia, 1971, 9, 307–315.

Chase, W. G., & Simon, H. A. Perception in chess. Cognitive Psychology, 1973, 4, 55–81.

Cherry, E. C. Some experiments on the recognition of speech, with one and with two ears. Journal of the Acoustical Society of America, 1953, 25, 975–979.

Cofer, C. N., Bruce, D. R., & Reicher, G. M. Clustering in free recall as a function of certain methodological variations. *Journal of Experimental Psychology*, 1966, *71*, 858–866.

Cohen, L. B., & Gelber, E. R. Infant visual memory. In L. B. Cohen and P. Salapatek (Eds.), *Infant perception: From sensation to cognition*. Vol. I. New York: Academic Press, 1975.

Cole, M., Frankel, F., & Sharp, D. Development of free recall learning in children. *Developmental Psychology*, 1971, *4*, 109–123.

Collins, A. M., & Quillian, M. R. Retrieval from semantic memory. *Journal of Verbal Learning and Verbal Behavior*, 1969, *8*, 240–247.

Conrad, R., & Hull, A. J. Input modality and the serial position curve in short-term memory. *Psychonomic Science*, 1968, *10*, 135–136.

Cooper, L. A., & Shepard, R. N. The time required to prepare for a rotated stimulus. *Memory & Cognition*, 1973, *1*, 246–250.

Corballis, M. C. Rehearsal and decay in immediate recall of visually and aurally presented items. *Canadian Journal of Psychology*, 1966, *20*, 43–51.

Corsi, P. M. Verbal memory impairment after unilateral hippocampal excisions. Paper presented at annual convention, Eastern Psychological Association, Philadelphia, April, 1969.

Craik, F. I. M. Short-term memory and the aging process. In G. A. Talland (Ed.), *Human aging and behavior*. New York: Academic Press, 1968.

Craik, F. I. M. Similarities between the effects of aging and alcoholic intoxication on memory performance, construed within a "levels of processing" framework. In I. M. Birnbaum and E. S. Parker (Eds.), *Alcohol and human memory*. New York: Wiley, 1977.

Craik, F. I. M. Human memory. *Annual review of psychology*. Vol. 30. Palo Alto, Calif.: Annual Reviews, Inc., 1979.

Craik, F. I. M., & Jacoby, L. L. A process view of short-term retention. In F. Restle, R. M. Shiffrin, N. J. Castellan, H. R. Lindman, and D. B. Pisoni (Eds.), *Cognitive theory*. Vol. 1. New York: Wiley, 1975.

Craik, F. I. M., & Lockhart, R. S. Levels of processing: A framework for memory research. *Journal of Verbal Learning and Verbal Behavior*, 1972, *11*, 671–684.

Craik, F. I. M., & Tulving, E. Depth of processing and the retention of words in episodic memory. *Journal of Experimental Psychology: General*, 1975, *104*, 268–294.

Craik, F. I. M., & Watkins, M. J. The role of rehearsal in short-term memory. *Journal of Verbal Learning and Verbal Behavior*, 1973, *12*, 599–607.

Crowder, R. G. The role of one's own voice in immediate memory. *Cognitive Psychology*, 1970, *1*, 157–178.

Crowder, R. G. Waiting for the stimulus suffix: Decay, delay, rhythm, and readout in immediate memory. *Quarterly Journal of Experimental Psychology*, 1971, *23*, 324–340. (a)

Crowder, R. G. The sound of vowels and consonants in immediate memory. *Journal of Verbal Learning and Verbal Behavior*, 1971, *10*, 587–596. (b)

Crowder, R. G. Visual and auditory memory. In J. F. Kavanagh & I. G. Mattingly (Eds.), *Language by ear and by eye: The relationships between speech and reading.* Cambridge, Mass.: MIT Press, 1972.

Crowder, R. G. Inferential problems in echoic memory. In P. Rabbitt & S. Dornic (Eds.), *Attention and performance V.* London: Academic Press, 1975.

Crowder, R. G. *Principles of learning and memory.* Hillsdale, N.J.: Erlbaum, 1976.

Crowder, R. G., & Morton, J. Precategorical acoustic storage (PAS). *Perception & Psychophysics,* 1969, *5,* 365–373.

D'Agostino, P. R. The blocked-random effect in recall and recognition. *Journal of Verbal Learning and Verbal Behavior,* 1969, *8,* 815–820.

D'Agostino, P. R., O'Neill, B. J., & Paivio, A. Memory for pictures and words as a function of level of processing: Depth or dual coding? *Memory & Cognition,* 1977, *5,* 252–256.

Daniels, A. H. The memory after-image and attention. *American Journal of Psychology,* 1895, *6,* 558–564.

Dark, V. J., & Loftus, G. R. The role of rehearsal in long-term memory performance. *Journal of Verbal Learning and Verbal Behavior,* 1976, *15,* 479–490.

Darley, C. F., & Glass, A. L. Effects of rehearsal and serial list position on recall. *Journal of Experimental Psychology: Human Learning and Memory,* 1975, *104,* 453–458.

Darwin, C. J., Turvey, M. T., & Crowder, R. G. An auditory analogue of the Sperling partial report procedure: Evidence for brief auditory storage. *Cognitive Psychology,* 1972, *3,* 255–267.

Davies, G., Ellis, H., & Shepherd, J. Cue saliency in faces as assessed by the "Photofit" technique. *Perception,* 1977, *6,* 263–269.

Davison, M. L., Fox, M. J., & Dick, A. O. Effect of eye movements on backward masking and perceived location. *Perception & Psychophysics,* 1973, *14,* 110–116.

Deese, J. Influence of inter-item associative strength upon immediate free recall. *Psychological Reports,* 1959, *5,* 305–312.

Deese, J. From the isolated verbal unit to connected discourse, In C. N. Cofer (Ed.), *Verbal learning and verbal behavior.* New York: McGraw-Hill, 1961.

DeGroot, A. D. *Thought and choice in chess.* The Hague: Mouton, 1965.

DeGroot, A. D. Perception and memory versus thinking. In B. Kleinmuntz (Ed.), *Problem solving.* New York: Wiley, 1966.

DeRosa, D. V., & Tkacz, S. Memory scanning of organized visual material. *Journal of Experimental Psychology: Human Learning and Memory,* 1976, *2,* 688–694.

Deutsch, J. A., & Deutsch, D. Attention: Some theoretical considerations. *Psychological Review,* 1963, *70,* 80–90.

Dhawan, M. & Pellegrino, J. W. Acoustic and semantic interference effects in words and pictures. *Memory & Cognition,* 1977, *5,* 340–346.

Dick, A. O. Iconic memory and its relation to perceptual processing and other memory mechanisms. *Perception & Psychophysics*, 1974, *16*, 575–596.

Dietze, G. Untersuchungen über den Umfang des Bewusstseins bei regelmässig aufeinander folgenden Schalleindrücken *Philosoph. Studien*, 1884, *2*, 362–393. (Cited in Murray, D. J. Research on human memory in the nineteenth century. *Canadian Journal of Psychology*, 1976, *30*, 201–220.)

Dodwell, P. C. *Visual pattern recognition*. New York: Holt, Rinehart and Winston, 1970.

Doerflein, R. S., & Dick, A. O. Eye movements and perceived location in iconic memory. Paper presented at Psychonomic Society Meetings, Boston, 1974.

Eagle, M., & Leiter, E. Recall and recognition in intentional and incidental learning. *Journal of Experimental Psychology*, 1964, *68*, 58–63.

Ebbinghaus, H. *Memory*. New York: Dover, 1964. (Originally published in 1885.)

Efron, R. The duration of the present. *Annals of the New York Academy of Science*, 1967, *138*, 713–729.

Efron, R. Effect of stimulus duration on perceptual onset and offset latencies. *Perception & Psychophysics*, 1970, *8*, 231–234.

Egeth, H. Atkinson, J., Gilmore, G., & Marcus, N. Factors affecting processing mode in visual search. *Perception & Psychophysics*, 1973, *13*, 394–402.

Egeth, H., & Bevan, W. Attention. In B. Wolman (Ed.), *Handbook of psychology*. New York: Prentice-Hall, 1973.

Egeth, H. E., Blecker, D. L., & Kamlet, A. S. Verbal interference in a perceptual comparison task. *Perception & Psychophysics*, 1969, *6*, 355–356.

Egeth, H., Jonides, J., & Wall, S. Parallel processing of multielement displays. *Cognitive Psychology*, 1972, *3*, 674–698.

Eichelman, W. H. Stimulus and response repetition effects for naming letters. *Perception & Psychophysics*, 1970, *7*, 94–96.

Eimas, P. D., Siqueland, E. P., Jusczyk, P., & Vigorito, J. Speech perception in infants. *Science*, 1971, *171*, 303–306.

Elias, C. S., & Perfetti, C. A. Encoding task and recognition memory: The importance of semantic encoding. *Journal of Experimental Psychology*, 1973, *99*, 151–156.

Enlow, D. H. *Handbook of facial growth*. Philadelphia: Saunders, 1975.

Erdelyi, M. H., & Becker, J. Incremental memory for pictures: Hypermnesia for pictures but not words in multiple recall trials. *Cognitive Psychology*, 1974, *6*, 159–171.

Erdelyi, M. H., Finkelstein, S., Herrell, N., Miller, B., & Thomas, J. Coding modality vs. input modality in hypermnesia: Is a rose a rose a rose? *Cognition*, 1976, *4*, 311–319.

Eriksen, C. W., & Hoffman, M. Form recognition at brief durations as a function of adapting field and interval between stimulations. *Journal of Experimental Psychology*, 1963, *66*, 485–499.

Eriksen, C. W., & Johnson, H. J. Storage and decay characteristics of nonattended auditory stimuli. *Journal of Experimental Psychology,* 1964, *68,* 28–36.

Eriksen, C. W., & Rohrbaugh, J. W. Some factors determining efficiency of selective attention. *American Journal of Psychology,* 1970, *83,* 330–343.

Erikson, C. W., & Spenser, T. Rate of information processing in visual perception: Some results and methodological considerations. *Journal of Experimental Psychology Monograph,* 1969, *72,* No. 2, Part 2.

Estes, W. K. An associative basis for coding and organization in memory. In A. W. Melton and E. Martin (Eds.), *Coding processes in human memory.* New York: Wiley, 1972.

Estes, W. K. The locus of inferential and perceptual processes in letter identification. *Journal of Experimental Psychology: General,* 1975, *104,* 122–145.

Estes, W. K. On the interaction of perception and memory in reading. In D. LaBerge and S. J. Samuels (Eds.), *Basic processes in reading: Perception and comprehension.* New York: Wiley, 1977.

Estes, W. K., & DaPolito, F. Independent variation of information storage and retrieval processes in paired-associate learning. *Journal of Experimental Psychology,* 1967, *75,* 18–26.

Fagan, J. F. Infant's delayed recognition memory and forgetting. *Journal of Experimental Child Psychology,* 1973, *16,* 424–450.

Fantz, R. L. Pattern vision in newborn infants. *Science,* 1963, *140,* 296–297.

Fantz, R. L. Visual experience in infants: Decreased attention to familiar patterns relative to novel ones. *Science,* 1964, *146,* 668–670.

Fechner, G. T. *Elements of psychophysics.* Vol. 2. Leipzig: Breitkopf & Härtel, 1860.

Fischler, I., & Juola, J. F. Effects of repeated tests on recognition time for information in long-term memory. *Journal of Experimental Psychology,* 1971, *91,* 54–58.

Fisher, G. H., & Cox, R. L. Recognizing human faces. *Applied Ergonomics,* 1975, *6,* 104–109.

Flavell, J. H. First discussant's comments: What is memory development the development of? *Human Development,* 1971, *14,* 272–278.

Flavell, J. H., Beach, D. R., & Chinsky, J. M. Spontaneous verbal rehearsal in a memory task as a function of age. *Child Development,* 1966, *37,* 283–299.

Flavell, J. H., Friedrichs, A. G., & Hoyt, J. D. Developmental changes in memorization processes. *Cognitive Psychology,* 1970, *1,* 324–340.

Flavell, J. H., & Wellman, H. M. Metamemory. In R. V. Kail, Jr., and J. W. Hagen (Eds.), *Perspectives on the development of memory and cognition.* Hillsdale, N.J.: Erlbaum, 1977.

Flexser, A. J., & Tulving, E. Retrieval independence in recognition and recall. *Psychological Review,* 1978, *85,* 153–171.

Fodor, J. A., & Bever, T. G. The psychological reality of linguistic segments. *Journal of Verbal Learning and Verbal Behavior*, 1965, *4*, 414–420.

Freud, S. *The psychopathology of everyday life*. (A. P. Brill, Trans.) New York: Mentor, 1951.

Friedman, A., & Bourne, L. E., Jr. Encoding the levels of information in pictures and words. *Journal of Experimental Psychology: General*, 1976, *105*, 169–190.

Friedman, S., & Carpenter, G. C. Visual response decrement as a function of age in human newborn. *Child Development*, 1971, *42*, 1967–1973.

Galton, F. Composite portraits, made by combining those of many different persons into a single, resultant figure. *Journal of the Anthropological Institute*, 1879, *8*, 132–144.

Gardiner, J. M. Levels of processing in word recognition and subsequent free recall. *Journal of Experimental Psychology*, 1974, *102*, 101–105.

Garrett, M. F., Bever, T., & Fodor, J. A. The active use of grammar in speech perception. *Perception & Psychophysics*, 1966, *1*, 30–32.

Gastaut, H., & Fischer-Williams, M. The physiopathology of epileptic seizures. In J. Field, H. W. Magoun, and V. E. Hall (Eds.), *Handbook of physiology, Section 1: Neurophysiology*. Vol. 1. Washington, D.C.: American Physiological Society, 1959.

Gazzaniga, M. S. The split brain in man. *Scientific American*, 1967, *217*, 24–29.

Gazzaniga, M. S. *The bisected brain*. New York: Appleton-Century-Crofts, 1970.

Geffen, G., Bradshaw, J. L., & Wallace, G. Interhemispheric effects on reaction time to verbal and nonverbal visual stimuli. *Journal of Experimental Psychology*, 1971, *87*, 415–422.

Gehring, R. E., Toglia, M. P., & Kimble, G. A. Recognition memory for words and pictures of short and long retention intervals. *Memory & Cognition*, 1976, *4*, 256–260.

Gholson, B., & Hohle, R. H. Verbal reaction times to hues vs. hue names and forms vs. form names. *Perception & Psychophysics*, 1968, *3*, 191–196.

Gibson, E. *Principles of perceptual learning and development*. New York: Appleton-Century-Crofts, 1969.

Gibson, J. J. *The senses considered as perceptual systems*. Boston: Houghton Mifflin, 1966.

Glanzer, M., & Clark, W. H. Accuracy of perceptual recall: An analysis of organization. *Journal of Verbal Learning and Verbal Behavior*, 1963, *1*, 289–299.

Glanzer, M., & Cunitz, A. R. Two storage mechanisms in free recall. *Journal of Verbal Learning and Verbal Behavior*, 1966, *5*, 351–360.

Glanzer, M., & Koppenaal, L. The effect of encoding tasks on free recall: Stages and levels. *Journal of Verbal Learning and Verbal Behavior*, 1977, *16*, 21–28.

Glucksberg, S., & Cowan, G. N. Memory for nonattended auditory material. *Cognitive Psychology,* 1970, *1,* 149–156.

Goldensohn, E. S. Seizures and convulsive disorders. In B. B. Wolman (Ed.), *Handbook of clinical psychology.* New York: McGraw-Hill, 1965.

Goldstein, A. G., & Chance, J. E. Recognition of complex visual stimuli. *Perception & Psychophysics,* 1971, *9,* 237–241.

Gombrich, E. H. The mask and the face. In E. H. Gombrich, J. Hochberg, and M. Black (Eds.), *Art, perception and reality.* Baltimore: Johns Hopkins Press, 1972.

Gough, P. B., & Cosky, M. J. One second of reading again. In N. J. Castellan, Jr., D. B. Pisoni, and G. R. Potts (Eds.), *Cognitive theory.* Vol. 2. Hillsdale, N.J.: Erlbaum, 1977.

Gray, C. R., & Gummerman, K. The enigmatic eidetic image: A critical examination of methods, data, and theories. *Psychological Bulletin,* 1975, *82,* 383–407.

Gray, J. A., & Wedderburn, A. A. I. Grouping strategies with simultaneous stimuli. *Quarterly Journal of Experimental Psychology,* 1960, *12,* 180–184.

Gregory, R. L. *Eye and brain* (2nd ed.). New York: McGraw-Hill, World University Library, 1973.

Gruneberg, M. M., Colwill, S. J., Winfrow, P., & Woods, R. W. Acoustic confusion in long term memory. *Acta Psychologica,* 1970, *32,* 394–398.

Guilford, J. P., & Dallenbach, K. M. The determination of memory span by the method of constant stimuli. *American Journal of Psychology,* 1925, *36,* 621–628.

Guthrie, G., & Wiener, M. Subliminal perception or perception of partial cue with pictorial stimuli. *Journal of Personality and Social Psychology,* 1966, *3,* 619–628.

Guy, C. L., Converse, J. M., & Morello, D. C. Esthetic surgery for the aging face. In J. M. Converse (Ed.), *Reconstructive plastic surgery.* Vol. 3. Philadelphia: Saunders, 1977.

Haber, R. N. Eidetic images. *Scientific American,* 1969, *220,* 36–44.

Haber, R. N. How we remember what we see. *Scientific American,* 1970, *222,* 104–112.

Haber, R. N., & Hershenson, M. *The psychology of visual perception.* New York: Holt, Rinehart and Winston, 1973.

Haber, R. N., & Nathanson, L. S. Post-retinal storage? Park's camel as seen through the eye of a needle. *Perception & Psychophysics,* 1968, *3,* 349–355.

Haber, R. N., & Standing, L. G. Clarity and recognition of masked and degraded stimuli. *Psychonomic Science,* 1968, *13,* 83–84.

Haber, R. N., & Standing, L. G. Direct measures of short-term visual storage. *Quarterly Journal of Experimental Psychology,* 1969, *21,* 43–54.

Haber, R. N., & Standing, L. G. Direct estimates of apparent duration of a flash followed by visual noise. *Canadian Journal of Psychology,* 1970, *24,* 216–229.

Hacker, M. J., & Hinrichs, J. V. Multiple predictions in choice reaction time: A serial memory scanning interpretation. *Journal of Experimental Psychology,* 1974, *103,* 999–1005.

Hagen, J. W. Strategies for remembering. In S. Farnham-Diggery (Ed.), *Information processing in children.* New York: Academic Press, 1972.

Hale, G. A., Miller, L. K., & Stevenson, H. W. Incidental learning in film content: A developmental study. *Child Development,* 1968, *39,* 69–77.

Hall, J. F. Learning as a function of word frequency. *American Journal of Psychology,* 1954, *67,* 138–140.

Hardyck, C. A model of individual differences in hemispheric functioning. In H. Whitaker and H. A. Whitaker (Eds.), *Studies in neurolinguistics.* Vol. 3. New York: Academic Press, 1977.

Harmon, L. D. The recognition of faces. *Scientific American,* November, 1973.

Hart, J. T. Memory and the memory-monitoring process. *Journal of Verbal Learning and Verbal Behavior,* 1967, *6,* 685–691.

Hawkins, H. L., Thomas, G. B., Presson, J. C., Conzic, A., & Brookmire, D. Precategorical selective attention and tonal specificity in auditory recognition. *Journal of Experimental Psychology,* 1974, *103,* 530–538.

Hebb, D. O. *The organization of behavior.* New York: Wiley, 1949.

Hebb, D. O. Distinctive features of learning in the higher animals. In J. F. Delafresnaye, A. Fessard, R. W. Gerard, and J. Konorski (Eds.), *Brain mechanisms and learning.* New York: Oxford University Press, 1961.

Hebb, D. O., & Foord, E. N. Errors of visual recognition and the nature of the trace. *Journal of Experimental Psychology,* 1945, *35,* 335–348.

Hécaen, H., & Angelerques, R. Agnosia for faces (prosopagnosia). *Archives of Neurology,* 1962, *1,* 92–100.

Hilgard, E. R. *Divided consciousness: Multiple controls in human thought and action.* New York: Wiley, 1977.

Hinrichs, J. V., & Krainz, P. L. Expectancy in choice reaction time: Anticipation of stimulus or response? *Journal of Experimental Psychology,* 1970, *85,* 330–334.

Hintzman, D. L. Repetition and memory. In G. H. Bower (Ed.), *The psychology of learning and motivation.* Vol. 10. New York: Academic Press, 1976.

Hochberg, J. Attention, organization and consciousness. In D. I. Mostofsky (Ed.), *Attention: Contemporary theory and analysis.* New York: Appleton-Century-Crofts, 1970. (a)

Hochberg, J. Attention in perception and reading. In F. A. Young and D. B. Lindsley (Eds.), *Early experience and visual information processing in perceptual and reading disorders.* Washington, D.C.: National Academy of Sciences, 1970. (b)

Hock, H. W., & Egeth, H. Verbal interference with encoding in a perceptual classification task. *Journal of Experimental Psychology,* 1970, *83,* 299–303.

Horowitz, L. M., & Manelis, L. Recognition and cued recall of idioms and phrases. *Journal of Experimental Psychology*, 1973, *100*, 291–296.

Hubel, D. H., & Wiesel, T. N. Receptive fields, binocular interaction and functional architecture in the cat's visual cortex. *Journal of Physiology*, 1962, *160*, 106–154.

Hubel, D. H., & Wiesel, T. N. Shape and arrangement of columns of cat's striate cortex. *Journal of Physiology*, 1963, *165*, 559–568.

Hubel, D. H., & Wiesel, T. N. Receptive fields and functional architecture of monkey striate cortex. *Journal of Physiology*, 1965, *195*, 215–243.

Hultsch, D. F. Adult age differences in retrieval: Trace dependent and cue dependent forgetting. *Developmental Psychology*, 1975, *11*, 197–201.

Hyde, T. S., & Jenkins, J. J. Differential effects of incidental tasks on the organization of recall of a list of highly associated words. *Journal of Experimental Psychology*, 1969, *82*, 472–481.

Ingalls, R. P. Effects of same-different patterns on tachistoscopic recognition of letters. *Journal of Experimental Psychology*, 1974, *102*, 209–214.

Ingram, T. T. S. The nature of dyslexia. In F. A. Young and D. B. Lindsley (Eds.), *Early experience and visual information processing in perceptual and reading disorders*. Washington, D.C.: National Academy of Sciences, 1970.

Jacobs, J. Experiments on 'prehension.' *Mind*, 1887, *12*, 75–79.

Jacoby, L. L. Physical features vs. meaning: A difference in decay. *Memory & Cognition*, 1975, *3*, 247–251.

Jacoby, L. L., & Bartz, W. H. Rehearsal and transfer to LTM. *Journal of Verbal Learning and Verbal Behavior*, 1972, *11*, 561–565.

James, W. *The principles of psychology*. New York: Dover, 1950. (Originally published in 1890.)

Jarvella, R. J. Syntactic processing of connected speech. *Journal of Verbal Learning and Verbal Behavior*, 1971, *10*, 409–416.

Jenkins, J. J. Remember that old theory of memory? Well, forget it! *American Psychologist*, 1974, *29*, 785–795.

Jenkins, J. J., & Russell, W. A. Associative clustering during recall. *Journal of Abnormal and Social Psychology*, 1952, *47*, 818–821.

Jenkins, J. J., Wald, J., & Pittenger, J. B. Apprehending pictorial events: An instance of psychological cohesion. In C. W. Savage (Ed.), *Minnesota studies in the philosophy of science*. Vol. 9, 1978.

Johnson, N. F. Sequential verbal behavior. In T. R. Dixon & D. L. Horton (Eds.), *Verbal learning and general behavior theory*. Englewood Cliffs, N.J.: Prentice-Hall, 1968.

Johnson, N. F. Organization and the concept of a memory code. In A. W. Melton and E. Martin (Eds.), *Coding processes in human memory*. New York: Wiley, 1972.

Johnson, R. E. Recall of prose as a function of the structural importance of the linguistic units. *Journal of Verbal Learning and Verbal Behavior*, 1970, *9*, 12–20.

Johnston, W. A., Wagstaff, R. R., & Griffith, D. Information-processing analysis of verbal learning. *Journal of Experimental Psychology*, 1972, *96*, 307–314.

Jonides, J., & Gleitman, H. A conceptual category effect in visual search: 0 as a letter or a digit. *Perception & Psychophysics*, 1972, *12*, 457–460.

Jonides, J., Kahn R., & Rozin, P. Imagery instruction improves memory in blind subjects. *Bulletin of the Psychonomic Society*, 1975, *5*, 424–426.

Judd, C. H., & Buswell, G. T. Silent reading. *Supplementary Educational Monographs*, 1922, *23*. (From P. A. Kolers, Some modes of representation.) In P. Pliner, L. Krames, and T. Alloway (Eds.), *Communication and affect: Language and thought*. New York: Academic Press, 1973.

Juola, J. F., Fischler, I., Wood, C. T., & Atkinson, R. C. Recognition time for information stored in long-term memory. *Perception & Psychophysics*. 1971, *10*, 8–14.

Kahneman, D. *Attention and effort*. Englewood Cliffs, N.J.: Prentice-Hall, 1973.

Kail, R. V., Jr., & Siegel, A. W. The development of mnemonic encoding in children: From perception to abstraction. In R. V. Kail, Jr., and J. W. Hagen (Eds.), *Perspectives on the development of memory and cognition*. Hillsdale, N.J.: Erlbaum, 1977.

Kaplan, I. T., & Carvellas, T. Scanning for multiple targets. *Perceptual & Motor Skills*, 1965, *21*, 239–243.

Katona, G. *Organizing and memorizing*. New York: Columbia University Press, 1940.

Keenan, J. M., MacWhinney, B., & Mayhew, D. Pragmatics in memory: A study of natural conversation. *Journal of Verbal Learning and Verbal Behavior*, 1977, *16*, 549–560.

Keeney, A. H. Introduction. In J. Hartstein (Ed.), *Current concepts in dyslexia*, St. Louis: Mosby, 1971.

Keeney, T. J., Cannizzo, S. R., & Flavell, J. H. Spontaneous and induced verbal rehearsal in a recall task. *Child Development*, 1967, *38*, 953–966.

Keppel, G., & Underwood, B. J. Proactive inhibition in short-term retention of single items. *Journal of Verbal Learning and Verbal Behavior*, 1962, *1*, 153–161.

Kerr, B. Processing demands during mental operations. *Memory & Cognition*, 1973, *1*, 401–412.

Kimura, D. Right-temporal lobe damage. *Archives of Neurology*, 1963, *8*, 264–271.

Kingsley, P. R., & Hagen, J. W. Induced versus spontaneous rehearsal in short-term memory in nursery school children. *Developmental Psychology*, 1969, *1*, 40–46.

Kinney, G. C., Marsetta, M., & Showman, D. J. Studies in display symbol legibility, Part XII. The legibility of alphanumeric symbols for digitalized television. Bedford, Mass.: The Mitre Corporation, ESD-TR-66-117, 1966.

Kintsch, W. Recognition and free recall of organized lists. *Journal of Experimental Psychology*, 1968, *78*, 481–487.

Kintsch, W. Memory for prose. In C. N. Cofer (Ed.), *The structure of human memory*. San Francisco: Freeman, 1976.

Kintsch, W. *Memory and cognition*. New York: Wiley, 1977.

Kintsch, W., & Bates, E. Recognition memory for statements from a classroom lecture. *Journal of Experimental Psychology: Human Learning and Memory*, 1977, *3*, 150–159.

Kirschner, L. A. Dissociative reactions: An historical review and clinical study. *Acta Psychiatrica Scandinavica*, 1973, *49*, 698–711.

Kirsner, K. Naming latency facilitation: An analysis of the encoding component of RT. *Journal of Experimental Psychology*, 1972, *95*, 171–176.

Kolers, P. A. Three stages of reading. In H. Levin and J. P. Williams (Eds.), *Basic studies on reading*. New York: Basic Books, 1970.

Kolers, P. A. Some modes of representation. In P. Pliner, L. Krames, and T. Alloway (Eds.), *Communication and affect: Language and thought*. New York: Academic Press, 1973.

Kolers, P. A. Memorial consequences of automatized encoding. *Journal of Experimental Psychology: Human Learning and Memory*, 1975, *1*, 689–701.

Kolers, P. A., & Ostry, D. J. Time course of loss of information regarding pattern analyzing operations. *Journal of Verbal Learning and Verbal Behavior*, 1974, *13*, 599–612.

Kosslyn, S. M. Can imagery be distinguished from other forms of internal representation? Evidence from studies of information retrieval times. *Memory & Cognition*, 1976, *4*, 291–297.

Kral, V. A. Memory disorders in old age and senility. In G. A. Talland and N. C. Waugh (Eds.), *The pathology of memory*. New York: Academic Press, 1969.

Kreutzer, M. A., Leonard, C., & Flavell, J. H. An interview study of children's knowledge about memory. *Monographs of the Society for Research in Child Development*, 1975, *40* (1, Serial No. 159).

Kristofferson, M. W. The effects of practice with one positive set in a memory scanning task can be completely transferred to a different positive set. *Memory & Cognition*, 1977, *5*, 177–186.

Külpe, O. *Outlines of psychology*. New York: Macmillan & Co., 1895.

LaBerge, D., & Samuels, S. J. Toward a theory of automatic information processing in reading. *Cognitive Psychology*, 1974, *6*, 293–323.

Ladefoged, P., & Broadbent, D. E. Perception of sequences in auditory events. *Quarterly Journal of Experimental Psychology*, 1960, *12*, 162–170.

Lashley, K. S. The problem of serial order in behavior. In L. A. Jeffress (Ed.), *Cerebral mechanisms in behavior*. New York: Wiley, 1951.

Latour, P. L. Visual threshold during eye movements. *Vision Research*, 1962, *2*, 261–262.

Lesgold, A. M., & Bower, G. H. Inefficiency of serial knowledge for associative responding. *Journal of Verbal Learning and Verbal Behavior,* 1970, *9,* 456–466.

Lewis, M., & Brooks, J. Infants' social perception: A constructivist view. In L. B. Cohen and P. Salapatek (Eds.), *Infant perception: From sensation to cognition.* Vol. 2. New York: Academic Press, 1975.

Liberman, A. M., Cooper, F. S., Schankweiler, D. P., & Studdert-Kennedy, M. Perception of the speech code. *Psychological Review,* 1967, *74,* 431–461.

Liggett, J. *The human face.* New York: Stein and Day, 1974.

Lindsay, P. H., & Norman, D. A. *Human information processing.* New York: Academic Press, 1972.

Linn, L. Clinical manifestations of psychiatric disorders. In A. M. Freedman and H. I. Kaplan (Eds.), *Comprehensive textbook of psychiatry.* Baltimore: Williams & Wilkins, 1967.

Livingston, R. B. Reinforcement. In G.C. Quarton, T. Melnechuck, and F. O. Schmitt (Eds.), *The neurosciences: A study program.* New York: Rockefeller University Press, 1967.

Loftus, E. Reconstructing memory: The incredible eyewitness. *Psychology Today,* 1974, *8,* 117–119.

Loftus, E. F., & Palmer, J. C. Reconstruction of automobile destruction: An example of the interaction between language and memory. *Journal of Verbal Learning and Verbal Behavior,* 1974, *13,* 585–589.

Lorayne, H., & Lucas, J. *The memory book.* New York: Stein and Day, 1974.

Luria, A. R. *The mind of a mnemonist.* New York: Basic Books, 1968.

Mackworth, J. F. The duration of the visual image. *Canadian Journal of Psychology,* 1963, *17,* 62–81.

Mackworth, N. H., & Bruner, J. S. How adults and children search and recognize pictures. *Human Development,* 1970, *13,* 149–177.

Mackworth, N. H., & Morandi, A. J. The gaze selects informative details within pictures. *Perception & Psychophysics,* 1967, *2,* 547–552.

Malt, B. C., & Seamon, J. G. Peripheral and cognitive components of eye guidance in filled-space reading. *Perception & Psychophysics,* 1978, *23,* 399–402.

Mandler, G. Organization and memory. In K. W. Spence and J. T. Spence (Eds.), *The psychology of learning and motivation.* Vol. 1. New York: Academic Press, 1967.

Mandler, G. Organization and recognition. In E. Tulving and W. Donaldson (Eds.), *Organization of memory.* New York: Academic Press, 1972.

Mandler, G., & Boeck, W. J. Retrieval processes in recognition. *Memory & Cognition,* 1974, *2,* 613–615.

Marmor, G. S., & Zaback, L. A. The role of visual imagery in mental rotation. Paper presented at Annual Convention, Eastern Psychological Association, April, 1976.

Martin, E., & Noreen, D. L. Serial learning: Identification of subjective subsequences. *Cognitive Psychology,* 1974, *6,* 421–435.

Massaro, D. W. Preperceptual auditory images. *Journal of Experimental Psychology*, 1970, *85*, 411–417.

Massaro, D. W. Preperceptual images, processing time, and perceptual units in auditory perception. *Psychological Review*, 1972, *79*, 124–145. (a)

Massaro, D. W. Preperceptual and synthesized auditory storage. Studies in human information processing, University of Wisconsin, 72-1, 1972. (Cited in Massaro, 1975.) (b)

Massaro, D. W. A comparison of forward versus backward recognition masking. *Journal of Experimental Psychology*, 1973, *100*, 434–436.

Massaro, D. W. Perceptual units in speech recognition. *Journal of Experimental Psychology*, 1974, *102*, 199–208.

Massaro, D. W. *Experimental psychology and information processing.* Chicago: Rand McNally, 1975.

Massaro, D. W., & Kahn, B. J. Effects of central processing on auditory recognition. *Journal of Experimental Psychology*, 1973, *97*, 51–58.

McCormack, P. D. Recognition memory: How complex a retrieval system? *Canadian Journal of Psychology*, 1972, *26*, 19–41.

McCormack, P. D., & Swenson, A. L. Recognition memory for common and rare words. *Journal of Experimental Psychology*, 1972, *95*, 72–77.

McLean, R. S., & Gregg, L. W. Effects of induced chunking on temporal aspects of serial recitation. *Journal of Experimental Psychology*, 1967, *74*, 455–459.

McNulty, J. A. Short-term retention as a function of method of measurement, recording time, and meaningfulness of the material. *Canadian Journal of Psychology*, 1965, *19*, 188–195.

Mechanic, A. The distribution of recalled items in simultaneous intentional and incidental learning. *Journal of Experimental Psychology*, 1962, *63*, 593–600.

Melton, A. W. Implications of short-term memory for a general theory of memory. *Journal of Verbal Learning and Verbal Behavior*, 1963, *2*, 1–21.

Meyer, D. E., Schvaneveldt, R. W., & Ruddy, M. G. Loci of contextual effects in visual word recognition. In P. Rabbitt (Ed.), *Attention and performance V.* New York: Academic Press, 1974.

Miller, G. A. The magical number seven, plus or minus two: Some limits on our capacity for processing information. *Psychological Review*, 1956, *63*, 81–97.

Miller, G. A., Galanter, E., & Pribram, K. H. *Plans and the structure of behavior.* New York: Holt, Rinehart & Winston, 1960.

Miller, G. A., & Isard, S. Some perceptual consequences of linguistic rules. *Journal of Verbal Learning and Verbal Behavior*, 1963, *2*, 217–218.

Milner, B. Brain mechanisms suggested by studies of temporal lobes. In F. L. Darley (Ed.), *Brain mechanisms underlying speech and language.* New York: Grune & Stratton, 1967.

Milner, B. Visual recognition and recall after right temporal-lobe excisions in man. *Neuropsychologia,* 1968, *6,* 191–210.

Milner, B. Memory and the medial temporal regions of the brain. In K. H. Pribram and D. E. Broadbent (Eds.), *Biology of memory.* New York: Academic Press, 1970.

Milner, B., Corkin, S., & Teuber, H. L. Further analysis of the hippocampal amnesic syndrome: 14-year follow-up study of H. M. *Neuropsychologia,* 1968, *6,* 215–234.

Modigliani, V., & Seamon, J. G. Transfer of information from short- to long-term memory. *Journal of Experimental Psychology,* 1974, *102,* 768–772.

Moely, B. E. Organizational factors in the development of memory. In R. V. Kail and J. W. Hagen (Eds.), *Perspectives on the development of memory and cognition.* Hillsdale, N.J.: Erlbaum, 1977.

Moely, B. E., Olsen, F. A., Hawles, T. G., & Flavell, J. H. Production deficiency in young children's clustered recall. *Developmental Psychology,* 1969, *1,* 26–34.

Mohs, R. C., Wescourt, K. T., & Atkinson, R. C. Search processes for associative structures in long-term memory. *Journal of Experimental Psychology: General,* 1975, *104,* 103–121.

Moray, N. Attention in dichotic listening: Affective cues and the influence of instructions. *Quarterly Journal of Experimental Psychology,* 1959, *11,* 56–60.

Moray, N., Bates, A., & Barnett, T. Experiments on the four-eared man. *Journal of the Acoustical Society of America,* 1965, *38,* 196–201.

Morris, C. D., Bransford, J. D., & Franks, J. J. Levels of processing versus transfer appropriate processing. *Journal of Verbal Learning and Verbal Behavior,* 1977, *16,* 519–533.

Morton, J., Crowder, R. G., & Prussin, H. A. Experiments with the stimulus suffix effect. *Journal of Experimental Psychology,* 1971, *91,* 169–190.

Moscovitch, M., & Craik, F. I. M. Depth of processing, retrieval cues, and uniqueness of encoding as factors in recall. *Journal of Verbal Learning and Verbal Behavior,* 1976, *15,* 447–458.

Moyer, R. S. Comparing objects in memory: Evidence suggesting an internal psychophysics. *Perception & Psychophysics,* 1973, *13,* 180–184.

Muensterburg, H. *On the witness stand.* New York: McClure, 1908.

Müller, G. E., & Schumann, F. Experimentelle Beiträge zur Untersuchung des Gedächtnisses. *Zeitschrift für Psychologie,* 1893, *6,* 192 pp. (Cited in Murray, D. J. Research on human memory in the nineteenth century. *Canadian Journal of Psychology,* 1976, *30,* 201–220.)

Murdock, B. B., Jr. The retention of individual items. *Journal of Experimental Psychology,* 1961, *62,* 618–625.

Murdock, B. B., Jr. The serial position effect in free recall. *Journal of Experimental Psychology,* 1962, *64,* 482–488.

Murray, D. J. Vocalization-at-presentation and immediate recall, with varying recall methods. *Quarterly Journal of Experimental Psychology,* 1966, *18,* 9–18.

Murray, D. J. Research on human memory in the nineteenth century. *Canadian Journal of Psychology*, 1976, *30*, 201–220.

Nebes, R. D. Hemispheric specialization in commissurotimized man. *Psychological Bulletin*, 1974, *81*, 1–14.

Neimark, E., Slotnick, N. S., & Ulrich, T. Development of memorization strategies. *Developmental Psychology*, 1971, *5*, 427–432.

Neisser, U. Visual search. *Scientific American*, 1964, *210*, 94–102.

Neisser, U. *Cognitive psychology*. New York: Appleton-Century-Crofts, 1967.

Neisser, U. *Cognition and reality*. San Francisco, Calif.: Freeman, 1976.

Neisser, U., & Becklen, R. Selective looking: Attending to visually specified events. *Cognitive Psychology*, 1975, *7*, 480–494.

Neisser, U., & Kerr, N. Spatial and mnemonic properties of visual images. *Cognitive Psychology*, 1973, *5*, 138–150.

Neisser, U., Novick, R., & Lazar, R. Searching for ten targets simultaneously. *Perceptual & Motor Skills*, 1963, *17*, 955–961.

Nelson, D. L., & Reed, V. S. On the nature of pictorial encoding: A levels-of-processing analysis. *Journal of Experimental Psychology: Human Learning and Memory*, 1976, *2*, 49–57.

Nelson, T. O. Repetition and depth of processing. *Journal of Verbal Learning and Verbal Behavior*, 1977, *16*, 151–171.

Nelson, T. O., & Vining, S. K. Effect of semantic versus structural processing on long-term retention. *Journal of Experimental Psychology: Human Learning and Memory*, 1978, *4*, 198–209.

Nickerson, R. S. Short-term memory for complex meaningful visual configurations, a demonstration of capacity. *Canadian Journal of Psychology*, 1965, *19*, 155–160.

Nickerson, R. S. A note on long-term recognition memory for pictorial materials. *Psychonomic Science*, 1968, *11*, 58.

Nickerson, R. S. Binary-classification reaction time: A review of some studies of human information-processing capabilities. *Psychonomic Monograph Supplements*, 1972, *4*, Whole No. 65.

Norman, D. A. Toward a theory of memory and attention. *Psychological Review*, 1968, *75*, 522–536.

Norman, D. A. *Memory and attention*. New York: Wiley, 1976.

Norman, D. A., & Bobrow, D. G. On data-limited and resource-limited processes. *Cognitive Psychology*, 1975, *7*, 44–64.

Ornstein, P. A., Trabasso, T., & Johnson-Laird, P. N. To organize is to remember: The effects of instructions to organize and to recall. *Journal of Experimental Psychology*, 1974, *103*, 1014–1018.

Pachella, R. G. The interpretation of reaction time in information processing research. In B. H. Kantowitz (Ed.), *Human information processing: Tutorials in performance and cognition*. Hillsdale, N.J.: Erlbaum, 1974.

Pachella, R. G. The effect of set on the tachistoscopic recognition of pictures. In P. M. A. Rabbitt and S. Dornic (Eds.), *Attention and performance V*. New York: Academic Press, 1975.

Paivio, A. *Imagery and verbal processes*. New York: Holt, Rinehart & Winston, 1971.

Paivio, A. Perceptual comparisons through the mind's eye. *Memory & Cognition*, 1975, *3*, 635–647.

Paivio, A., & Csapo, K. Concrete-image and verbal memory codes. *Journal of Experimental Psychology*, 1969, *80*, 279–285.

Paivio, A., Rogers, T. B., & Smythe, P. C. Why are pictures easier to recall than words? *Psychonomic Science*, 1968, *11*, 137–138.

Palmer, S. E. Visual perception and world knowledge: Notes on a model of sensory cognitive interaction. In D. A. Norman, D. E. Rumelhart, and the LNR Research Group, *Explorations in cognition*. San Francisco: Freeman, 1975.

Parks, T. E. Post-retinal visual storage. *American Journal of Psychology*, 1965, *78*, 145–147.

Parks, T. E., & Kroll, N. E. A. Enduring visual memory despite forced verbal rehearsal. *Journal of Experimental Psychology: Human Learning and Memory*, 1975, *1*, 648–654.

Patterson, K. E., & Baddeley, A. D. When face recognition fails. *Journal of Experimental Psychology: Human Learning and Memory*, 1977, *3*, 406–417.

Pellegrino, J. W., & Battig, W. F. Relationships among higher order organizational measures and free recall. *Journal of Experimental Psychology*, 1974, *102*, 463–472.

Penfield, W. Memory mechanisms. *American Medical Association Archives of Neurology and Psychiatry*, 1952, *67*, 178–191.

Penfield, W. *The mystery of the mind*. Princeton, N.J.: Princeton University Press, 1975.

Peterson, L. R., & Peterson, M. J. Short-term retention of individual verbal items. *Journal of Experimental Psychology*, 1959, *58*, 193–198.

Peterson, M. J., & Graham, S. E. Visual detection and visual imagery. *Journal of Experimental Psychology*, 1974, *103*, 509–514.

Pezdek, K. Cross-modality semantic integration of sentence and picture memory. *Journal of Experimental Psychology: Human Learning and Memory*, 1977, *3*, 515–524.

Piaget, J. *The child's conception of the world*. New York: Harcourt, Brace, and World, 1929.

Pisoni, D. B. Perceptual processing time for consonants and vowels. *Journal of the Acoustical Society of America*, 1973, *53*, 369.

Pisoni, D. B., & Tash, J. Reaction times to comparisons within and across phonetic categories. *Perception & Psychophysics*, 1974, *15*, 285–290.

Pittenger, J. B., & Shaw, R. E. Aging faces as viscal-elastic events: Implications for a theory of non-rigid shape perception. *Journal of Experimental Psychology: Human Perception & Performance*, 1975, *1*, 374–382.

Posner, M. I., & Boies, S. J. Components of attention. *Psychological Review*, 1971, *78*, 391–408.

Posner, M. I., Boies, S. J., Eichelman, W. H., & Taylor, R. L. Retention of visual and name codes of single letters. *Journal of Experimental Psychology Monograph,* 1969, *79,* No. 1, Part 2.

Posner, M. I., & Keele, S. W. Time and space as measures of mental operations. Paper presented at Annual Convention, American Psychological Association, September, 1970.

Posner, M. I., & Mitchell, R. F. Chronometric analysis of classification. *Psychological Review,* 1967, *74,* 392–409.

Posner, M. I., & Nissen, M. J. Visual dominance: An information-processing account of its origins and significance. *Psychological Review,* 1976, *83,* 157–171.

Posner, M. I., & Rossman, E. Effect of size and location of informational transforms upon short-term retention. *Journal of Experimental Psychology,* 1965, *70,* 496–505.

Posner, M. I., & Taylor, R. L. Subtractive method applied to separation of visual and name components of multiletter arrays. In W. G. Koster (Ed.), *Attention and Performance II.* Amsterdam: North Holland, 1969.

Postman, L. Short-term memory and incidental learning. In A. W. Melton (Ed.), *Categories of human learning.* New York: Academic Press, 1964.

Postman, L. A pragmatic view of organization theory. In E. Tulving and W. Donaldson (Eds.), *Organization of memory.* New York: Academic Press, 1972.

Postman, L. Tests of the generality of the principle of encoding specificity. *Memory & Cognition,* 1975, *3,* 663–672.

Postman, L., & Phillips, L. W. Short-term temporal changes in free recall. *Quarterly Journal of Experimental Psychology,* 1965, *17,* 132–138.

Powell, G. D., Hamon, T. G., & Young, R. K. Selective encoding interference in paired-associate learning. *Journal of Experimental Psychology: Human Learning and Memory,* 1975, *1,* 473–479.

Pribram, K. H., & Broadbent, D. E. *Biology of memory.* New York: Academic Press, 1970.

Pritchard, R. M. Stabilized images on the retina. *Scientific American,* 1961, *204,* 72–78.

Psotka, J., Norris, R. G., & Currie, J. L. Recognizing Galton's composite faces. Paper presented at Annual Convention, Eastern Psychological Association, March, 1978.

Pylyshyn, Z. W. What the mind's eye tells the mind's brain: A critique of mental imagery. *Psychological Bulletin,* 1973, *80,* 1–24.

Rabinowitz, J. C., Mandler, G., & Patterson, K. E. Determinants of recognition and recall: Accessibility and generation. *Journal of Experimental Psychology: General,* 1977, *106,* 302–329.

Raymond, B. J. Free recall among the aged. *Psychological Reports,* 1971, *29,* 1179–1182.

Reder, L. M., Anderson, J. R., & Bjork, R. A. A semantic interpretation of encoding specificity. *Journal of Experimental Psychology,* 1974, *102,* 648–656.

Reese, H. W. The development of memory: Life-span perspectives. In H. W.

Reese (Ed.), *Advances in child development and behavior.* Vol. II. New York: Academic Press, 1976.

Reese H. W. Imagery and associative memory. In R. V. Kail and J. W. Hagen (Eds.), *Perspectives on the development of memory and cognition.* Hillsdale, N.J.: Erlbaum, 1977.

Reicher, G. M. Perceptual recognition as a function of meaningfulness of stimulus material. *Journal of Experimental Psychology,* 1969, *81,* 275–280.

Reicher, G. M., Snyder, C. R. R., & Richards, J. T. Familiarity of background characters in visual scanning. *Journal of Experimental Psychology: Human Perception and Performance,* 1976, *2,* 522–530.

Reiff, R., & Scheerer, M. *Memory and hypnotic age regression.* New York: International Universities Press, 1959.

Reitman, J. S. Mechanisms of forgetting in short-term memory. *Cognitive Psychology,* 1971, *2,* 185–195.

Reitman, J. S. Without surreptitious rehearsal, information in short-term memory decays. *Journal of Verbal Learning and Verbal Behavior,* 1974, *13,* 365–377.

Reitman, W. What does it take to remember? In D. A. Norman (Ed.), *Models of human memory.* New York: Academic Press, 1970.

Restle, F., & Brown, E. Organization of serial pattern learning. In G. H. Bower (Ed.), *The psychology of learning and motivation.* Vol. 4. New York: Academic Press, 1970.

Riggs, L. A., Ratliff, F., Cornsweet, J. C., & Cornsweet, T. N. The disappearance of steadily fixated visual test objects. *Journal of the Optical Society of America,* 1953, *43,* 495–501.

Rips, L. J., Shoben, E. J., & Smith, E. E. Semantic distance and the verification of semantic relations. *Journal of Verbal Learning and Verbal Behavior,* 1973, *12,* 1–20.

Rock, I. *An introduction to perception.* New York: Macmillan, 1975.

Rosch, E. Cognitive representations of semantic categories. *Journal of Experimental Psychology: General,* 1975, *104,* 192–233.

Rosenbaum, D. A. Rule use in character classification: Are serial and parallel processing discrete? *Memory & Cognition,* 1974, *2,* 249–254.

Ross, J., & Lawrence, K. A. Some observations on memory artifice. *Psychonomic Science,* 1968, *13,* 107–108.

Rossi, S. I., & Wittrock, M. C. Developmental shifts in verbal recall between mental ages two and five. *Child Development,* 1971, *42,* 333–338.

Rubin, D. C. Very long-term memory for prose and verse. *Journal of Verbal Learning and Verbal Behavior,* 1977, *16,* 611–621.

Rundus, D. Analysis of rehearsal processes in free recall. *Journal of Experimental Psychology,* 1971, *89,* 63–77.

Rundus, D., & Atkinson, R. C. Rehearsal processes in free recall: A procedure for direct observation. *Journal of Verbal Learning and Verbal Behavior,* 1970, *9,* 99–105.

Russell, W. R., & Nathan, P. W. Traumatic amnesia. *Brain,* 1946, *69,* 280–300.

Sabo, R. A., & Hagen, J. W. A developmental study of perceptual and cognitive factors affecting selective attention. Paper presented at Biennial Meetings, Society for Research in Child Development, Minneapolis, 1971.

Sachs, J. S. Recognition memory for syntactic and semantic aspects of connected discourse. *Perception & Psychophysics*, 1967, *2*, 437–442.

Sakitt, B. Locus of short-term visual storage. *Science*, 1975, *190*, 1318–1319.

Santa, J. L., & Lamwers, L. L. Encoding specificity: Fact or artifact. *Journal of Verbal Learning and Verbal Behavior*, 1974, *13*, 412–423.

Sarason, I. G. *Abnormal psychology* (2nd ed.). Englewood Cliffs, N.J.: Prentice-Hall, 1976.

Schnorr, J. A., & Atkinson, R. C. Repetition versus imagery instructions in the short- and long-term retention of paired-associates. *Psychonomic Science*, 1969, *15*, 183–184.

Schulman, A. I. Memory for words recently classified. *Memory & Cognition*, 1974, *2*, 47–52.

Scoville, W. B. Amnesia after bilateral mesial temporal-lobe excision: Introduction to Case H. M. *Neuropsychologia*, 1968, *6*, 211–213.

Seamon, J. G. Retrieval processes for organized long-term storage. *Journal of Experimental Psychology*, 1973, *97*, 170–176.

Seamon, J. G. Effects of generative processes on probe identification time. *Memory & Cognition*, 1976, *4*, 759–762.

Seamon, J. G. Rehearsal, generative processes, and the activation of underlying stimulus representations. *Perception & Psychophysics*, 1978, *23*, 381–390.

Seamon, J. G. Dynamic facial recognition: Preliminary studies and theory. Unpublished manuscript, 1980.

Seamon, J. G., & Chumbley, J. I. Retrieval processes for serial order information. *Memory & Cognition*, 1977, *5*, 709–715.

Seamon, J. G., & Gazzaniga, M. S. Coding strategies and cerebral laterality effects. *Cognitive Psychology*, 1973, *5*, 249–256.

Seamon, J. G., & Murray, P. Depth of processing in recall and recognition memory: Differential effects of stimulus meaningfulness and serial position. *Journal of Experimental Psychology: Human Learning and Memory*, 1976, *2*, 680–687.

Seamon, J. G., Stolz, J. A., Bass, D. H., & Chatinover, A. I. Recognition of facial features in immediate memory. *Bulletin of the Psychonomic Society*, 1978, *12*, 231–234.

Seamon, J. G., & Virostek, S. Memory performance and subject-defined depth of processing. *Memory & Cognition*, 1978, *6*, 283–287.

Seamon, J. G., & Wright, C. E. Generative processes in character classification: Evidence for a probe encoding set. *Memory & Cognition*, 1976, *4*, 96–102.

Seitz, M. R., & Weber, B. A. Effects of response requirements on the location of clicks superimposed on sentences. *Memory & Cognition*, 1974, *2*, 43–46.

Selfridge, O. G. Pandemonium: A paradigm for learning. In *Symposium on the mechanization of thought processes*. London: H. M. Stationery Office, 1959.

Selfridge, O. G., & Neisser, U. Pattern recognition by machine. *Scientific American*, 1960, *203*, 60–68.

Shaffer, L. H. Multiple attention in continuous verbal tasks. In P. M. A. Rabbitt and S. Dornic (Eds.), *Attentional performance V*. New York: Academic Press, 1975.

Shapiro, I. L. Visual perception and reading. In L. A. Faas (Ed.), *Learning disabilities: A book of readings*. Springfield, Ill.: Charles C. Thomas, 1972.

Shepard, R. N. Learning and recall as organization and search. *Journal of Verbal Learning and Verbal Behavior*, 1966, *5*, 201–204.

Shepard, R. N. Recognition memory for words, sentences, and pictures. *Journal of Verbal Learning and Verbal Behavior*, 1967, *6*, 156–163.

Shepard, R. N. The mental image. *American Psychologist*, 1978, *33*, 125–137.

Shepard, R. N., & Chipman, S. Second-order isomorphism of internal representations: Shapes of states. *Cognitive Psychology*, 1970, *1*, 1–17.

Shepard, R. N., & Metzler, J. Mental rotation of three-dimensional objects. *Science*, 1971, *171*, 701–703.

Shiffrin, R. M. Information persistence in short-term memory. *Journal of Experimental Psychology*, 1973, *100*, 39–49.

Shiffrin, R. M. Short-term store: The basis for a memory system. In F. Restle, R. M. Shiffrin, N. J. Castellan, H. R. Lindman, and D. B. Pisoni (Eds.), *Cognitive theory*. Vol. 1. Hillsdale, N.J.: Erlbaum, 1975.

Shiffrin, R. M., Craig, J. C., & Cohen, U. On the degree of attention and capacity-limitations in tactile processing. *Perception & Psychophysics*, 1973, *13*, 328–336.

Shiffrin, R. M., & Gardner, G. T. Visual processing capacity and attentional control. *Journal of Experimental Psychology*, 1972, *93*, 72–82.

Shiffrin, R. M., & Grantham, D. W. Can attention be allocated to sensory modalities? *Perception & Psychophysics*, 1974, *15*, 460–474.

Shiffrin, R. M., & Schneider, W. An expectancy model for memory search. *Memory & Cognition*, 1974, *2*, 616–628.

Shuell, T. J. Clustering and organization in free recall. *Psychological Bulletin*, 1969, *72*, 353–374.

Shulman, H. G. Encoding and retention of semantic and phonemic information in short-term memory. *Journal of Verbal Learning and Verbal Behavior*, 1970, *9*, 499–508.

Shulman, H. G., & Greenberg, S. N. Perceptual deficit due to division of attention between memory and perception. *Journal of Experimental Psychology*, 1971, *88*, 171–176.

Simon, H. A. How big is a chunk? *Science*, 1974, *183*, 482–488.

Skinner, B. F. *About behaviorism*. New York: Alfred A. Knopf, 1974.

Skoog, T. *Plastic surgery: New methods and refinements.* Philadelphia: Saunders, 1974.

Smith, E. E. Theories of semantic memory. In W. K. Estes (Ed.), *Handbook of learning and cognitive processes.* Vol. 6. Hillsdale, N.J.: Erlbaum, 1978.

Smith, E. E., Shoben, E. J., & Rips, L. J. Structure and process in semantic memory: A feature model for semantic decision. *Psychological Review,* 1974, *81,* 214–241.

Smith, E. E., & Spoehr, K. T. The perception of printed English: A theoretical perspective. In B. H. Kantowitz (Ed.), *Human information processing: Tutorials in performance and cognition.* Hillsdale, N.J.: Erlbaum, 1974.

Sperling, G. The information available in brief visual presentations. *Psychological Monographs,* 1960, *74* (11, Whole No. 498).

Sperling, G. A model for visual memory tasks. *Human Factors,* 1963, *5,* 19–31.

Sperling, G. Successive approximation to a model for short-term memory. *Acta Psychologica,* 1967, *27,* 285–292.

Sperling, G. Short-term memory, long-term memory, and scanning in the processing of visual information. In F. A. Young and D. B. Linsley (Eds.), *Early experience and visual information processing in perceptual and reading disorders.* Washington, D.C.: National Academy of Sciences, 1970.

Sperry, R. W. Hemisphere deconnection and unity in conscious experience. *American Psychologist,* 1968, *23,* 723–733.

Squire, L. R., Slater, P. C., & Chace, P. M. Retrograde amnesia: Temporal gradient in very long term memory following electroconvulsive therapy. *Science,* 1975, *187,* 77–79.

Standing, L. Learning 10,000 pictures. *Quarterly Journal of Experimental Psychology,* 1973, *25,* 207–222.

Stanley, G. Visual memory processes in dyslexia. In D. Deutsch and J. A. Deutsch (Eds.), *Short-term memory.* New York: Academic Press, 1975.

Stanners, R. F., Meunier, G. F., & Headley, D. B. Reaction time as an index of rehearsal in short-term memory. *Journal of Experimental Psychology,* 1969, *82,* 566–570.

Sternberg, R. J., & Tulving, E. The measurement of subjective organization in free recall. *Psychological Bulletin,* 1977, *84,* 539–556.

Sternberg, S. High-speed scanning in human memory. *Science,* 1966, *153,* 652–654.

Sternberg, S. Two operations in character recognition: Some evidence from reaction-time measurements. *Perception & Psychophysics,* 1967, *2,* 45–53.

Sternberg, S. Memory scanning: new findings and current controversies. *Quarterly Journal of Experimental Psychology,* 1975, *27,* 1–32.

Stromeyer, C. F., III Eidetikers. *Psychology Today,* 1970, *4,* 76–80.

Stromeyer, C. F., III, & Psotka, J. The detailed texture of eidetic images. *Nature*, 1970, *225*, 346–349.

Stroop, J. R. Studies of interference in serial verbal reactions. *Journal of Experimental Psychology*, 1935, *18*, 643–662.

Studdert-Kennedy, M., Shankweiler, D., & Shulman, S. Opposed effects of a delayed channel on perception of dichotically and monotically presented CV syllables. *Journal of the Acoustical Society of America*, 1970, *48*, 599–602.

Sumby, W. H. Word frequency and serial position effects. *Journal of Verbal Learning and Verbal Behavior*, 1963, *1*, 443–450.

Sutherland, N. S. Object recognition. In E. C. Carterette and M. P. Friedman (Eds.), *Handbook of perception*. Vol. 3. New York: Academic Press, 1972.

Talland, G. A., & Waugh, N. C. (Eds.), *The pathology of memory*. New York: Academic Press, 1969.

Taylor, R. L., & Reilly, S. Naming and other methods of decoding visual information. *Journal of Experimental Psychology*, 1970, *83*, 80–83.

Teuber, H. L., Milner, B., & Vaughan, H. G., Jr. Persistent anterograde amnesia after stab wound of the basal brain. *Neuropsychologia*, 1968, *6*, 267–282.

Theios, J., & Muise, J. G. The word identification process in reading. In N. J. Castellan, Jr., D. B. Pisoni, and G. Potts (Eds.), *Cognitive theory*. Vol. 2. Hillsdale, N.J.: Erlbaum, 1977.

Thomson, D. M., & Tulving, E. Associative encoding and retrieval: Weak and strong cues. *Journal of Experimental Psychology*, 1970, *86*, 255–262.

Till, R. E., & Jenkins, J. J. The effects of cued orienting tasks on the free recall of words. *Journal of Verbal Learning and Verbal Behavior*, 1973, *12*, 489–498.

Titchener, E. B. *Lectures on the elementary psychology of feeling and attention*. New York: Macmillan & Co., 1908.

Townsend, J. T. A note on the identifiability of parallel and serial processes. *Perception & Psychophysics*, 1971, *10*, 161–163.

Townsend, J. T. Some results concerning the identifiability of parallel and serial processes. *British Journal of Mathematical and Statistical Psychology*, 1972, *25*, 168–199.

Treisman, A. M. Verbal cues, language and meaning in selective attention. *American Journal of Psychology*, 1964, *77*, 215–216.

Tresselt, M. E., & Mayzner, M. S. A study of incidental learning. *Journal of Psychology*, 1960, *50*, 339–347.

True, R. M. Experimental control in hypnotic age regression states. *Science*, 1949, *110*, 583–584.

Trumbo, D., & Milone, F. Primary task performance as a function of encoding, retention, and recall in a secondary task. *Journal of Experimental Psychology*, 1971, *91*, 273–279.

Tulving, E. Subjective organization in free recall of unrelated words. *Psychological Review*, 1962, *69*, 344–354.

Tulving, E. Episodic and semantic memory. In E. Tulving and W. Donaldson (Eds.), *Organization of memory*. New York: Academic Press, 1972.

Tulving, E., & Arbuckle, T. Y. Sources of intratrial interference in immediate recall of paired associates. *Journal of Verbal Learning and Verbal Behavior*, 1963, *1*, 321–334.

Tulving, E., & Gold, C. Stimulus information and contextual information as determinants of tachistoscopic recognition of words. *Journal of Experimental Psychology*, 1963, *66*, 319–327.

Tulving, E., & Osler, S. Effectiveness of retrieval cues in memory for words. *Journal of Experimental Psychology*, 1968, *77*, 593–601.

Tulving, E., & Pearlstone, Z. Availability versus accessibility of information in memory for words. *Journal of Verbal Learning and Verbal Behavior*, 1966, *5*, 381–391.

Tulving, E., & Thomson, D. M. Encoding specificity and retrieval processes in episodic memory. *Psychological Review*, 1973, *80*, 352–373.

Tulving, E., & Watkins, O. C. Recognition failure of words with a single meaning. *Memory & Cognition*, 1977, *5*, 513–522.

Turvey, M. T. On peripheral and central processes in vision: Inferences from an information processing analysis of masking with patterned stimuli. *Psychological Review*, 1973, *80*, 1–52.

Turvey, M. T. Visual processing and short-term memory. in W. K. Estes (Ed.), *Handbook of learning and cognitive processes*. Vol. V. Hillsdale, N.J.: Erlbaum, 1977.

Tversky, B. Pictorial and verbal encoding in a short-term memory task. *Perception & Psychophysics*, 1969, *6*, 225–233.

Underwood, B. J., & Schulz, R. W. *Meaningfulness and verbal learning*. Philadelphia: Lippincott, 1960.

Varley, W. H., Levin, J. R., Severson, R. A., & Wolff, P. Training imagery production in young children through motor involvement. *Journal of Educational Psychology*, 1974, *66*, 262–266.

Vernon, M. D. *Backwardness in reading*. Cambridge, England: Cambridge University Press, 1958.

Volkman, F. C. Vision during voluntary saccadic eye movements. *Journal of the Optical Society of America*, 1962, *52*, 571–578.

von Wright, J. M. On the problems of selection in iconic memory. *Scandanavian Journal of Psychology*, 1972, *13*, 159–171.

Vurpillot, E. The development of scanning strategies and their relation to visual differentiation. *Journal of Experimental Child Psychology*, 1968, *6*, 637–650.

Walker, N. S., Garrett, J. B., & Wallace, B. Restoration of eidetic imagery via hypnotic age regression: A preliminary report. *Journal of Abnormal Psychology*, 1976, *85*, 335–337.

Walker-Smith, G. J., Gale, A. G., & Findlay, J. M. Eye movement strategies involved in face perception. *Perception*, 1977, *6*, 313–326.

Watkins, M. J., Watkins, O. C., Craik, F. I. M., & Mazuryk, G. Effect of nonverbal distraction on short-term storage. *Journal of Experimental Psychology*, 1973, *101*, 296–300.

Wattenbarger, B. L. Speed and accuracy set in visual search performance. Paper presented at Annual Convention, Midwestern Psychological Association, 1967.

Waugh, N. C., & Norman, D. A. Primary memory. *Psychological Review*, 1965, *72*, 89–104.

Weizmann, F., Cohen, L. B., & Pratt, R. J. Novelty, familiarity, and the development of infant attention. *Developmental Psychology*, 1971, *4*, 149–154.

Wheeler, D. D. Processes in word recognition. *Cognitive Psychology*, 1970, *1*, 59–85.

Wickelgren, W. A. Sparing of short-term memory in an amnesic patient. Implications for strength theory of memory. *Neuropsychologia*, 1968, *6*, 235–244.

Wickelgren, W. A. The long and the short of memory. *Psychological Bulletin*, 1973, *80*, 425–438.

Wickelgren, W. A. Speed-accuracy tradeoff and information processing dynamics. Paper presented at Annual Convention, Psychonomics Society, 1974.

Wickens, D. D. Encoding categories of words: An empirical approach to meaning. *Psychological Review*, 1970, *77*, 1–15.

Wickens, D. D., Born, D. G., & Allen, C. K. Proactive inhibition and item similarity in short-term memory. *Journal of Verbal Learning and Verbal Behavior*, 1963, *2*, 440–445.

Wilkes, A. L., & Kennedy, R. A. Relationship between pausing and retrieval latency in sentences of varying grammatical form. *Journal of Experimental Psychology*, 1969, *79*, 241–245.

Wilkes, A. L., & Kennedy, R. A. The relative accessibility of list items within different pause-defined groups. *Journal of Verbal Learning and Verbal Behavior*, 1970, *9*, 197–201.

Williams, M. Traumatic retrograde amnesia and normal forgetting. In G. A. Talland and N. C. Waugh (Eds.), *The pathology of memory*. New York: Academic Press, 1969.

Winograd, E. Recognition memory for faces following nine different judgments. *Bulletin of the Psychonomic Society*, 1976, *8*, 419–421.

Wolfe, H. K. Untersuchungen über das Tongedächtniss. *Philosoph. Studen.*, 1886, *3*, 534. (Cited in Murray, D. J. Research on human memory in the nineteenth century. *Canadian Journal of Psychology*, 1976, *30*, 201–220.)

Wood, G. Organizational processes and free recall. In E. Tulving and W. Donaldson (Eds.), *Organization of memory*. New York: Academic Press, 1972.

Woodward, A. E., Jr., Bjork, R. A., & Jongeward, R. H., Jr. Recall and recognition as a function of primary rehearsal. *Journal of Verbal Learning and Verbal Behavior*, 1973, *12*, 608–617.

Yarbus, A. L. *Eye movements and vision*. New York: Plenum Press, 1967.

Yarmey, A. D. Hypermnesia for pictures but not for concrete or abstract words. *Bulletin of the Psychonomic Society,* 1976, *8,* 115–117.

Yates, F. A. *The art of memory.* Middlesex, England: Penguin, 1966.

Yuille, J. C., & Catchpole, M. J. Associative learning and imagery training in children. *Journal of Experimental Child Psychology,* 1973, *16,* 403–412.

Name Index

Aaronson, D., 159
Aderman, D., 98
Allen, C. K., 81
Allport, F. H., 156, 157
Alpern, M., 26
Anderson, J. R., 143, 183, 185, 189, 190, 193–96, 198
Anderson, R. C., 185, 186
Angelergues, R., 214
Arbuckle, T. Y., 116
Arenberg, D., 212
Aristotle, 4, 5
Arnheim, R., 35
Atkinson, J., 95
Atkinson, R. C., 24, 80, 95, 108–12, 119–21, 124, 126, 129–31, 138, 182, 187
Ault, R. L., 201
Averbach, E., 25, 28

Bach, M. J., 205
Bachrach, A. J., 73
Baddeley, A. D., 77, 117, 118, 125, 129, 139, 149
Bahrick, H. P., 136, 218
Bahrick, P. O., 136
Barber, T. X., 216
Barbizet, J., 117, 118, 210, 212, 215, 216
Barclay, J. R., 137, 138
Barlow, H. B., 33
Barnett, T., 44
Bartlett, F. C., 8, 11, 98, 188, 191, 193
Bartz, W. H., 121
Bass, D. H., 150
Bates, A., 44
Bates, E., 190
Battig, W. F., 167
Baxt, N., 7, 21

Beach, D. R., 205
Becker, J., 136
Becklen, R., 65
Belmont, J. M., 116
Bernbach, H. A., 114
Bevan, W., 135, 181
Bever, T. G., 158
Biederman, I., 97, 98
Birnbaum, I. M., 210
Bjork, R. A., 115, 123, 185
Blake, M., 183
Blake, R. R., 103
Blecker, D. L., 67
Bobrow, D. G., 74
Bobrow, S. A., 127
Boeck, W. J., 187
Boies, S. J., 69, 70, 103, 104
Bolton, L. S., 163
Boring, E. G., 181
Born, D. G., 81
Bourne, L. E., Jr., 147
Bousfield, W. A., 155, 164, 165
Bower, G. H., 127, 138, 139, 143, 145, 149, 161–66, 168, 169, 183, 187, 190, 193–96
Bracey, G. W., 179
Bradshaw, J. L., 215
Bransford, J. D., 129, 189, 190
Brewer, W. F., 189
Broadbent, D. E., 63, 64, 158, 210
Brooks, J., 151
Brooks, L. R., 139
Brown, A. L., 207, 208
Brown, E., 168
Brown, J. A., 77, 186, 188
Brown, R., 174, 183
Bruce, D. R., 112, 164
Bruner, J. S., 204
Buchanan, M., 7
Buchman, H., 148
Buckhout, R., 192

Burrows, D., 179, 180
Burtt, H. E., 217
Buschke, H., 167, 208, 212
Busse, E. W., 213
Buswell, G. T., 33
Butterfield, E. C., 116
Butters, N., 118

Calfee, R. C., 87
Cannizzo, S. R., 206
Carey, S., 152
Carmichael, L., 134
Carpenter, G. C., 202
Carvellas, T., 95
Catchpole, M. J., 206
Cermak, L. S., 118, 125
Chace, P. M., 211
Chance, J. E., 145
Chase, W. G., 77
Chatinover, A. I., 150
Cherry, E. C., 59, 62, 63
Chinsky, J. M., 205
Chipman, S., 146
Chumbley, J. I., 169
Clark, M. C., 165
Clark, W. H., 135
Cofer, C. N., 164, 165
Cohen, L. B., 60, 201, 202
Cohen, U., 62
Cole, M., 206
Collins, A. M., 193, 194, 196, 198
Colwill, S. J., 112
Conrad, R., 41
Converse, J. M., 148
Cooper, L. A., 140
Corballis, M. C., 39, 40
Coriell, A. S., 28
Corkin, S., 118
Corsi, P. M., 214
Cosky, M. J., 100
Cowan, G. N., 47, 48
Cox, R. L., 150, 152
Craig, J. C., 62
Craik, F. I. M., 77, 121–23, 125–31, 187, 188, 212
Crowder, R. G., 21, 24, 39–43, 45, 46, 50, 53–56, 116, 125
Crowley, J. J., 112

Csapo, K., 136
Cunitz, A. R., 24, 113–16
Currie, J. L., 152

D'Agostino, P. R., 146, 187
Dallenbach, K. M., 76
Daniels, A. H., 7
DaPolito, F., 186
Dark, V. J., 121, 122
Darley, C. F., 121–23
Darwin, C. T., 45, 46
Davies, G., 150
Davison, M. L., 34
Deese, J., 164, 186
DeGroot, A. D., 76
DeRosa, D. V., 180
Descartes, 4, 5
Deutsch, D., 64
Deutsch, J. A., 64
Dhawan, M., 146
Diamond, R., 152
Dick, A. O., 34, 35
Dietz, G., 7
Dodwell, P. C., 91
Doerflein, R. S., 34

Eagle, M., 186
Ebbinghaus, H., 7, 11, 134, 153, 167, 217
Efron, R., 14, 50–52, 56
Egeth, H., 67, 95, 181
Eichelman, W. H., 103, 104
Eimas, P. D., 61
Elias, C. S., 127
Ellis, H., 150
Enlow, D. H., 148, 151
Erdelyi, M. H., 136, 138
Eriksen, C. W., 26, 30, 47, 69
Estes, W. K., 168, 186

Fagan, J. F., 151, 202–4
Fantz, R. L., 60, 202
Fechner, G. T., 19
Findlay, J. M., 150
Finkelstein, S., 138
Fischer-Williams, M., 67
Fischler, I., 181, 182

Fisher, G. H., 150, 152
Flavell, J. H., 205, 206, 208
Flexser, A. J., 187, 188
Fodor, J. A., 158
Foord, E. N., 135
Fox, M. J., 34
Fox, R., 103
Frankel, F., 206
Franks, J. J., 129, 189
Freud, S., 209
Friedman, A., 147
Friedman, S., 202
Friedrichs, A. G., 208

Galanter, E., 161, 164
Gale, A. G., 150
Galton, F., 152
Gardiner, J. M., 128
Gardner, G. T., 69
Garrett, J. B., 217
Garrett, M. F., 158
Gastaut, H., 67
Gazzaniga, M. S., 139, 214, 215
Geffen, G., 215
Gehring, R. E., 136, 145
Gelber, E. R., 201, 202
Gholson, B., 67
Gibson, E., 90, 91
Gibson, J. J., 35
Gilmore, G., 95
Glanzer, M., 24, 113–16, 126, 135
Glass, A. L., 97, 98, 121–23
Gleitman, H. A., 95
Glucksberg, S., 47, 48
Gold, C., 98
Goldensohn, E. S., 68
Goldstein, A. G., 145
Gombrich, E. H., 152
Goodglass, H., 118
Gough, P. B., 100
Graham, S. E., 105
Grant, S., 139
Grantham, D. W., 62
Gray, C. R., 143
Gray, J. A., 63
Greenberg, S. N., 71
Gregg, L. W., 169
Gregory, R. L., 35
Griffith, D., 71

Gruneberg, M. M., 112
Guiford, J. P., 76
Gummerman, K., 143
Guthrie, G., 30, 31
Guy, C. L., 148

Haber, R. N., 15, 16, 18, 20, 21, 24,
    27, 29, 31, 50, 51, 135, 142
Hacker, M. J., 181
Hagen, J. W., 204, 206
Hale, G. A., 205
Hall, J. F., 186
Hamon, T. G., 139
Hardyck, C., 215
Harmon, L. D., 152, 153
Hart, J. T., 183
Hawkins, H. L., 52
Hawles, T. G., 206
Headley, D. B., 70, 72
Hebb, D. O., 108, 124, 135
Hécaen, H., 214
Herrell, N., 138
Herrmann, D. J., 111, 182
Hershenson, M., 24, 27, 31
Hilgard, E. R., 216
Hinrichs, J. V., 105, 181
Hochberg, J., 31, 34, 64, 65, 98, 99,
    105
Hock, H. W., 67
Hoffmann, M., 30
Hogan, H. P., 134
Hohle, R. H., 67
Holmgren, J. E., 95
Horowitz, L. M., 185
Hoyt, J. D., 208
Hubel, D. H., 91
Hull, A. J., 41
Hultsch, D. F., 212
Hyde, T. S., 127

Ingalls, R. P., 103
Ingram, T. T. S., 35
Isard, S., 98

Jacobs, J., 7, 75
Jacoby, L. L., 121, 128, 130
James, W., 6, 24, 108, 112, 130, 181

Jarvella, R. J., 159
Jenkins, J. J., 125, 127, 164, 165, 190, 191
Johnson, H. J., 47
Johnson, M. K., 190
Johnson, N. F., 159, 168
Johnson, R. E., 188
Johnson-Laird, P. N., 167
Johnston, W. A., 71
Jongeward, R. H. Jr., 123
Jonides, J., 95, 144
Judd, C. H., 33
Juola, J. F., 95, 181, 182, 187
Jusczyk, P., 60

Kahn, B. J., 50
Kahn, R., 144
Kahneman, D., 67
Kail, R. V., Jr., 205
Kamlet, A. S., 67
Kaplan, I. T., 95
Karlin, M. B., 149, 187
Katona, G., 164
Keele, S. W., 61
Keenan, J. M., 190
Keeney, A. H., 34
Keeney, T. J., 206
Kennedy, J. F., 173
Kennedy, R. A., 159, 169
Keppel, G., 81
Kerr, B., 68, 74
Kerr, N., 143, 144
Kimble, G. A., 136, 145
Kimura, D., 214
Kingsley, P. R., 206
Kinney, G. C., 91, 92
Kintsch, W., 147, 187, 190, 191
Kirschner, L. A., 209
Kirsner, K., 104
Koffka, K., 156
Köhler, W., 156
Kolers, P. A., 33, 99, 130, 190
Koppenaal, L., 126
Kosslyn, S. M., 146
Krainz, P. L., 105
Kral, V. A., 213
Kreutzer, M. A., 208
Kristofferson, M. W., 179

Kroll, N. E. A., 103
Kulik, J., 174
Külpe, O., 181

LaBerge, D., 24, 69, 72, 73, 101–5
Ladefoged, P., 158
Lamwers, L. L., 185
Lappin, J. S., 103
Lashley, K. S., 167
Latour, P. L., 34
Lawrence, K. A., 163
Lazar, R., 95
Leiter, E., 186
Leonard, C., 208
Lesgold, A. M., 165, 168
Levin, J. R., 206
Lewis, M., 151
Liberman, A. M., 55
Liggett, J., 147
Lincoln, A., 152
Lindsay, P. H., 100
Linn, L., 209
Livingston, R. B., 173
Locke, J., 4
Lockhart, R. S., 125, 126, 129–31
Loftus, E. F., 192, 193
Loftus, G. R., 121, 122
Lorayne, H., 163
Lucas, J., 163
Luria, A. R., 141, 142

Mackworth, J. F., 26
Mackworth, N. H., 33, 204
MacWhinney, B., 190
Malt, B. C., 99
Mandler, G., 167, 187, 188
Manelis, L., 185
Marcus, N., 95
Marmor, G. S., 145
Marsetta, M., 91
Martin, E., 168, 169
Massaro, D. W., 6, 39, 46–50, 52, 55, 56
Mayhew, D., 190
Mayzner, M. S., 125
Mazuryk, G., 77
McCormack, P. D., 186, 187
McLean, R. S., 169

McNeill, D., 183
McNulty, J. A., 186
Mechanic, A., 127
Melton, A. W., 76, 78, 124, 125
Metzler, J., 139–41
Meunier, G. F., 70, 72
Meyer, D. E., 104
Miller, B., 138
Miller, G. A., 76, 98, 161, 164
Miller, L. K., 205
Milner, B., 118, 119, 214
Milone, F., 71
Mitchell, R. F., 103, 104
Modigliani, V., 121
Moely, B. E., 206
Mohs, R. C., 182
Morandi, A. J., 33
Moray, N., 44, 45, 64, 66
Morello, D. C., 148
Morris, C. D., 129
Morton, J., 40–43, 46, 50, 53, 54,
    125
Moscovitch, M., 129
Moyer, R. S., 146
Muensterberg, H., 192
Muise, J. G., 100
Müller, G. E., 164
Murdock, B. B., Jr., 78–80, 82, 113,
    179, 180
Murray, D. J., 21, 41
Murray, P., 116, 128, 130, 186

Nathan, P. W., 210
Nathanson, L. S., 15, 16
Nebes, R. D., 215
Neimark, E., 206
Neisser, U., 14, 35, 39, 64, 65, 87,
    90, 92, 93, 95, 96, 99, 125, 143,
    144, 217, 218
Nelson, D. L., 147
Nelson, T. O., 128, 130
Nickerson, R. S., 135, 177, 207
Nissen, M. J., 147
Noreen, D. L., 169
Norman, D. A., 24, 64, 74, 80, 96,
    97, 100, 108–10, 156
Norris, R. G., 152
Novick, R., 95

Olsen, F. A., 206
O'Neill, B. J., 146
Ornstein, P. A., 167
Osler, S., 183
Ostry, D. J., 130

Pachella, R. G., 95, 181
Paivio, A., 136, 138, 146
Palmer, J. C., 192, 193
Palmer, S. E., 97
Parker, E. S., 210
Parks, T. E., 15, 103
Patterson, K., 125, 149, 188
Paulson, R., 189
Pavlov, I., 5
Pearlstone, Z., 183, 209
Pellegrino, J. W., 146, 167
Penfield, W., 200, 201, 215
Perfetti, C. A., 127
Peterson, L. R., 77, 80–82
Peterson, M. J., 77, 80–82, 105
Pezdek, K., 189
Phillips, L. W., 115
Piaget, J., 201
Pichert, J. W., 185, 186
Pisoni, D. B., 52, 55
Pittenger, J. B., 151, 191
Plato, 4, 5
Posner, M. I., 61, 69, 70, 78, 82,
    103–5, 147, 179
Postman, L., 115, 127, 170, 185
Powell, G. D., 139
Pratt, R. J., 60
Pribram, K. H., 161, 164, 210
Pritchard, R. M., 33
Proust, M., 134
Prussin, H. A., 42
Psotka, J., 142, 152
Pylyshyn, Z. W., 143

Quillian, M. R., 193, 194, 196,
    198

Rabinowitz, J. C., 98, 188
Raymond, B. J., 212
Reder, L. M., 185

Reed, V. S., 147
Reese, H. W., 206, 207, 212, 213
Reicher, G. M., 95, 98, 164
Reiff, R., 216
Reilly, S., 103
Reitman, J. S., 81, 82
Reitman, W., 174
Restle, F., 168
Richards, J. T., 95
Riggs, L. A., 33
Rips, L. J., 193, 194, 196, 197
Rock, I., 35
Rogers, T. B., 136
Rohrbaugh, J. W., 26
Rosch, E., 104
Rosenbaum, D. A., 180, 181
Ross, J., 163
Rossi, S. I., 206
Rossman, E., 78, 82
Rozin, P., 144
Rubin, D. C., 190
Ruddy, M. G., 104
Rundus, D., 119–21
Russell, W. A., 164, 165
Russell, W. R., 210

Sabo, R. A., 206
Sachs, J. S., 188, 189
Sakitt, B., 19–21, 50
Samuels, S. J., 24, 69, 72, 73,
    101–5
Santa, J. L., 185
Sarason, I. G., 209
Scarborough, H. S., 159
Scheerer, M., 216
Schenov, 5
Schneider, W., 181
Schnorr, J. A., 138
Schulman, A. I., 128
Schulz, R. W., 134
Schumann, F., 164
Schvaneveldt, R. W., 104
Scott, M. S., 207
Scoville, W. B., 118
Seamon, J. G., 99, 104, 105, 116,
    121, 128, 130, 139, 148–51, 169,
    179, 181, 186, 215
Sedgewick, C. H., 155
Seitz, M. R., 159

Selfridge, O. G., 87–91, 125
Severson, R. A., 206
Shaffer, L. H., 72
Shapiro, I. L., 35
Sharp, D., 206
Shaw, R. E., 151
Shepard, R. N., 135, 137, 139–41,
    146, 186
Shepherd, J., 150
Shiffrin, R. M., 24, 62, 69, 80–82,
    108–12, 119, 120, 124, 126,
    129–31, 181
Shoben, E. I., 193, 194, 196, 197
Showman, D. J., 91
Shuell, T. J., 167
Shulman, H. G., 71, 112
Siegel, A. W., 205
Simon, H. A., 76, 77
Siqueland, E. P., 61
Skinner, B. F., 6
Skoog, T., 148
Slater, P. C., 211
Slotnick, N. S., 206
Smith, E. E., 91, 98, 193, 194, 196,
    197
Smythe, P. C., 136
Snyder, C. R. R., 95
Sophocles, 217
Spenser, T., 69
Sperling, G., 21–29, 31, 35, 44, 48
Sperry, R., 214
Spoehr, K. T., 91
Springston, F., 164
Squire, L. R., 211
Stacy, E. W., Jr., 97, 98
Standing, L. G., 16, 18, 20, 21, 29,
    50, 51, 135
Stanley, G., 34
Stanners, R. F., 70–72
Stegar, J. A., 135
Sternberg, R. J., 167
Sternberg, S., 177, 179
Stevenson, H. W., 205
Stolz, J. A., 150
Stromeyer, C. F., III, 142, 143
Stroop, J. R., 66, 67
Studdert-Kennedy, M., 55
Sumby, W. H., 116
Sutherland, N. S., 96
Swenson, A. L., 186

Talland, G. A., 210
Tash, J., 55
Taylor, R. L., 103, 179
Teuber, H. L., 118
Theios, J., 100
Thomas, J., 138
Thomson, D. M., 183–85
Thomson, N., 77, 139
Tieman, D., 168
Till, R. E., 127
Titchner, E. B., 181
Tkacz, S., 180
Toglia, M. P., 136, 145
Townsend, J. T., 175
Trabasso, T., 167
Treisman, A. M., 64, 125
Tressett, M. E., 125
True, R. M., 216
Trumbo, D., 71
Tulving, E., 98, 116, 127–30, 166,
    167, 183–85, 187, 188, 193, 209
Turvey, M. T., 21, 30, 36, 45, 46
Tversky, B., 105

Ulrich, T., 206
Underwood, B. J., 81, 134, 205

Varley, W. H., 206
Vaughan, G. H., Jr., 118
Vernon, M. D., 35
Vining, S. K., 130
Virgorito, J., 61
Virostek, S., 128
Volkman, F. C., 34
von Wright, J. M., 27, 28, 44
Vurpillot, E., 204

Wagstaff, R. R., 71
Wald, J., 191
Walker, N. S., 217
Walker-Smith, G. J., 150
Wall, S., 95

Wallace, B., 217
Wallace, G., 215
Walter, A. A., 134
Warrington, E. K., 117, 118
Watkins, M. J., 77, 121–23
Watkins, O. C., 77, 185, 187
Wattenbarger, B. L., 95
Waugh, N. C., 24, 80, 108–10, 210
Weber, B. A., 159
Wedderburn, A. A. I., 63
Weizmann, F., 60
Wellman, H. M., 208
Wertheimer, M., 156
Wescourt, K. T., 111, 182
Wheeler, D. D., 98
Whitten, W. B., 115
Wickelgren, W. A., 95, 112, 118
Wickens, D. D., 81, 83
Wiener, G., 30, 31
Wiesel, T. N., 91
Wight, E., 139
Wilkes, A. L., 159, 169
Williams, M., 210
Winfrow, P., 112
Winograd, E., 149
Winzenz, D., 165, 168, 169
Wittlinger, R. P., 136
Wittrock, M. C., 206
Wolfe, H. K., 7
Wolff, P., 206
Wood, C. T., 182
Wood, G., 170
Woods, R. W., 112
Woodward, A. E., Jr., 123
Wright, C. E., 181

Yarbus, A. L., 31, 32, 65, 150
Yarmey, A. D., 136, 138
Yates, F. A., 163
Young, R. K., 139
Yuille, J. C., 206

Zaback, L. A., 145

Subject Index

Abstraction, 101–4. *See also* Memory for gist and details
Activation of memory representations, 104, 105
Afterimages, 17–19
Alcoholism. *See* Korsakoff's syndrome
Amnesia. *See* Neuropathology; Psychopathology
Attention, basis of
filter model, 62–64
information pick up, 64, 65
Attention, capacity of, 61, 73–83
encoding, 68–70
recall, 71, 72
rehearsal, 70, 71
Attention, failures
epilepsy, 67, 68
response competition, 66, 67
Attention, selectivity
bases, 62–66
necessity, 61, 62
origins, 60, 61
Automaticity. *See* Practice

Brain damage, 118, 119. *See also* Neuropathology
Brain stimulation, electrical, 200, 201, 215, 216

Central and peripheral processes, 19–21, 52, 53, 61, 62
Cerebral hemispheres. *See* Neuropathology
Children and adults, memory differences
attentional processes, 204, 205
recognition, 207, 208
strategy use, 205–7

Chunking, 76, 77
Clustering, semantic, 164, 165
Cocktail party phenomenon, 59, 60
Coding, 111. *See also* Control processes
Color mixture, 14, 15
Conceptually driven processing, 96–101
Context effects
in object identification, 97, 98
in memory, 190, 191
in reading, 98–101
Contiguity, principle of, 4, 5
Control processes, 108
Cues. *See* Recall processes in long-term storage

Data driven and conceptually driven processing, 96–101
Dual coding theory. *See* Mental imagery
Dualism, mind-body, 4, 5
Dyslexia, 34, 35

Echoic memory
duration of, 43–51
locus of, 52, 53
model of, 53, 54
speech perception, 54–56
Eidetic imagery. *See* Mental imagery
Encoding processes, 68. *See also* Attention
Encoding specificity. *See* Recall processes in long-term storage
Epilepsy, 67, 68
Eye movements
recording of, 31, 32
types of, 33
Eyewitness testimony, 8, 192, 193

Faces
  changes over time, 147, 151
  recognition, 136, 147–53
Feature analysis in pattern recognition, 90–96
  extraction and interpretation, 90, 91
  neurological basis, 91
  types of features, 96
Flashbulb memories, 173, 174
Forgetting, immediate memory
  decay, 81, 82
  interference, 80, 81
  limited capacity, 82, 83
Forgetting, long-term storage, 182–86
Free recall
  primacy and recency, 112–17
  serial position function, 113
Fugue states. See Psychopathology

Generative processes and expectancies, 104, 105
Gestalt laws of organization. See Organizational processes

HAM. See Semantic memory
Hypermnesia, 136
Hypnotic age regression. See Memory permanence

Iconic memory
  capacity of, 25–27
  duration of, 16, 17
  locus of, 19–21
  model of, 21–27
Immediate memory
  and attention, 73–83
  capacity of, 75–77
  duration of, 77–79
  forgetting, 80–83
  iconic memory and, 24, 36
Infant memory, 201–4
Inference in memory, 193, 194
Interference, 80, 81
Introspection. See Mental imagery

Korsakoff's syndrome, 112, 117, 118, 131, 210

Labeling, 134, 135
Learning and information transfer, 110
Levels of processing, 125–29
Long-term storage, 108–24

Masking
  auditory, 48–50
  visual, 28–30
Memory for gist and details
  abstraction, 188–90
  context effects, 190, 191
  reconstructive processes, 191–93
Memory permanence
  early experience, 217
  electrical stimulation, 215, 216
  hypnotic age regression, 216, 217
Memory scanning, 177–79
  expectancy effects, 181
  practice effects, 179, 180
  organization effects, 180, 181
Memory span, 75–77
Memory structures, 108
Mental imagery
  experimental evidence, 138–41
  introspection, 138
  picture metaphor and, 143–45
  subjective experience, 137, 138
  supernormal, 141–43
  theories of, 145–47
Mental rotation, 139–41. See also Mental imagery
Mnemonics
  method of loci, 159–61
  plans, 161–63
  rhymes and rules, 163, 164
Modality effect, 39–41

Neuropathology
  anterograde and retrograde amnesia, 210–12
  cerebral accidents and surgery, 213–15
  old age and senility, 212, 213
Nonsense syllables, 8, 134

Organizational processes
  grammatical, 158, 159
  visual, 156–58
Organization in memory
  free recall, 164–67
  locus of, 170
  serial learning, 167–69

Pandemonium model of pattern
    recognition, 88–91
Perceptual confusions, 91, 92
Peripheral processes. *See* Central
    and peripheral processes
Philosophers, Greek, 3, 4
Practice
  and automaticity, 72, 73
  and memory scanning, 179, 180
  and visual search, 95
Precategorical acoustic storage, 43
Primacy and recency, 112–17
Primary memory. *See* Immediate
    memory
Proactive interference, release from,
    81, 83. *See also* Interference
Processing, serial and parallel,
    175–77
Psychopathology, 208–9

Reading, 98–101
Reading problems, 34, 35
Recall and recognition differences
  organization and search, 187
  recall of unrecognized stimuli,
    187, 188
  stimulus and instructional vari-
    ables, 186, 187
Recall of unrecognized stimuli,
    187, 188
Recall processes in long-term stor-
    age
  available but inaccessible traces,
    182, 183
  cues and encoding specificity,
    183–86
Recency effects
  long-term, 115, 116
  short-term, 112–17
Recoding, 101. *See also* Abstraction
Recognition memory
  long-term storage, 181, 182

pictures and words, 134–36
  short-term storage, 174–81
Reconstructive processes. *See*
    Memory for gist and details
Rehearsal and long-term storage
  frequency, 119–21
  interpretation difficulties, 121,
    122
  types of, 122–24
Rehearsal processes, 41, 53, 54,
    110, 111
Repetition effects, 124, 125
Representations in memory, 101–3,
    179. *See also* Abstraction
Retardation and recall, 116, 117

Saccadic eye movements. *See* Eye
    movements
Schemas, 36, 98, 191
Scientific method, 6, 7
Secondary memory, 108–24
Semantic memory
  feature comparison model, 196–
    98
  network model, 193, 194
  propositional model, 194–96
Sensory memory. *See* Echoic mem-
    ory; Iconic memory
Serial order information, 167–69
Serial position effect, 113
Shadowing, 62, 63
Shock, electroconvulsive, 210, 211
Short-term and long-term storage
    distinction, 112–19
Short-term storage, 108–24. *See
    also* Immediate memory
Simultaniety judgment, 50, 51
Slit viewing, moving, 15
Stroop effect, 66, 67. *See also* Atten-
    tion
Suffix effect, 41–43

Tabula rasa, 4
Tachistoscope, 22
Template matching, 86–90

Visual fixations, brief, 31
Visual search, 92–95